NEVER FIGHT FAIR!

NEVER FIGHT FAIR!

Navy SEALs' Stories of
Combat and Adventure

ORR KELLY

★
PRESIDIO

Published by Presidio Press
505 B San Marin Dr., Suite 300
Novato, CA 94945-1340

Library of Congress Cataloging-in-Publication Data

Kelly Orr.
    Never fight fair! : Navy SEALs' stories of combat and adventure / Orr Kelly.
       p.   cm.
    Includes index.
    ISBN 0-89141-519-X
    1. United States. Navy. SEALs—History. 2. United States. Navy. SEALs—Anecdotes. 3. United States. Navy—Commando troops.
I. Title.
VG87,K453   1995
  359.9—dc20   94-26976
                                        CIP

Typography by ProImage

For the brave men who go where others dare not go and do what others dare not do and for those among them who have given their lives for their country.

Contents

Preface   ix

Introduction   SEALs: What Makes Them Tick?   1

PART 1   THE EARLY DAYS   9

    Chapter 1   MacArthur's Frogmen   11

    Chapter 2   UDT Sixteen—A Bum Rap?   21

    Chapter 3   Fishnets in Korea   28

    Chapter 4   The Iceberg Caper   35

    Chapter 5   Big War in a Small Place   37

PART 2   THE GLORY DAYS   45

    Chapter 6   Welcome Back for *Gemini*   47

    Chapter 7   Alone in the Mid-Atlantic   51

    Chapter 8   First Men from the Moon   54

    Chapter 9   Unlucky Thirteen   58

PART 3   FROGMEN IN VIETNAM   65

    Chapter 10   Good Fun in North Vietnam   67

    Chapter 11   Operation Jackstay   72

    Chapter 12   "Heaviest Load I've Ever Carried"   78

PART 4   THE SEALs' WAR   83

    Chapter 13   A Greek Tragedy   85

    Chapter 14   A Narrow Escape   102

    Chapter 15   First Blood For Squad 2-Bravo   109

    Chapter 16   The Bullfrog   123

    Chapter 17   More VC Than You'll Ever Want   131

    Chapter 18   "My Worst Disaster"   136

Chapter 19   The Sting   141
Chapter 20   Like a Shooting Gallery   144
Chapter 21   "Everything Is Written Down"   149
Chapter 22   Blowing Bunkers   153
Chapter 23   "Something's Happened to Mike"   155
Chapter 24   "I Don't Want You Operating . . ."   159
Chapter 25   They Called It Bright Light   165
Chapter 26   A Taste for Ears   170
Chapter 27   "Vous les Américains Sont Pires
             que les Français"   173
PART 5   SEALs UNDER THE SEAS   185
Chapter 28   "Dead Before Sunrise"   187
Chapter 29   One of Our Dolphins (SDVs) Is Missing   195
Chapter 30   Blocking Haiphong Harbor   200
Chapter 31   Operation Thunderhead   205
Chapter 32   "An Electrical Shock . . ."   220
Chapter 33   Target: Libya   223
Chapter 34   Shadowing the *Achille Lauro*   227
Chapter 35   A World-Class Swim   230
PART 6   SEALs FROM THE SKIES   249
Chapter 36   A Shocking Takeoff   251
Chapter 37   "I Started to Black Out"   255
Chapter 38   "Your Adrenaline Pumps"   258
Chapter 39   "I'm Going to Jump"   262
Chapter 40   "I Hated Every One . . ."   266
Chapter 41   When Your Eyes Freeze Shut   272
PART 7   SEALs IN ACTION   281
Chapter 42   Jump into a Dark Sea   283
Chapter 43   A Beautiful Day to Go to War   289
PART 8   THE INNOVATORS   297
Chapter 44   Birth of the STAB   299
Chapter 45   Dogs on Patrol   306
Chapter 46   What Do You Wear to War?   311
Chapter 47   SEALs: A New Generation   316
Chapter 48   Letting Go   321
Glossary   323
Index   331

Preface

When I began research on *Brave Men, Dark Waters,* my history of navy special warfare—the frogmen—I naively gave the book the subtitle *The Untold Story of the Navy SEALs.*

As I quickly learned, there is no single untold story of the SEALs or of their predecessors. Instead, there are many more stories than there are frogmen.

You cannot devote your career to swimming onto enemy beaches, climbing in and out of submarines under water, navigating through dark seas in tiny SEAL delivery vehicles (SDV), or jumping out of airplanes into the dark and cold six or eight miles in the air without having some stories to tell.

Often, what SEALs do in training or in exercises is just as challenging and almost as dangerous as what they do in combat. It will be difficult for anyone to read the chapter, "A World-Class Swim," describing going in and out of a submarine through the torpedo tubes, or "Dead Before Sunrise," in which one of the survivors describes being trapped underwater in a wrecked SDV, without getting a severe, if vicarious, case of claustrophobia.

Many stories still remain untold except perhaps when frogmen gather and exchange reminiscences among themselves. Some of them are stories men would rather forget or have deliberately held in. Many of them are classified secret and will remain that way. Sometimes, it is simply that no one asks.

These, then, are some of the stories SEALs tell. I met with many of them with my tape recorder running. I then transcribed the tapes and edited the transcripts into the stories that appear in this volume. In many cases, those with whom I spoke turned out to be excellent storytellers. Their accounts flowed smoothly from tape to paper. In other cases, I edited the transcripts to make the stories easier for the reader to follow. In some cases, several men gave slightly different versions of the same event. In every case these are the words of the men themselves although I have limited the degree of profanity and obscenity to about the level you might read in your daily newspaper.

In a few chapters, I have not used the names of those who spoke with me. In other cases, in fairness, I have left out the names of some of those referred to critically by those telling the stories. If there is hyperbole in the telling of these stories, I am sure the reader will recognize it as such.

SEALs, like members of any military organization, use many acronyms in talking about their work. I have inserted parenthetical explanations for terms and phrases that may not be familiar to the reader the first time they are used and have also provided a glossary of terms.

For those readers not familiar with the history of naval special warfare, it should be noted that the American frogmen first operated in World War II. A training base was set up at Fort Pierce, Florida, in 1943 to train naval combat demolition units (NCDU) to clear obstacles during the Normandy invasion in Europe, and many of those men died in the operation in June 1944. At Omaha Beach, 31 died and 60 more were wounded, 52 percent of the 175 men involved. At Utah Beach, the toll was much lower—4 killed and 11 wounded.

Many of those trained at Fort Pierce were sent to the Pacific, where they went through another training session in a base on the Hawaiian island of Maui. Known as underwater demolition teams (UDT), they paved the way as American forces made their island-hopping way toward Japan. As noted in chapter 1, a small group of men was assigned to work under Gen. Douglas MacArthur in the southwest Pacific and they continued to use the NCDU designation. Also considered part of the frogman fraternity are those who served in the World War II Scouts and Raiders, with a mobile support team or special boat unit, in a SEAL delivery vehicle team, or as part of a naval special warfare staff or unit.

The SEALs (for sea, air, land) were formed from the UDT veterans in 1962. They were trained not so much for clearing obstacles along the shoreline, the specialty of the UDT units, as for land combat. The SEALs almost immediately became involved in what was then a small-scale counterinsurgency war in Vietnam and remained for a decade as the American role grew into a major involvement.

In 1983, the distinction between the work of the UDT units and the SEALs had become so slight that the underwater demolition teams were converted into SEAL teams.

The SEAL headquarters is now in Coronado, California, with teams based there and at Little Creek and Dam Neck, Virginia. They routinely operate overseas, often in exercises with special operations forces of other nations. The Naval Special Warfare Command is a part of the larger U.S. Special Operations Command, based at MacDill Air Force Base, Florida.

Those interviewed for this book, with the few exceptions noted above, are identified as their stories are introduced. I am grateful to all of them for taking the time to share their stories with me and with my readers.

I would also like to thank those who have been helpful in getting me together with other SEALs: Robert P. Clark and Thomas Hawkins in Virginia Beach, Virginia; Norman Olson in Panama City, Florida; and Maynard Weyers in Alexandria, Virginia. Thanks are also due to RAdm. Raymond C. Smith Jr., commander of the Naval Special Warfare Command; his deputy, Capt. Timothy Holden; Comdr. Glen King, director of public affairs for the command; and especially his stalwart aide, JO1 Mike Hayden.

I am especially thankful to Capt. Ronald E. Yeaw, who saved the records kept by the SEAL Team TWO platoons in Vietnam just as they were about to be burned and permitted me to use them to establish dates of operations and the names of those involved. Unfortunately, the similar records kept by the SEAL Team ONE platoons were apparently discarded during a housecleaning at Coronado some years ago.

Maynard Weyers, who retired as a captain after serving as commodore of Naval Special Warfare Command Group Two, in Little Creek, Virginia, and Comdr. James Eugene "Gene" Wardrobe, a member of the staff at Coronado, read the manuscript of the book, double-checking for errors, and I am grateful for their help.

This book would not have been possible without the patient understanding of my wife, Mary; the guidance provided by my agent, Mike Hamilburg, and the professional expertise of my editor, Bob Tate, and his colleagues at Presidio Press.

Introduction
SEALs: What Makes Them Tick?

The idea for the title for this volume—*Never Fight Fair!*— came to me as I was reading comments by several SEALs in *Full Mission Profile,* the professional bulletin of Naval Special Warfare. In a list of "operator principles," Lt. Comdr. T. L. Bosiljevac, then executive officer of SEAL Team EIGHT, wrote, "There is no such thing as a fair fight. Never plan a fair operation." And in another issue, Comdr. Larry W. Simmons, then commander of SEAL Team FIVE, wrote, "Be SNEAKY, STEALTHY and do the UNEXPECTED."

Because SEALs often operate in units as small as half a dozen men, and sometimes smaller, they must always plan to have the advantage against any adversary. If the enemy expects attack tomorrow, hit him tonight. If he expects you to come by sea, arrive by parachute. If he watches for you in a helicopter, arrive as a tourist in an airliner. If he expects hand-to-hand combat or a knife fight, shoot him. If he expects you to fight by some set of rules, throw the rule book away.

This is not to say that SEALs are outlaws, except perhaps for an occasional rogue warrior. They are a highly disciplined force, and they abide by the rules of engagement set down by higher authorities and the internationally recognized laws of warfare. But within those limits, they can be expected to do whatever they can think of to tilt the outcome of any encounter in their favor.

SEALs, as I learned from talking to many of them, are different from other fighting men and different, in fact, from most other men.

During interviews for this book, two veteran SEALs, Capt. Ronald E. "Ron" Yeaw, and Command Master Chief Hershel Davis, each drawing on his own experiences, reflected on those differences— what it is that makes a SEAL different from other human beings.

When Ron Yeaw went to war as assistant commander of a SEAL Team TWO platoon in Vietnam in 1967, he was an idealistic young man who fought to defend freedom and to save South Vietnam from communism. He was wounded and medevaced after putting in five months of his six-month deployment.

He went back again for a second tour as a platoon commander. This time, it was "because I really enjoyed what I was doing and hadn't gotten a full deployment the first time." He returned once more as officer in charge of all the SEAL Team TWO platoons in country and brought the last three platoons home with him as part of the U.S. withdrawal in 1971. Few SEAL officers spent as much time in the war zone as he did.

Later, he served as commanding officer of SEAL Team SIX, the elite special unit set up in 1980 to deal with terrorists and carry out the most difficult hostage-rescue operations.

During his career, he has had a rare opportunity to observe SEALs in action in a variety of roles, from death-defying peacetime exercises to actual combat, where death was a constant danger.

During an interview in his office at the Pentagon, where he is presently stationed, Captain Yeaw drew on his experience to reflect on what makes a SEAL different from other mortals:

A lot of words have been written about training, but nothing that really gets into: Who are these guys? And what makes them tick? Particularly at SIX [SEAL Team SIX] and I think in the other teams, you really see it in the enlisted and junior officers. There's ah—these guys, all they want to do is be assigned a mission.

That's what the military is for, to go play war. If you've got a war going on, the name of the game is to get involved in it. Which is the standard response of SEALs. To be a young guy in a SEAL team— you've got no business there if that's not what you want to do.

They really, really, really want to go into life-threatening, extremely dangerous situations. They want to go up to Father Death and look him right square in the face and give him a knockout punch in the eye. Father Death will rise again—he must, so they again can meet him in a true test of spirit, will, skill, determination, and guts.

They want to go to the Grim Reaper, get right up next to him and punch him out—do it three or four times a day. That's what they really want to do. And the whole unit is like that, because of what you have to go through to get into the SEALs and stay there, what you have to endure mentally and psychologically. If you really don't want to do that, then you're going to get weeded out. Our training attempts to simulate combat through a variety of techniques, whether sleep deprivation or food deprivation or sheer misery. That whole process is not just to simulate hardship in combat, it's to see who is willing to absorb all that and keep going.

The standard line is, if you gave the SEAL operators a standard psychology test to see if they're normal, they'd all flunk. The real essence is overcoming the challenge, doing what—not so much doing what very few other people can do; that is a reality—the guys don't do this because nobody else can do it. It's their psyche. It's their makeup. They feed on this. Whether it's parachute jumping or locking out of a submarine. [SEALs go in and out of a submerged submarine through a chamber originally designed to permit crew members to escape. The chamber, or lock, permits a safe transition from the sea-level pressure inside the vessel to the heavier pressure under the ocean water and keeps water from getting into the submarine.] They enjoy putting themselves in situations where, if it weren't for their individual mental stability, physical prowess, and dependence on one another, they wouldn't make it.

I've been around it for twenty-eight years and I'm not really sure I can put my finger on it. A psychiatrist or a psychologist would probably put it in book terms, but that would lose the essence. I had a psychologist there at SIX and there had been one before. I'm not sure those guys had a clue what was really going on. These guys got their psychology out of a book. The SEALs are different psychologically and they're proud of it. They have ways of looking at things and ways of putting things in perspective for themselves that would cause "normal" people to throw up their hands.

This psyche of the SEAL does a couple of things. It bonds team members together. It destroys marriages. It fractures relationships, in some cases, between SEALs and their sons or daughters if, for example, the son doesn't measure up.

You ask yourself what comes first, the chicken or the egg. I think the individual starts out with a desire to do something different. And then he gets into training and that reaches parts of his mind that tell him, no, this is nuts, but yeah, I really want to do this.

And then you get on a team where you can share this with a lot of other people who have this same motivation and then it really starts to feed and build. You go through these experiences of a night free fall and get this feeling that is off the top of the chart. It satisfies the hidden need—the itch that needs to be scratched, that you never really could put your finger on before. It feeds the SEALs' psyches to overcome the ultimate challenge, which is, of course, the challenge to your life. Overcoming that challenge provides the ultimate high and the ultimate satisfaction.

It doesn't require medals and award citations and demonstrations of public support. It doesn't require pats on the back. It ends with the accomplishment of that personal need of overcoming this extreme danger and then being able to share that with the other folks who have overcome the same challenge. The experience of being with the team, just looking at each other and saying, "We did that! And we beat it!" But once that's over, it's over.

Then you move on to the next one. "What are we going to do tomorrow? Let's cook up something so we can kick ass tomorrow." The average person is going to look at them and say, "These guys are crazy."

This is not necessarily what it takes to become a SEAL. But this is what a guy becomes. It starts as an individual desire. Then he learns the kind of situations he can get in that tap whatever portions of his brain and his gut and his heart need to be tapped for these things to come out and to get this sense of satisfaction. Then he gets in with a group and the shared experience and the camaraderie just feed it.

All he wants is to be able to display his skill on the battlefield. You can train only so much. And you can train as realistically as you want. You can try and add realism. But there is only one arena to really get the ultimate and that's when you're going against somebody who can shoot back at you. That's what every SEAL seeks.

I've talked a lot about the individual and his open and hidden motivations. There are also pressures on a SEAL from his platoon mates.

In more cases than not, the individual requires those pressures, and it is those pressures which keep him going by justifying his actions.

For example, group loyalty is extremely strong in the teams. You are either in or you are out. If you are in, you must act in the stereotyped way and support the platoon norms and mores. The environment is rough and unforgiving. It is better to die than look bad or lose. It's all for one and one for all. If you aren't in XYZ Platoon, you are shit!

Most in the organization have these pressures and they stay because of them. They want them, they need them. They require the approval, respect, and support of their small, select group. When your life will (not may) someday depend on the performance of the guy next to you in the line of march, HALO [high altitude, low opening parachute jump] formation, ambush path, lockout chamber, or vertical board and search team, you need to know that he will sacrifice himself for the group if need be. That he will accomplish the mission without regard for his personal safety. This is personal, very personal. Either you have it or you don't.

If you ever got down and had a real discussion with them [guys on active duty] they would scare you. I've been in discussion with some of them when I was in the teams, and it started to scare me a little bit. All this guy wants to do is go into combat, as though nothing else in the world matters.

This is what they are at the entry level, the first eight to ten years. Then time in the teams increases, other aspects of their lives start to open up: they get married, have kids, start relating with other people outside their own platoons. As they get older, some of this focus starts to erode. They don't remain as sharp or combat ready as they were. They get into positions of responsibility and cannot maintain the daily rigors of SEAL platoon readiness training. Instead of going to the rifle range or going jumping, they've got to do paperwork. There is a natural regression over time away from combat.

This is truer of the officers than the enlisted and it is very individualistic. Some put the training aside quickly and easily. Others hang on for as long as they can. You never really lose the desire to maintain great physical shape. It is just too ingrained, and does too many positive things for you.

The family puts a lot of pressure on. But what comes across loud and clear is duty first, family second. It takes a special woman to put up with what is nonverbally expected. A guy doesn't sit down with his girlfriend, fiancée, or newly married wife and say, "This is what I expect of you. By the way, I can leave at any time and not tell you where I am going or when I'm coming back and I just expect you to take care of the kids, the yard, the bills, and the house. I'll come back when I can and then I'll say, 'Well, I'm going to go again.'"

SEALs aren't the most brilliant in the military. Maybe the nuclear submariners are. But these guys are the sharpest. They have a mental agility and an ability to get right through to the bottom line, right now. They are not good for a lot of talk or a lot of fluff. They will get right down to it.

These guys are different from other people. They're not your average military. They're not your average human being. They're SEALs.

Hershel Davis retired in the fall of 1993 after twenty-eight years in the navy, eighteen of them in the senior enlisted rank of master chief. He served in Vietnam as a member of SEAL Team TWO in 1969. A tall, broad-shouldered man who sports a wide, ferocious-looking mustache with its tips neatly twirled, Davis still speaks with the strong midwestern accent of his native Missouri.

You want a description of Hershel Davis? He's loud and obnoxious and likes to jump and shoot. I love it. Jumping's my first love, shooting my second love.

If I was going to stand up and volunteer for something, I'd volunteer for most of the jumping and most of the shootin'. And swimming. I fancy myself as a frogman. I prefer the title "frogman." There are a lot of SEALs in the navy but damn few frogmen.

This is a high-speed, high-adrenaline, very exciting life when it's just the normal, everyday routine. It can scare the shit out of you. You brush old Death, sometimes, on a daily basis. You see the old Grim Reaper over there and he's grinnin' and taking a swipe at you with that big scythe but he's missed me, thank God. I don't seek after him but it does come with the territory. Every time you leave the ramp of an airplane in the middle of the night on a jump or you get in the water for a ship attack, you don't know if you're going to come out unscathed.

If you don't have a reputation as an operator, you don't have a reputation. The assets are those boys out there going in harm's way. The assets are those boys putting their fins on in the dark of night in the Gulf of Thailand with all the goddamn sea snakes. The assets are the boys going out with the tiger sharks charging over the reefs at you.

We were some bad son of a bitches. That's a fact of life. I will be eternally grateful, as long as I live, to the men who trained me. You cannot take Judeo-Christian principles into a goddang war when you're fighting atheistic, cold-blooded butchering bastards. You cannot. It's easy to sit back here and say this and that and the other thing and talk about atrocities and shit. But when you go in that field and you're behind enemy lines and you're outnumbered three hundred or four hundred to one, you better be one bad dude. You don't waste no time giving quarter and being a nice guy. If you're not badder than the bad guys, you lose. I ain't going to tell you no more than that.

They were terrified of us. That's why we were called "the men with green faces." They considered us evil spirits. They were afraid of us. They would not make contact with us if they could help it. Unless they had us outnumbered a zillion to one. Every time they tangled with us, they got their ass handed to them.

I was just so proud to be a part of that. I was a Stoner machine gunner in Bravo Squad. Joe Shit the ragman is who I was. I just shot my machine gun until it broke, sometimes. And then I'd try to fix it.

SEALs are gunslingers. That's what we do. SEALs are trained to hurt folks and blow things up. That's what we do. And if you don't like guns, what the sam hill are you doing in a SEAL team?

We still have SEALs just as bad as we've ever had. We're a mirror image of the civilian population. Every shittin' thing that exists in the civilian population that's not good exists in a SEAL team— certainly to a lesser degree because of our screening process. We still get a lot of turkeys. You bet your sweet bippy. We've had murderers, rapists, robbers. For a long time we had Jesus freaks. Bible thumpers. They thought I was the devil. Told me I was possessed.

If you can't accept the responsibility for taking a human life, if you've got to kneel down and pray on it—you've got to get all that done way before. I pray. I pray to the Lord to protect me and I pray that every time I fire a shot I kill something. If he would just bless me with those two things—which he has so far.

Those are the kinds of things a man should be interested in. If you are a navy SEAL, you should be in pursuit of harm's way. Avidly pursuing harm's way. If there's something going on in the world and there's going to be SEALs there, by God I want to be one of them.

The Early Days

PART ONE

Chapter 1
MacArthur's Frogmen

William L. "Bill" Dawson, retired after a twenty-five-year career as a fireman in the District of Columbia, now lives in the quiet little town of La Plata a few miles south of Washington, D.C. For two years during World War II, Dawson was one of a tiny group of sailors who helped pave the way for Gen. Douglas MacArthur's campaign northward through the western Pacific toward his return to the Philippines.

While the fabled underwater demolition teams—the "naked warriors"—grew dramatically in size until they were able to put a thousand men in the water in preparation for the landings on Okinawa and were ready to send even more if an invasion of the main Japanese islands had been necessary, the units in which Dawson served totalled a mere dozen men, under the command of Lt. Francis Riley "Frank" Kaine, who became a leader in naval special warfare into the Vietnam War era.

Dawson was seventeen years old when he enlisted in the navy on 14 April 1943 in his hometown of Washington, D.C. While most of the millions of Americans who enlisted or were drafted to serve during World War II signed on for "the duration plus six months," Dawson enlisted for a "minority cruise"—agreeing to serve until he was twenty-one years old.

From the date of his enlistment until his arrival back in Honolulu after nearly two years in the South Pacific, Dawson kept a carefully printed log of his travels. Here is the story of his experience, a view of war from the vantage point of a young and very junior enlisted man, interspersed with entries from his diary:

I joined the navy on April 14, 1943, when I was seventeen, for a minority cruise. You get out when you're twenty-one. I was waiting at Bainbridge, Maryland, to go to submarine school when two officers gave a speech about a new outfit. Another fellow and I figured this was a chance to get out of there [waiting to go to sub school].

We went up to volunteer but they told us the place was closed. They had over five hundred applicants. So we went around back, piled up some crates, climbed in the window, and got at the end of the line. We filled out the applications. The officer asked us a bunch of questions.

One question I asked was, "Is there any chance of getting in submarines after I take this training?" He didn't think so. Well, that's come to pass. The SEALs operate out of submarines all the time now.

They picked forty-two men out of the five hundred that applied and we were two of them.

There were thirty-six Seabees and forty-two of us navy men from Bainbridge, with officers from the Mine Disposal School in Washington, D.C., along with Commander Kauffman.

Draper L. Kauffman, an Annapolis graduate who served with both the French and British in the early days of World War II, before the U.S. became involved, established a bomb disposal school in Washington, D.C., in 1942 and, in June 1943, set up another school at Fort Pierce, Florida, to train members of what became naval combat demolition units and underwater demolition teams.

We went to Fort Pierce in July 1943 and went through training in July and August. We had quite a training. Commander Kauffman trained right along with us when he wasn't in Washington. The men liked him pretty well.

Down there in Florida, they weeded out some of the men in training. Many a time I wanted to lie down and cry but the sand flies and mosquitoes wouldn't let me. Lots of times when we were swimming, the sea nettles were so bad we were pulling guys out of the water. I was a lifeguard on one of the rubber boats. Guys were screaming. They were great big, hard jellyfish, thousands of them. We didn't have any rubber suits or any equipment.

Originally, we came out of Fort Pierce with five men and an officer. Quite a few of the men I trained with in the first class at Fort Pierce went to Normandy. Three units in our group stayed and went to Europe. We were lucky to go to the Pacific.

We went to California and were sent to different places. Lieutenant Kaine was our officer. Our two units—Units Two and Three—stayed together and they sent us to the southwest Pacific. [Dawson's diary lists the members of Unit Two, commanded by Kaine, as himself, William J. Armstrong, Alan H. Pierce, Dillard J. Williams, and Jonny N. Wilhide. Members of Unit Three, commanded by Lt. Lloyd G. Anderson, were Cornelius C. DeVries, Harrison G. Eskridge, Edward A. Messall, Sam Pandopony, and James D. Sandy.]

We went all through New Guinea, the Philippine Islands, and Borneo and made twelve different operations. Some of the other units went to different parts of the Pacific and merged with the UDT teams. They had eighty men and fifteen officers. We stayed individual units—five men and an officer, a total of twelve men. I don't know of any others that stayed individual units.

It's funny, now the SEALs are back to operating in squads. [A SEAL team is made up of ten platoons of sixteen men, divided into two squads of eight men. However, for certain operations, larger units are employed.]

We were called naval combat demolition units. We never became underwater demolition teams.

We went directly to the Pacific from California. We boarded ship on November 3, 1943, at Port Hueneme with two hundred tons of TNT on board. We left Hueneme on the *Frank C. Emerson,* a Liberty ship. We crossed the equator, crossed the international date line, and arrived in Brisbane [Australia] on December 26.

I didn't keep track [in the diary] of the various jobs we did because everything was top secret. But I have all the dates of where we went and when we went.

When we left Australia, we went to Milne Bay [New Guinea]. We were under a marine colonel who sent us on a thirty-six-mile hike through the jungles to keep us in training.

The first operation we went on was in the Admiralty Islands [in the

South Pacific north of New Guinea]. We went ashore with the army and slept in foxholes for a night or two. We lined the foxholes with bangalore torpedoes, if you want to believe that, to keep the sand from coming in on us. We had what we called "Washing Machine Charlie," who used to come over every night, same time, right on schedule, and drop a couple of bombs. We used to kid, if he hit us, we'd wave as we passed over the States.

Dawson made the following succinct diary entry:
   April 22. Arrived at Aitape, saw plenty of action.

Then we went over to the harbor and blasted a coral reef out of the channel coming in to the big harbor there. We had to knock the top off the coral reef so the deeper drafted ships could get in.

We were diving in about twenty feet of water with shallow diving gear.

What kind?

We had training at Fort Pierce with the Momsen lung, which was used for escaping from a submarine. When we went overseas, we had rebreathers.

The rebreathers were a canvas rig that came down over your head, front, and back, with a full face mask. It was a self-contained breathing apparatus. It had a tank of oxygen and a tank of lime. The lime would help repurify the air. You would give yourself a shot of oxygen every so often as you needed it. We could stay down half an hour, three quarters of an hour, depending on how hard you were breathing.

We also had a mask and hand pump. They could pump air to you from the surface. We used those a couple of times.

We used the rebreathers for diving on those coral reefs in the Admiralty Islands. The coral reef dropped off to sixty fathoms on both sides. Looking down, it got pretty dark down there. The current, coming in and out of the inlet, would kind of move you over to the edge once in a while. It would shake you up a little bit.

We were using a lot of bangalore torpedoes, in boxes. And the rubber hose. We used that to more or less blow everything even. We set like four tons a shot. We'd get these boxes laid on the coral reef and we could step from box to box to keep from sinking into the coral.

A couple of times, I must have been getting low on oxygen, I thought

I saw different things under the water, like coral snakes and rays swimming around. But I couldn't swear to it.

Did you see sharks when swimming with lungs?

Not too much. But there were sharks in the water. We threw grenades and everything else trying to run them off. In the water, you could see a hundred feet. It was beautiful, with the coral reef and the tropical fish. When we got to the Philippines, it started getting murky and hard to see.

I never worried too much about what was in the water, for some reason. We knew there were sharks and octopus and stingrays or manta rays, because we'd see 'em. I never gave too much thought about sharks bothering us. We were very fortunate.

We were swimming off the side of the ship one day. The current was pretty swift. This officer came out and had a pretty blue elastic bathing suit on.

I said, "Why don't you go in?"

He said, "I can't swim."

I said, "Hell, don't worry about it. We'll pull you out."

He dove over and he couldn't swim a stroke. I looked at this other fellow and we both went in at the same time, one on each side. We had a hell of a time getting back to the ship with that current. We got him out and he never so much as thanked us. I don't know what the hell he was thinking about but he took us at our word.

One of our shots didn't go off one day. We went out in the rubber boat. I was one of the better divers, the swimmers. So they gave me the job of making a straight dive with a rope line to go down and wrap the rope around the explosive hose so we could pull it up and recap it. Well, just before I went off the boat, this sea snake came by. He was as big around as the rubber hose and half as long. They were thirty-foot sections if I remember right. He was about half as long as that hose. I looked at that snake and the guys looked at me and I looked at them. Well, I went off and got it done, but I wasn't feeling too easy about it.

We laid our explosive on the coral reef and blew two or three shots in the couple—two or three—days we were out there.

We killed a mess of jewfish [a name given to several species of very large fish found in warm seas]. The first blast we set off, we killed a small one. We took it in to the army. They told us they would take all of them we could get because they were good eating.

So we set off about a four-ton blast. And we killed about a dozen of these jewfish. I understand they are deep sea fish. They looked like a regular scale fish that someone had stuck an air hose in and blew them up. We took three of them in to the beach, lowered the ramp on the landing craft, and pulled them in.

They took an army truck, with an A-frame hoist on the back, and it pulled one of them to the top of the frame. His tail was still on the ground. They told us they fed over nine hundred men with that one fish.

The other two fed the whole Seabee battalion. Everyone was eating rations [packaged C- or K-rations similar to today's meals, ready-to-eat (MREs)]. Those boys were glad to get that fresh fish!

Was your landing opposed by the Japanese?

The Japs still had the island but the landing itself wasn't that bad. There was fighting going on but we were fortunate none of us got hurt.

Did you reconnoiter the beach before the landing?

No. We just went in on the beach in an LST [landing ship, tank]. Later on, we did recon on different jobs.

Did the army know what you were supposed to be doing?

Not really. We operated under secret orders for damn near two years. I guess only the top brass really knew who we were and what our job was supposed to be. Because when we talked to people, they didn't know what we were or who we were or anything else. It was kept secret pretty well.

Reportedly, Kaine was called to brief General MacArthur personally.

Kaine was called before most of our ops. Where he went and who he went to see, I couldn't tell you. Then he'd come back and he had our orders.

What was your understanding of your job?

We knew exactly what we were supposed to do from our training in Florida. Our training covered disposing of all obstacles, sand bars, or anything like that. We even had training in mines and booby traps, disassembling or trying to locate them.

All we wore was trunks and we did have these canvas jungle boots. They even did away with those later on. They had rubber soles. We used them for diving because the coral would cut you. If it was real bad coral, we would wear our pants and tuck 'em in. Sometimes you'd sink in coral up to your knees, laying explosives. The main thing was trunks, boots, and a knife strapped to us was all we had.

We actually didn't run into too many obstacles in the water other than sand bars and coral reefs until later on in the Philippines and Borneo. We ran into obstacles in Borneo and worked with some of the Australian demolition teams.

From the Admiralty Islands, the frogmen moved west to the island of Biak in what is now Indonesia in LCI-448, a large landing ship. The diary records frequent air raids:

May 27. Arrived Biak, 2 air raids, 5 Jap planes.

May 28. Biak, 2 air raids. One Billy Mitchel.

May 29. Biak, 2 air raids, 2 Jap planes, L.C.I. 448 got one.

May 30. Biak, 2 air raids, 1 Jap plane shot down.

May 31. Biak, 2 air raids, 2 Jap planes shot down.

June 1. Finished Blasting Channel, 2 air raids, bombing at night.

June 2. Three air raids, 10 planes shot down, "Jap," L.C.I. 448 got one.

June 3. 2 air raids, dive bombers. Jest missed can. One man killed.

June 4. Jap task force headed this way, Biak, two air raids, night bombing, our force arrived.

June 5. 2 air raids, early morning bombing. Left Biak, ship slightly damaged.

Did you ever see MacArthur?

I took a picture of him and his crew. But when I changed my scrapbook, that picture got away from me.

We were in the Philippines before he was. We went in three or four days before D day and made a recon of the beach, checked the depth of the water.

The frogmen left Hollandia 13 October in a 130-ship convoy, headed toward the Philippines. The diary records the landing there:

Oct. 20. Made reconnaissance of beach. Arrived in San Pedro Bay at dawn, landing made on Leyte, L.C.I. 71 and 72 hit from beach. Philippines.

We were walking up the damn beach after one of our recons—on Leyte—and firing started. Christ, I buried my nose in the sand, I'll tell you. I wanted to dig a hole. When the army hit the beach, they passed by all these pillboxes. And the Japs were still in them. They just went right by them and the Japs opened up. We were walking down the beach after checking the depth of the water. This was about the same time they hit the beach. We were in the water taking soundings and the army hit the beach and we came up out of the water and started walking up the beach and they started shooting.

Did the Japanese fire at you while you were in the water?

Occasionally. There were places where we went in with explosives on our rubber boats—explosive hose, bangalore torpedoes—and snipers fired at us. You could only stay underwater so long. Sometimes we actually hid behind a rubber boat of explosives. There was nowhere else to hide, I tell you.

One operation we were supposed to go on in the Philippines when they were getting ready to invade Manila. We were supposed to take a PT boat down one night. They picked six of us out. We were all ready to go. This PT boat was going to take us in to the harbor in Manila and drop us off. There were some pontoons and cables and buoys and they thought maybe it was a submarine net. And we were going to blow the pontoons and such, drop the cable on the bottom, if that's what it was.

But the PT boat we were supposed to go on made a run on the beach earlier and got all shot up. So they canceled that trip for us.

Were you attacked by enemy planes?

We were attacked a number of times by planes, in convoys and in the harbors, especially in the Philippines. When we got up to the Philippines—all through the Philippines—the Jap suicide planes, the kamikaze, they'd come in and pick out the biggest ship and head straight for it. We knocked a few of them out of the air. I had the job of painting them on the conning tower when we shot a plane down.

The APD [a destroyer converted for use as a small troop carrier] we were on going to Lingayen Gulf had three Jap planes come in, using us as a shield. They came in real low on the water. Just before they got to us, they had to go up to go over us. They were trying to get to the carriers, the bigger ships. They weren't interested in the guys running on the sides of the convoy, like us. But we shot all three of them down and one of them almost got us, almost crash-dived us. In Lingayen Gulf, they were just shooting them down all over the place.

Dawson's diary records a hectic period when the American ships were battered by air attacks, gunfire from the shore, and typhoons:

Oct. 24. One air raid after another, (L.C.I. 1065 sunk.) (L.C.I. 65 crashed by plane.) (Tug sunk.) 29 Jap planes shot down. Think we got one.

Oct. 26. Air raids all day. Bombing and strafing. Big naval battle.

Oct. 27. Seven air raids. Liberty hit by crashdive. Total Jap planes to date 200.

Oct. 29. Three air raids at dawn. A typhoon started at 2330.

Oct. 30. What a night. Typhoon eased off at 0500.

Nov. 3. Air raids all night long. 10 planes shot down.

Nov. 4. Air raid in morning. A P.T. hit.

Nov. 8. Typhoon started 1200.

Nov. 9. Typhoon quit 0200. We were nearly on the beach.

Nov. 12. Three air raids. 7 ships hit, 4 liberties, 2 L.C.I. one L.S.T. 12 Japs shot down.

Nov. 14. Three air raids. 9 Japs shot down. Blasted P.B.Y.

Nov. 16. Have been blasting the last few days for P.B.Y. slip. [The PBY was a flying boat.] 9 Japs shot down the 14th.

We heard some of the pilots were chained in the cockpit. You really don't know. They'd just fly over and dive straight into a ship.

Did you lose any members of your two units?

No, we were very fortunate. We got cut by coral a couple of times. Some of the fellows got infected pretty bad. It laid 'em up for a few weeks.

We were training one night in New Guinea, practicing for an invasion. We were diving at night with shallow water diving gear. We used to put rubbers [condoms] over flashlights to waterproof them. When we were underwater, we'd put them under your arm so you could use both hands to tie knots in your primacord [explosive cord that sets off the explosives].

One man's light didn't move. We got suspicious after a while. So Kaine and I dove in and pulled him out and got him up on the beach and pulled his mask off. He looked like he had seen a ghost and it froze on his face. It took about twenty-four hours before the doctor brought him around. He was out colder than hell. We still don't know what it was—lack of oxygen, just froze up from fear, what it was.

Did you have any contact with the underwater demolition teams?

I didn't even know they were around until we got to Borneo. Then one of the teams did come over, in June 1945. I think it was UDT Thirteen, but I'm not sure of it. [Unit histories show that both UDT Eleven and UDT Eighteen operated in that area in June 1945.] They more or less relieved us so we could go home.

They tried to send us to Maui because they hadn't invaded Japan yet. Fortunately, we had been over there for two years and deserved our leave so they sent us back home. We were on thirty days' leave when the war ended.

Chapter 2
UDT Sixteen: A Bum Rap?

If the legend is true, most navy frogmen would just as soon forget about what happened to Underwater Demolition Team Sixteen during the battle of Okinawa in World War II.

According to the legend, the team broke and swam back out to sea, leaving a row of obstacles to be cleared by members of UDT Eleven the following day.

But, while the legend has some basis in fact, the truth of what happened on 30 March 1945 is a more complex story.

The basic facts are agreed upon.

UDT Sixteen was one of three UDT units recruited directly from the Pacific amphibious forces as the navy carried out its island-hopping strategy that was expected to culminate in a bloody invasion of the Japanese home islands. Earlier UDT units had been formed from new recruits and members of the Seabee construction battalions.

UDT Sixteen began its training at Maui in the Hawaiian Islands on 1 November 1944 and left Maui for Okinawa on 13 February 1945—a remarkably short period of time compared with the year or more that it now takes a young man to qualify as a SEAL.

Arriving off Okinawa on 23 March, the frogmen began a reconnaissance of three beaches designated Red Three, Blue One, and Blue Two. They found a maze of obstacles. One account tells of twelve hundred posts, each six feet high and eight inches in diameter, that had been hammered into the reef by the Japanese about forty yards out from the high-water mark. One participant remembers, instead, rows of metal tetrahedrons made of lengths of steel welded together.

During the days immediately preceding the invasion, a thousand frogmen were in the water at one time or another. Some were assigned to beaches where there would be no landings, as a diversion. But the three beaches where UDT Sixteen and UDT Eleven had the responsibility for clearing the way were the real thing: this is where the troops would storm ashore. If the obstacles remained standing, they would be trapped at the reef line.

Each team sent more than eighty officers and men in toward the beach. They swam toward the obstacles, each burdened by three to five packs of explosives. Hiding behind the posts and swimming underwater from post to post, they placed the explosives, linking them by explosive cord.

To protect the swimmers, the navy provided an awesome barrage of gunfire from 4 landing craft, 3 destroyers, 2 aircraft carriers, and 3 battleships.

"Fire support was very satisfactory and it kept the Nips well in their holes. . . ." the official history of UDT Eleven reports. "The air support was very satisfactory and contributed much in keeping the enemy fire to a minimum."

When the explosives were triggered, the beaches where UDT Eleven had the responsibility erupted in a sheet of water, torn pieces of the obstacles, chunks of coral, and bits of fish.

But, in the area where UDT Sixteen had worked, there was silence. The official history of UDT Sixteen says nothing about this. It simply states: "Working with Team Eleven, placed charges and cleared the beaches."

Word went around that the reason for the failure of the charges to explode on UDT Sixteen's beaches was that, after one of its members had been killed, the team members abandoned the job and swam out to sea.

Draper L. Kauffman, who had set up the school for training frogmen at Fort Pierce, Florida, two years earlier, watched as one section of the beach exploded but the other didn't. In an oral history interview years later, he recalled watching as one whole beach failed to go:

It had been badly done. The southern beaches went beautifully. We had one man killed by a sniper in the morning operation, but very little fire. We did have some and, of course, we were in there a long time. This was not a quick job.

The next day I really made a group of enemies because I refused to send back the team that had botched the job to fix it. Naturally, they wanted very much to go in, but I didn't dare take a chance because this was almost our last opportunity. I sent my best team back in and they did a very fine job.

The UDT Eleven history gives this version of events on the day after the failure to clear obstacles on one section of the beach:

On 31 March, the team received word that "the job must be done." Four boats with eighty-nine officers and men moved toward the obstacle line. Landing craft sailed up and down, as close in as they could come, hammering the shore with gunfire. But this failed to stifle the Japanese marksmen.

The commanding officer UDT Eleven called commander UDT teams requesting highly intensified fire support 100 to 500 yards inland along the entire operational area. For the next 20 minutes, the area specified was covered by the heaviest supporting fire imaginable. Enemy fire diminished considerably. One 5-inch projectile was observed to hit at the root of a tree. The tree broke off about halfway up the trunk and a body was seen blown from the upper branches.

In this operation over 1,000 charges were carried to the obstacles, all were placed and some 50 or more others were salvaged from the previous day's work and used. It is estimated over 1,000 obstacles were demolished in this operation. Combined with the previous day's result, it appeared that UDT Eleven had cleared some 1,300 yards of beach of nearly 1,400 obstacles. There were no casualties, which seems miraculous. Either the Nips were poor shots or it can be accredited to the defensive measures used by the swimmers.

John A. Devine, who now lives in Saint James, New York, has a different recollection of what happened in those two days before the

Okinawa invasion. Devine, who retired from the navy in 1959 as a chief warrant officer, was a first class petty officer, the senior enlisted man in one of the UDT Sixteen platoons at Okinawa. This is his account of what happened:

It has been reported that UDT Sixteen did not do their job and were observed swimming out from the beach before their job was completed. This is entirely untrue. What really happened, I suspect, was that one man was observed swimming out from the beach. This was the one man that was killed from UDT Sixteen—Coxswain Frank Lynch.

I was his platoon leader and, as I had all the obstacles on my section of the beach loaded with explosives and this one man still had explosive left, I sent him to the platoon operating on my right flank to use up his explosives with them. After he used his explosives, he was directed to report back to me.

After we were picked up and I reported him missing, the leader of the other platoon told me that he had seen Lynch swimming out to the pickup line instead of reporting back to me. He said that, some time later, one of our five-inch shells landed short. He looked out to see where it landed and he said it appeared to land in the approximate location where the swimmer would be.

We didn't know the swimmer was killed until the next morning (D day) when we received word that his body was found on the beach with a hole in his forehead.

Team Eleven's contention that Team Sixteen didn't complete its job because of sorrow over one of its men being killed doesn't hold up. It was twenty-four hours later before we knew he had been killed.

I don't know if the reason the obstacles on Team Sixteen's portion of the beach were not blown was ever established. My own suspicion is that the trunk line was cut by wave action or, possibly, was not properly connected to the main trunk line.

One fact that has not been mentioned is that approximately fifteen men and a few officers from our team volunteered to swim back in that afternoon, to wipe the remaining obstacles out.

I was one of the men that swam back in, after the tide had receded and without any gunfire support. With the Japanese firing at us, we crawled on our bellies across the coral to get to the obstacles. We did blow some of them out but again left some still standing—for whatever reason, only God knows.

Those were the obstacles that UDT Eleven went in and destroyed.

I've heard the Team Sixteen record showed that five officers from Team Sixteen received the Silver Star medal and fifteen enlisted men were awarded the Bronze Star.

I was a member of Team Sixteen from the day of commissioning upon completion of training at Maui until the day of decommissioning at Oceanside, California, and I don't remember any man from Team Sixteen receiving any awards.

Robert Fisher, a retired judge of the New York Supreme Court, has a somewhat different recollection of those events of half a century ago. Fisher, who lives in a suburb of Binghamton, New York, was then a lieutenant junior grade and the executive officer of UDT Sixteen.

I was already a lawyer, working for a Wall Street firm, when the war started. I was 4-F because of some injuries from playing football in college but a doctor told me how to get around that and I was able to join the navy.

I became executive officer of UDT Sixteen when it was formed at Maui. The CO was a fellow named Eddie Mitchell. He could swim—but not very far—so he pretty much let me run the team.

The team was made up of volunteers from the fleet. When we got their records, we could see that most of them weren't volunteering for UDT. They were volunteering off the ship they were on because they were in trouble. Some of them had had deck court-martials.

They were tough kids. But they are the kind of guys you want when the going gets tough. We instilled a sense of pride in them. They were a tough, proud outfit.

When we got to Okinawa, we did a reconnaissance. It was pretty much pro forma, nothing exciting although there were some people shooting at us. Then we were set to go in the next day and blow the obstacles.

We asked for firepower support and we got everything except the atom bomb. We would have asked for that, too, if we knew about it.

The Japanese had put tetrahedrons in the water. These were made of steel rails, welded together, so three rails stuck up in the air. If a boat hit one, it would hang up.

The guys put their packs [of explosives] on and we went in. I went with them. It's pretty safe, if you dare admit it. One of the things is that only your head is showing. And then you can get under the water. We had it much better than the marines.

We put on the explosives, we put on the primacord, and then we pulled the fuse and nothing happened.

That afternoon I asked for volunteers to go back in to finish the job. The ships that were providing us cover were pulling out and the tide was going out. I had to ask them to go in bare ass with a receding tide. Everyone except one man volunteered. I took fourteen guys.

We went back in, hooked it up, and blew it. We got it cleared this time.

The history of UDT Eleven says they had to go in the next day to clear the obstacles.

If UDT Eleven went in the next day, it was unbeknownst to me. I went on a destroyer that morning and they sent me over by breeches buoy to an amphibious ship to brief the commander of the 6th Marine Division. I met the CO of the division and told him about the beach, what equipment he could use, what the terrain was like. I never heard that UDT Eleven went back in. We were the ones that went back in and we finally got it to work.

Did you find out why the explosives didn't go off the first time?

We had some five-inch fire from a destroyer and some of those shots were short. I believe one of those shorts cut the line and also killed the Lynch kid.

Draper Kauffman says in his oral history that he had to send in another team to finish your job. Did he ever tell you he was unhappy?

No.

After Okinawa, UDT Sixteen was sent back to Oceanside, California, while other teams continued operations in the Pacific. Did you feel that the team was in some sort of disgrace?

I can't think of anything that would make me think that. We went to Oceanside to prepare for the invasion of Kyushu [the southernmost of the major Japanese home islands]. We knew about the cold water up there and we tested some rubber suits but they were no good.

The UDT Sixteen history says medals were awarded to members of the team after Okinawa. Did you receive one?

After the war, I got some sort of medal. The recruiting officer called me up and told me to come down and get it.

Did you go back to the Wall Street firm after the war?

No, I came home and hung up my shingle. When we were there in Okinawa with our butts showing, the second time we went in, I was thinking: How did I get in this position? I decided when I went back home, I'd do something about the process.

I ran for district attorney. I served as a special prosecutor for both Governors [Averell] Harriman and [Nelson] Rockefeller and I started an organized crime task force. And I'm retired now after serving on the state supreme court. I trace it all back to that day at Okinawa fifty years ago.

Chapter 3
Fishnets in Korea

James L. "Gator" Parks became a frogman nearly half a century ago and then spent his entire career in naval special warfare. Now retired, he lives in Panama City, Florida, and works at the Naval Coastal Warfare Center, improving the SEAL delivery vehicles (SDVs) used to transport today's underwater warriors.

A round-faced man with a full head of silvery blond hair, Parks still speaks with the soft accent of his native Texas. He was in training at Coronado, California, when the Korean War broke out and he soon found himself in hostile waters off the North Korean coast. This is his story of those early days:

I lived on a farm in Texas outside of Dallas. We grew peanuts. I decided early on in life that wasn't a real good way to make a livin'. I joined the navy when I was seventeen. That was in January of '48.

I went from boot camp to the Philippines for two years. Subic Bay and the Philippines was a terrible place, particularly for a young man. I think they had three bars in Olongapo at that time and unless you were twenty-one—and I was far from that—they wouldn't let you within a mile of it. There wasn't much to do except drink Red Cap ale at the EM club, which gets old.

Every month when they came out with this list of schools on the bulletin board, I would go put in for all of them. I rotated on a normal rotation. When I got back to San Francisco for reassignment they said I had been selected to go to the underwater demolition team. Nobody knew where it was at. They were going to send me to Fort Pierce, Florida, which had been closed down for a number of years.

Finally somebody heard about them having one in Coronado and I went there. Training was not under a formalized training unit as it is now. We had interteam training. They would hold people in the team until they had enough to have a training class. So I worked with the team for perhaps six months before we started training. That was really kind of a leg up.

There was very little in academics but you certainly did need a strong back. The folks putting you through were folks that you knew and they were trying to see how bad they could hurt you. And even for an eighteen year old, that was pretty bad.

Did you have Hell Week then?

I don't remember much about Hell Week. It doesn't stand out as something all that awful to me. But we went to San Clemente Island [off the California coast] in the winter. I was cold when I got there and we stayed about five weeks and I continued to get colder all the time I was there. That was the most miserable month of my life, no question. There was no hot food. There was no hot shower. You lived in pup tents. That was long before the days of wet suits. We would have dawn recons every morning. In late evening, we would put demolition charges on obstacles and blow 'em.

We wore dry suits when it was cold enough. But most of us didn't wear anything to keep warm. I found these old black wool diving underwear were pretty good. After I finally got a wet suit, I wouldn't let it out of my sight for years.

In June 1950, the Korean War started. Detachments from UDT One and Three went before us. We were still in training. As soon as we were finished—I think it was about July—we caught up with Team Three in Japan. In that class, there were about twenty of us left. We started with a whole bunch of people. Most of 'em dropped out right away.

I was in the teams for five or six years before I wasn't a new guy. It was a pretty clannish thing, pretty hard to break in. Most of them were from World War II. They were very different from the people in the teams today. They were more hell raisers. I suspect if you'd transplant all of us as young men into the teams today, they'd kick us all out in a week or ten days.

After training with the team, we started doing recons up in Korea. One of the things I remember most about is the fishnet cutting. In your last book, you gave that mostly to Team One. But Team Three probably did the vast majority of the net cutting.

As background for Parks's recollections, the official histories of Teams One and Three, which later became UDT Eleven and Twelve, give these accounts of their operations in Korea:

Members of Team Three made the first UDT reconnaissance in the Korean War on a beach beside the fishing village of P'ohang in order to determine if reinforcements could be landed. Shortly after this, small amphibious raiding parties were organized to harass the enemy by using demolitions at strategic points along his supply route. Combined with a detachment of marines, these raider groups were highly successful in penetrating the enemy's defenses. In September, UDT Three reconned the mud flats at Inch'on and buoyed the fast-flowing channel there. A week after the highly successful Inch'on landing, the team was employed as swimmer-raiders off the beach of Katsupoai-po where heavy enemy resistance was encountered. Did mine search and clearance in October and November for landings at Wonsan and Chinnampo.

By December 1950, UN troops were being redeployed. In the ensuing withdrawal, UDT Three demolished the dock area of Hungnam Harbor rather than leave it for the Chinese reds to use. UDT operations for the rest of the Korean conflict consisted mainly of raids behind the enemy's lines. . . .

Command history of UDT One:

Within a week after setting up base at Camp McGill in Japan, Team One combined forces with a detachment of U.S. Marines to form a raider group whose mission was to disrupt enemy logistics supplying the troops pressuring the UN toehold at Pusan, by destroying tunnels and bridges of coastal railroads and highways, a task at which they were highly successful. Next for UDT One came the familiar job of reconning beaches, including the mud flats at Inch'on, where the masterful amphibious landing occurred in mid-September, and where Team One men served as assault wave guides. During the mop-up of the operation, UDT One was called upon to set buoys, conduct bomb and mine disposal ops, assist in salvage work, and demolish hazardous wrecks.

Parks's account continues:

We had some excitement, we got shot at a couple of times. It was in that period that we lost the only two people we lost in Korea to hostile action. Fry and Satterfield. They were both in Team One. Fry I went through training with. Satterfield had been around for quite a while. As far as I know they were the only two deaths in Korea from hostile fire.

They were on a—this is secondhand, I guess, but it's true. They were on a beach. They were up talking to these Koreans. It was just an administrative recon. When they turned and went back to the boat, these people they had been talking to went up behind the dune line and broke out some automatic weapons and started shooting at them in the water.

Fry was getting in the boat when he got hit and they just got terrible lucky with Satterfield, hit him right in the head while he was swimming. That's really rare that that can happen.

They were not in my team and they were at another place. They were getting water depth in to the beach. UDT's primary mission in those days was from the three fathom curve in. We would gather information for a landing. That's primarily what they were doing. We did a god-awful amount of recon. We did both sides of the peninsula.

Early on in the war, we were doing raids because we were the only people they had. We would go in and blow up "radar sites." I went on a couple of those and I never saw a radar site. The intelligence was just terrible. Both raids that I went in on, there was just a farmhouse and a barn they thought was a radar installation. There wasn't nothing there.

Did you run into the North Koreans?

I think we thought we had a problem one night but I think we were shooting at ourselves. One time we did take some pretty heavy fire. We were in rubber boats. That caused a lot of people to go swimming in the cold water. We swam from the rubber boats on in. We got up on the beach and I think we ended up getting that guy or a couple of them. They brought in the thirty-six-foot landing craft we used and it had .30-caliber guns on it. That quieted it down pretty quick.

Did you ever blow up tunnels?

I only know of one time our team blew up a tunnel. There were some people got shot that night.

That was fairly effective, blowing tunnels. I think Team One did quite a lot of that, trying to knock a big bunch of rocks down in the tunnel. It takes a hell of a lot of demolition to do anything to a rock tunnel, as we found out.

We would just ride an APD up to Korea from Japan. Then when we got through we went back to Japan, to Camp McGill. One of our room boys was actually a kamikaze pilot. Obviously he never flew a mission. But he was a well-educated young man, very interesting to talk to. We also met a submarine commander who later became vice chief of staff of the Japanese navy. He had some real good sea stories.

It wasn't all that much of a shooting war for us in Korea. Consequently, I guess most of us thought that was a lot of fun. Most of us that stayed around learned it wasn't near that much fun when the real shootin' started.

You mentioned cutting fishnets. What did you do?

We were up north pretty far when we were doing the fishnets. We were up near the Soviet border and back down. In the evening—we had our schedule set up where we would work every night—we would go in in rubber boats. Generally we would leave the boats out a way from where the nets were. We would leave the rubber boats out where they wouldn't be so easily spotted and swim on in. We would have big bolt cutters and we would cut the top line, which would be a wire rope. We would cut that wire rope in as many places as we could. Then you'd take your knife and cut the rest of the netting that was there and try to leave it so it would be very difficult to repair.

They were using those nets to catch fish to feed troops with and that was what we were trying to curtail. We got a lot of bad publicity from the [North] Koreans because we were "criminals," coming in and cutting their fishnets and starving their people. It was rumored they even had rewards out for us, but I don't know that to be a fact.

We would do this all up and down the coast of North Korea. I think we were very effective. We cut a lot of fishnets up, I know that. We went in one night and sank some sampans, too, with demolition charges. None of that stuff seemed to be guarded to any extent at all. You could actually see people up on the beach. Either we were doing our job pretty well or they weren't paying much attention.

Another thing we did a lot of was take South Koreans up north and land them on the beach [behind enemy lines]. I often wondered what ever happened to all them people. There were a lot of folks. Probably half were North Korean to begin with.

After the Inch'on landing on 15 September 1950, United Nations forces under Gen. Douglas MacArthur recaptured Seoul, occupied the North Korean capital of P'yongyang and the port city of Wonsan and drove north nearly to the Chinese border. On 26 October, the Chinese entered the war, forcing some of MacArthur's forces to evacuate from Wonsan and others to retreat back nearly to Seoul.

The other exciting thing we did was in Wonsan Harbor. They had a lot of mines. The *Pirate* and the *Pledge,* two minesweepers, were sunk there. They wanted us to be human minesweepers. We would line up abreast in the channel and swim the channel every day, which was a long channel. And we never failed to find contact mines in it. Evidently they were bringing them out under sampans at night. We blew up a lot of mines. We'd just take a half-pound block and strap it under the mine and set it off. Rarely did the mine itself go off. It would just blow a hole in it and sink it.

By the way, these mines were U.S. mines, every one of them. Every one that I saw. They had probably gotten them out of China after World War II.

The old contact mines had lead horns on them with an acid vial inside. When you broke the horn, it would allow that acid to run down into a battery and cause an electric current and it would go off. Over these lead horns they had protectors that had soluble washers in them. They were supposed to come off in a day or so after you planted them.

Well, you know how you get, around anything like that. You get pretty brave after a while. We'd been working on these things for a couple of weeks. Generally, we would just loop a loop around a horn on each side of it for the half-pound pack [of explosives]. Well, I wasn't much of a mine man. At the time I didn't know anything about these protectors on the horns. I reached up and put the loop over the horn and one of those things hadn't come off. But as soon as I touched it, it shot way up out of the water. That caused several of the gray hairs I still have.

Weren't you concerned about breaking the horns?
They're not that easy to break. They're fairly heavy-duty.
How did you find the mines?
Just swim with a face mask. We'd line up abreast, use a whole team, about sixty people out there in the water. We did it every day for a month or so that they kept us there. They'd plant at night, we'd sweep in the daytime.

One of the strangest things, most profound things, I've ever witnessed was a big city without any people in it. It must have been Wonsan. I was a third class then. They didn't entrust me with a lot of information. Anyway, this huge city. There was absolutely nothing there. The animals were even gone. It was really an eerie thing. We came in there and evidently they moved out in anticipation of our landing.

Was there fighting during the landing there?
It was a pretty well secured area. There were no hostilities right on the beach. When we came out of there, when the Chinese came in, we pulled out of the same area. They were pursued pretty heavily. I was in the area but I wasn't on the beach. I was on an APD, just standing by, mainly doing lifeguard duty at that time.

How long were you out there during the Korean War?
Team One and Team Three were out there together for the first year of the war. And then they sent Team One back and six months later they sent Team One out and rotated us back. We were there when the war ended.

Chapter 4
The Iceberg Caper

Jack "Blackjack" Macione served briefly as a member of the underwater demolition teams before becoming a SEAL in the early 1960s. He recalled those early days during an interview at his home in Virginia Beach, Virginia:

When I got through training, I went to Tule, Greenland. I went up to Tule as a frogman—UDT—before I got "volunteered" as a SEAL. Not many people got to make that trip. Every year two or three guys go up there to put the Pinelli system around the pier.

The Pinelli system was a hose with a lot of holes in it. You would put it around the pier and air would come out and keep the ice from forming. That pier was their lifeblood. Ice breakers would bring the ships in but they had to tie up at that pier.

We were there a few weeks and this big berg breaks off the glacier and bottoms out right off the head of the pier. It stopped the ships from making their turns at the pier.

So the captain of the base asks us if we can go out and blow it up. There's not much in the demolition manuals on ice demolition. You'd be lucky to find a page and a half.

We got a rubber boat and we put three or four hundred pounds of explosives in it. We started paddling out to this berg. The whole base showed up to watch this happen. The berg was beautiful. It had two big pinnacles, with a natural bridge of ice connecting them.

This thing is big, a city block. And it was dangerous. These things will float around, they'll melt, the water density will change, and they'll roll over.

As we were coming up to the berg a piece the size of Wisconsin breaks off of it and this frigging ten-foot wave comes at us.

So finally we get up on the berg, right under the natural bridge. We put two or three hundred pounds of explosives in place. We back off, we fire the damn thing electrically. There's a big explosion, a lot of fire. We go back. There's a little hole I couldn't even lie in, it was so shallow.

So we take forty pounds each. We dive down sixty feet. It had bottomed out but there was a two-foot space underneath. It was rolling. It could squash you like a bug.

I motion: We've got to get the explosives in there. So my dive buddy is like this: big eyes. We put the explosives in as far as we can. We actually got them in maybe thirty feet. It was hairy.

We swam back out, got up on our rubber boat, and backed off. We fire the charge. We sit there. Nothing happens.

Then the berg crumbles and breaks apart. These people on shore all cheer.

While we were there, we saw there was a ridge between this village and the sea. The only time the people could get their boats in or out was at high tide. I was sitting on that ridge. The ice breaker was about a hundred yards away. Their Fathometer was off the scale. It was something like two thousand fathoms. That ridge was the top of a mountain.

We blew a slot about ten feet wide in that ridge. That meant these Eskimos could take their boats out anytime they wanted to. Their whole lives changed. They could get their boats in and out.

Well, if you're really, really good to an Eskimo, he'll give you his wife. But if you're incredibly good, he'll give you his dogs. All they wanted to do was give us their dogs. We didn't take them and they were offended. I believe somewhere in Eskimo lore, we're now in it.

Chapter 5
Big War in a Small Place

In April 1965, President Lyndon Johnson sent the army's 82d Airborne Division and U.S. Marines to the Dominican Republic to help quell a rebellion against the government of the small Caribbean nation. A small unit of the newly formed SEALs, under the command of Lt. "Blackjack" Macione, accompanied them. Macione's story of the Dominican Republic operation begins shortly before members of SEAL Team TWO left their base in Little Creek, Virginia:

I was thumbing through a *Popular Mechanics* magazine and I saw this passive night vision scope, supposedly being tested at Aberdeen [the army's Aberdeen Proving Ground north of Baltimore]. I called Aberdeen and asked if we could try it for a few days. They were more than happy to get it into the hands of an operator.

We took it to the drive-in movie, looked in other people's cars. It was phenomenal. I grabbed the Starlight Scope and off we went to the Dominican Republic.

There were government forces on one side, rebels on the other. The United Nations—predominantly the U.S.—had run a corridor between them. It was only a couple of blocks wide. We were supposed to keep the two forces apart.

The rebels were sandbagging in weapons during the day and hiding them near shutters and cupolas on buildings in the town. Some of the Americans were on rooftops at night, having a cigarette and walking around. The rebels would go up where they had hidden the weapons and fire off some shots. If I remember right, they had killed three and put the eye out on a fourth.

So the area commander asked if I could do something about it. I said, "Funny you should mention it but we've got a brand-new thing that might do it."

So Bruhmuller [BM1 William N. Bruhmuller II] or another guy was doing the shooting and I was doing the spotting. We had zeroed in on a cupola that was out maybe one hundred yards. Every night, almost at midnight, someone had fired off random shots and done the damage they did. We took a peek at that cupola and almost at the stroke of midnight the shutters opened up and there was a guy standing with his rifle. And whoever fired, that guy died of surprise. He also died of a bullet in the head. It was pitch-black—pitch-black—and he nailed him.

We were holed up in an automotive place, a new car showroom. We found a manikin and rigged him up on the roof with a set of pulleys and pulled him across the roof all night. If they took any shots, we'd nail the guy with the Starlight Scope. No more problems.

Another time we're camped in the jungle in a big tent. The Special Forces like to sleep in a pup tent on the ground. The hell with that. We took a case of K-bar knives. They'll get you anything.

I think it was Rudy Boesch [for many years the command master chief of SEAL Team TWO and higher commands]—I said, "Take a case of K-bars and get us some creature comforts."

Rudy comes back. He's got racks, mattresses, sheets, bookcases. He's got an air conditioner, a reefer, tables, folding chairs, television, generator. So we set our tent up. It's like a room at the Ramada. These Special Forces guys were coming over, doing a triple take. Then they'd come over and want to sit.

Another funny incident. A guy named [Mike] Boynton. There's a handful of guys I would take into combat with me. Boynton was one of them. Pierre Birtz, [Richard J.] "Hook" Tuure, Bob Gallagher. Yeah, those guys right there. If I had to pick a handful, that would be it. Cool fellows. Nice fellows to have around.

We were preparing for that radio station mission. [An assignment to blow up a radio station.] We had gone to a CIA briefing and they wanted to be sure we were nonattributable.

I said, "Look, I've got a guy who has a goddamn tattoo on his arm. I think it says 'God bless America.'"

The CIA guy says, "Don't worry. We'll take care of it."

It's like midnight, we're in a tent in the middle of the jungle. You hear the sound of the jungle and the hissing of the Coleman lanterns. We're getting sterilized clothing [with no marks to link it to the U.S.]. This Special Forces sergeant has all the clothing stacked out on the table and we're going down the line. The roar of the silence is only interrupted by this sergeant asking, us answering—one-word conversations. Hat? 9 1/2.

So I'm walking behind Boynton. He's six feet two or more, weighed 220. Big guy. The sergeant is asking him sizes. Hat. 10 1/2 large. Shirt? 54 extra wide. Pants? 62 extra long.

So he says, "Shoes?"

And Boynton says, "5 1/2."

The whole tent stopped. We're off to be killed and the whole tent stops.

This grizzly sergeant looks over the counter at his feet. He looks up at Boynton and says, "You fall down a lot?"

Suddenly, up shows an army Special Forces corpsman. The guy was in white. Here we are in the middle of the jungle, everybody in cammo, black face and here's this guy with the white smock.

He says, "Lieutenant Macione?"

I says, "Yes?"

"I understand you've got a guy with a tattoo on?"

"Yeah. Boynton, come here."

The guy says, "Roll up your sleeve."

I says, "Roll up your sleeve, Boynton."

He rolls up his sleeve.

The guy takes a can of ether spray, sprays his tattoo, takes his scalpel, goes choo, choo, choo choo, and pulls the tattoo right off.

Boynton is like, "What the f——?"

Another funny story:

A Cuban ship had docked—or Russian ship. It had docked and was unloading arms to the rebels. The 82d Airborne had a howitzer set up. They put a round or two right through the bridge of the ship. Well, the ship broke loose and caught fire. And then it kind of smoldered and floated out into the bay.

Their commander or the CIA, I can't remember who it was, asked me if we could send a couple of guys out to search the ship. Myself and a guy named Bump [AO2 Charles Bump], we swam out to the ship, me and him. The only thing we had on were our swimming trunks and our fins and our M16s.

We no sooner get up on the ship than we start taking automatic weapons fire from the rebel side of the house. So we just had to keep the ship's bulkhead between us and them. The 105 [mm howitzer shell] had gone right through the bridge and all we saw was just bones. It had burned them to a crisp. I picked up a belt buckle—I want to say it was Cuban—and kept it as a souvenir.

We couldn't find anything. We couldn't find any arms. There was some beer but we couldn't find any ammo or anything. Whether they had taken it all off or it was never there, I don't know. Anyways, the ship shouldn't have been there. It was in a bad area.

The ship had begun to leak bunker fuel, fuel oil. When that fuel hits salt water it gets like monkey shit. Clotty and sticky and black. We had to swim a quarter or half a mile. When we came out of the water, the rebels were shooting at us. I had my squad on the break-water firing back, just so we could get out of the water safely. This was broad daylight, maybe eleven o'clock in the morning.

We came out of the water; bullets were jumping all around us. I got behind a rock. I fired two shots. Couldn't see anything, just to shoot. And the third round jammed. I ejected it, slammed another one home, and fired and it exploded. I felt shit go by me like that—whizzz. With such force it blew the bottom right out of the magazine and flattened the rounds—flat sides on them. The bolt had exploded in the casing of the weapon and locked itself in. Later, I took that weapon back to Colt to see what had happened. They said they plug the barrels all the time and shoot and it blows the plug out.

Another guy who was in my platoon, he started laughing like hell. It turns out, in the rush, I had grabbed his weapon. It was his weapon that blew up.

We're caked with this oil and it sticks to you like snot. It's hot. It's sweaty. Bump and I, we go back to the 82d compound. The only thing we've got to get this shit off is gasoline. Here we are rubbing each other down with gasoline. It's hot and it's burning and we've just been shot at and I'm not in the greatest of moods.

I'm on one knee, bare ass as can be, rubbing this shit off me. Burning, my skin coming off.

I hear, off to the side, this squeaky little voice saying, "Just what do you think you're doing?"

I turn and first thing I see is shiny black jump boots. Impeccable. Starched and pressed fatigue pants. Shiny brass belt buckle, and this pure snowy white T-shirt. Little baby face with a cap on top of his head and he's got this butter bar on, a second lieutenant, 82d Airborne. Little kid.

I'm bare ass. He's in uniform.

I said, "Get the hell out of here."

He was like a little bantam hen. His feathers bristle up. "Do you know who you're talking to? You're talking to . . ."

I'm still on my knees. I say, "Better than that, do you know who you're talking to?"

A look comes over his face that says, Wait a minute. This guy is bare ass. He doesn't have any rank on. Who the hell am I talking to?

So I said—I think I called myself commander—I said, "You get in a lean and rest right now. You start doing push-ups until I tell you to stop."

We get ourselves washed off. This grizzly old sergeant is standing over there laughing. This guy's pumping away. He must have done two hundred push-ups.

I told this sergeant, "You turn him loose when you're ready."

He says, "Aye, aye, sir."

You mentioned plans for an attack on a radio station. Was that called off?

No, it wasn't. I'm concerned about going further with it. I'm going to deny I told you. This never happened.

The plan executed as follows:

We took two personnel carriers, rubber-tired vehicles. They were nonattributable [to the U.S.] vehicles. Dominican National Guard vehicles. Myself, one other guy. I don't remember who it was. This was the middle of the night, three o'clock in the morning.

We had six hundred pounds of high explosives in the first vehicle. We had a squad in the second one.

We drove up to the building, right through the front door, like storefront windows, into the lobby. We had forty-second fuses. We pulled the fuses, jumped into the second vehicle, and hauled ass.

The charge went off and blew the bottom floor out of the building. The building came down—a ten-story building or something like that. That took care of the radio station.

One other job wasn't any fun at all. We had to search the sewers. Covering everything were cockroaches as big as your thumb. We had to tape up our legs and wrists and necks and go in, with mosquito netting over you.

The cockroaches just crawling all over you. It was the toughest thing my guys ever did, where I thought I was going to lose 'em. It was crunchy, crunchy.

William Bruhmuller was one of the senior enlisted men in SEAL Team TWO during the Dominican Republic deployment. He recalls a strange little war:

If I remember correctly, we were on one side of the river and the bad guys were on the other side. Without too much effort, we could have walked through that ten-block area they had and corralled them— gotten the whole thing over with in the morning.

But that wasn't going to happen. We had destroyers. We had aircraft carriers. This was going to be a major battle. It was the only war we had going at the time. Everybody wanted to get involved in the thing.

Anyway, we convinced them to let us move downtown so we could at least observe enemy movements and maybe even do some penetration into their compounds or their areas. The rule was, you could not fire unless you were fired at. I mean, because there were so many civilians.

At noontime the whistle would blow—the dog is protecting the sheep and the wolf is trying to get them and the whistle blows at noontime and they all go to lunch together. Same situation. At noontime down there, it would be like a time-out. All the bad guys would jump over the barbed wire, have rice compliments of the government, and then go back to the war in the afternoon.

Being the instigators that we are, we got downtown and took the Starlight Scopes with us. We moved into a warehouse that had been an appliance and automobile sales place. They sold refrigerators and cars and TVs. Once we get in, we try to decide what to do. Well, we had to draw some fire.

So Macione said, "Let's make a couple of manikins up."

We got this stuff all together. We had snipers with Starlight Scopes looking out there, trying to find a target of opportunity. And these other couple of guys had these manikins on little dollies and we would roll them back and forth so we might be able to draw some fire. And if we could draw some fire, all hell would break loose.

Jack Macione tells how you used the Starlight Scope to shoot a man in the darkness.

I remember the roof and the manikin thing. I do remember shooting at someone. I got a chance to shoot at a couple of people. I think I did. I think we had to do that a couple of nights.

I've never shot anybody with the Starlight Scope. All I did was observe or spot somebody or somebody would spot for me. He would move the Starlight Scope real slowly. He would say, "I see something on that tall building," and try to give you some description and zero you in on it.

Once you zero in on it, with your night vision, you start to see some movement. I think that's what happened that night. I think we had seen somebody the night before. The rooftop had a sort of an entry, where you come up through this stairwell and out on the roof. I believe that's what it was like. I also believe that was a suspected case where they had a .50-caliber position. That was one of the points of interest.

In fact, later on, we took a recoilless rifle. Yes. I did shoot a guy up there. This was probably three or four days later. We observed them moving a .50 caliber up on the roof. And I recall this because we were able to see this during the daylight hours, people coming up through that little door area, obviously with ammunition, putting it up on the roof. We watched them load this sucker all day long. Obviously they were going to do something that night. It looked like they were setting up a position for a .50-caliber machine gun.

So we took a recoilless rifle and let them get all set up, even let them test fire a few rounds, and then with one shot we blew them right off the roof. Yeah, I did shoot that guy.

The Glory Days

Chapter 6
Welcome Back for *Gemini*

During the 1960s and 1970s, as American astronauts reached for, and finally landed on, the moon, the navy's underwater demolition teams played a vital role in the nation's space program.

While the more glamorous SEALs sometimes got the credit, the recovery of the space capsules of the Mercury, Gemini, and Apollo programs was always done by the UDT frogmen.

For men whose routine heroics—and plain hard work—usually went unheralded, those were the glory days. They saw themselves on television, in the pages of *Life* magazine, even in the *Encyclopedia Britannica.* One group was flown to Chicago on a private jet for a ticker tape parade through the city's downtown area.

Martin Every was a young frogman in the mid-60s. Every, whose son is now a member of SEAL Team EIGHT, recalled those days during an interview in his office in Northern Virginia:

I was operations officer for UDT Twenty-one in 1965 when they decided to put UDT people on the astronaut pickups after they had lost a capsule. They made me the training officer for the recoveries.

Other members of the team took the *Gemini III* [the first manned test of the two-man *Gemini* spacecraft crewed by Virgil I. Grissom and John W. Young].

I took *Gemini IV* [7 June 1965]. That was the one with McDivitt and White [James A. McDivitt and Edward W. White II]. They had done the first American space walk [a twenty-minute excursion by White]. The other guys in my pickup team were [Petty Officers] Neil G. Dow and Everett W. Owl.

We were on the USS *Wasp* about 390 miles east of Cape Kennedy in the Atlantic. We got a radio message from McDivitt. He says, "Don't forget, I want to be recovered in a hurry."

We had practiced and practiced with a JG helicopter pilot. The day of the big event, the commander comes out and says, "I'm going to fly this."

He doesn't know anything about all the techniques we had worked out. The big problem was how the rotor wash was going to blow the capsule and the flotation collar. These two guys would jump first. I'd go third.

I was hollering, "Go! Go!" Telling my guys to jump.

The helicopter pilot heard me and thought it was the crew chief telling him to get out of the area and took off. I jumped. It was twenty or twenty-five feet, from a moving helicopter, with a single tank on my back. I went ass over teakettle. Fortunately, the only thing that happened was I ran a tooth through my lip. You can get hurt real bad jumping out of a helicopter, and some guys have.

We jumped in the water, inflated the [flotation] collar, and got the astronauts out.

First, we had to find a wrench attached to the capsule and use it to unlock the door. The astronauts were eager to get out. They were trying to open it from the inside. One of them had a broken face plate on his mask and he was sick.

When we looked inside, it was the first time we had ever seen the inside of a real capsule. We'd always practiced with a dummy boilerplate capsule. We had been taught where to find things. But they had not put the ejection mechanism on "safe." If we had pulled the wrong lever when we were helping them out, it would have ejected these two astronauts in the ejection seat. If it had gone off, the astronauts, and probably a couple of us, would have been killed.

We helped McDivitt out and then White came out by himself and bounced off the collar into the raft. We could just imagine losing an astronaut in eight thousand feet of water.

We stayed with the capsule while the carrier approached from about sixty miles away. We had been out there about an hour and we couldn't get the door closed on the thing. When the carrier came, that was the hairiest part. We were nervous when they were trying to pick up the capsule because the carrier drifted down toward us and there was no way to get away. We thought we might have to swim under the carrier, but we might not have enough air. On the pickup of Gus Grissom and John Young [*Gemini III*], one frogman had to swim under the capsule to get out of the way.

When I got back on the carrier, I was really tired. We had to wear wet suits because the chemicals from the retro-rockets, in the water, might be corrosive to the skin. I would much rather jump in just wearing trunks.

A messenger came to my room—I was a JG—and said the admiral would like you to come up for dinner. I didn't know where his cabin was. I didn't have any whites. Had to borrow some whites. Maybe I should have worn my wet suit.

I got up there real early. There was a marine guard and I told him I was there to see the admiral. He let me in.

I got to watch pictures of the first walk in space with White and McDivitt. It was really exciting. They both wrote me personal letters. One is on the wall there.

I said I had enjoyed this and I mentioned that my wedding anniversary was the next day. They made arrangements to have a C-2 [small transport plane] pick me up and make sure I got back.

NASA just had lots of money in those days. These collars we put around the capsule, they cost ten thousand dollars or something. We'd say we used up a couple of CO_2 capsules and they'd give us a whole new collar.

The space program was big news in those days. They sent me up to New York to be interviewed by Mike Wallace.

They asked me to wear my wet suit. But it's summer—110 degrees. I tell them I can't do that.

I report to CBS. Mike Wallace says, "Hey Martin, is there anything you don't want to talk about on the air?"

I said, "Yeah, when I opened that door, one of the astronauts had cracked his face plate and was sick. I don't want to talk about anything that's medical."

First question, "When you opened that capsule . . ." I felt like I'd really been had.

They kept calling down, asking me to come talk about the next one, the next one. The guys are starting to go off to Vietnam and here I am getting orders for New York television.

One funny thing: The *Gemini IV* capsule is at the Air and Space Museum in Washington. The heat shield on the forward end of the capsule has some strange marks. The scientists puzzled over them. I could have told them they were scratches I made with my weight belt.

Chapter 7
Alone in the Mid-Atlantic

From 1964 to 1966, Christopher O. "Chris" Bent served as a member of UDT Twenty-one. More than two decades later, he recalled one of his most challenging experiences in an article written for *Fire In The Hole,* the newsletter of the UDT/SEAL Museum Association. Here is his account of what it was like to be alone, at night, in the mid-Atlantic, two thousand miles from land:

It was mid-February in 1966 when a small detachment from UDT Twenty-one was assigned to recover the first flight of the *Apollo* spacecraft (AS-201), to be launched from Cape Kennedy atop the newly developed mighty Saturn Booster. This would be unmanned, suborbital, otherwise a full-scale test with the recovery scheduled north of Ascension Island—just south of the equator, midway between Brazil and Africa. (Check map—this place is nowhere!)

We weren't all that excited as our egos were sufficiently stimulated from just having done the *Gemini VI* recoveries in December, and this assignment would keep us from joining the rest of the team in St. Thomas [the frogmen's winter training base in the Caribbean].

In any case, two weeks later aboard the USS *Wasp,* rain or shine we are the only personnel allowed to jog the flight deck and we do so with glee. Most of our time is spent studying this new three-man spacecraft which had a much larger "sail area" than the two-man *Gemini,* which floated on its side.

The upright *Apollo* silhouette presented a lot of surface to the wind, which made it drift much faster than we could swim. Rule One was to always exit the helicopter downwind so the spacecraft would drift to you. Smart, eh? The problem then became one of slowing the spacecraft down so you could work on it by attaching the flotation collar and then the support raft, all of which had to be dropped downwind and swum over. This could proceed relatively smoothly *if* there were no waves. Who ever heard of waves two thousand miles from shore?

The dubious honor of being in charge had its moments. It was necessary to develop night recovery techniques for contingency Plan Delta. Of course, my team felt I was eminently qualified for this command responsibility and that my mother would be so much prouder than their mothers.

So, a day later I singularly exited the helo into the pitch-black. With wet suit, fins, and SCUBA it is a momentary free fall quickly embraced by five-foot seas and infinite anonymity. The difficulty with all this was that the horizonless seas provided the pilot with no visual references; moreover, his altimeters were nonfunctional under thirty feet.

He could easily get too close and clip a wave or even worse (for us) drop a swimmer above ten feet, who, if wearing a tank, could rotate in the air and suffer serious injury on impact. Out with me came a parachute I was to attach and deploy as a sea anchor to the oncoming practice spacecraft, which was set adrift by the USS *Wasp* earlier, radio and light beacons armed.

The water was crystal clear, which added some comfort to the general eeriness. The helo's lights were intermittently screwing up my night vision. While trying to wave him off, I realized our ability to communicate was zero and I was really alone.

Oh, great!

So, back to work. I swam (thank God for duckfeet) to the approaching spacecraft, attached the parachute, and deployed it. However, it just drifted like a blob, billowing out as imagination would have it. I was down about ten to fifteen feet trying to arrange the canopy to inflate when suddenly I saw something off to the side, emerging from the darkness.

My mind says, B-I-G S-H-A-R-K and I A-M A-L-O-N-E! It's five miles deep and swimming to Africa gives the shark a slight edge.

Meanwhile, the helo pilot is probably eating Oreos and dozing on autohover or something.

My mouth was getting dry, causing the possibility of real fear. "What the ——— can I do?"

Well, until this moment, as you are reading, no one has known that I turned and swam right into that white parachute canopy and pulled it completely around me until only a face mask, two big eyeballs, and bubbles could finally witness a grotesque and menacing parachute deployment bag swim by. . . .

Oh, by the way, the actual recovery of the first *Apollo* spacecraft was performed flawlessly two days later.

Mother was proud.

Chapter 8
First Men from the Moon

Michel "Mike" Bennett, who retired as a boatswain's mate senior chief in 1990 after a quarter century in UDT and SEAL teams, was involved in three astronaut pickups, either as backup or on the prime crew. His participation in the recovery of the first men from the moon, the crew of *Apollo 11*, gave him a brief moment of fame. But in some ways his role in the backup crew for the *Apollo 14* recovery is more memorable.

Bennett, who now works for a security firm in the Washington, D.C., suburbs, recalled those days in an interview:

We were on the USS *Hornet*, in the Pacific, five hundred miles south of American Samoa, getting ready to recover the *Apollo 14* crew. We'd practice. The ship would drop the boilerplate [a mock-up of the space capsule] off. This one day, like three days before the burn-in, we were getting ready to practice.

The *Hornet* was moving at a pretty good clip when they put the boilerplate in the water. The elevator [used to lift aircraft to the flight deck] was lowered, with a ladder hanging down.

They wanted us to crawl down the Jacob's ladder into the water but that would put us right up close to the ship. We wanted to jump off that elevator. The elevator captain says, "No, you can't do that. You have to ask the bos'n."

He was up on the main deck. I went in, took the elevator up. We're in our jumpin'-in-the-water gear, fins and stuff, but no tanks. I asked him, "Hey, can we jump off the elevator so we can catch up with the boilerplate?"

He says, "Yeah, it's okay."

By that time, they turned the boilerplate loose and it was drifting on. I hollored, "Go!" The other guys jumped off the elevator. By the time I got back down, it would have been way aft. I would have had a mile or so to swim. So I jumped off the flight deck.

I heard the bos'n say, "You can't . . ."

How far were you from the water?

About eighty or ninety feet.

Anyway, just as I went off, I saw a wire from the flight deck, one of the antennas sticking out. I thought, oh shit, I'm going to hit it. I hit something and my arm was flailing back. When I flailed back, my watch—this Rolex they had issued us—came off.

And man, I hit the water and boom, my head hurt. Oh, Jesus.

By that time, the ship took a turn to come back to look at the boilerplate. I'm swimming and my head's hurting, boom, boom, boom.

I had a strobe light attached to my life jacket. When I hit the water, I brought my head down and it hit me right up here [points to his right forehead]. In the salt water that cut bleeds real big. As I come up to the boilerplate, one of the guys looks down and his eyes are this big.

I say, "Oh, man! I hit that wire when I went off."

He said, "Holy cow!"

I just knew I'd hit my nose. My whole face was numb. I just knew my nose was ripped off. I looked down and I had blood all over me. I thought my whole face was torn off. I reached up and felt and it was still there.

He said, "Man, you've got a little cut over your eye."

Just as the ship came by, I see two marines on deck with M16s. They were there for shark shooters. And here I was bleeding.

The day *Apollo 14* came down, I was in the backup crew. We were out in the helicopter and it was maxed out. We were flying at seventeen thousand feet so we could see the burn-in.

We started getting odd vibrations.

The crew tells us, "Buckle up. We're going in to the ship."

I'm sitting at the door, enjoying the scenery. I was on the outboard side as we came to the ship. The wheel on my side just barely made it onto the hangar deck and the rotor blade stops—whrr, whrr.

They say, "Get off! Get off!"

We're in full wet suits and had our tanks on.

I took my seat belt off and ran out.

What happened is, he was losing hydraulics and the rotor blades were locking up and he just made it to the ship before the rotor blades locked up. Or else we would have, boom, gone down into the water.

This was **Apollo 14.** *Were you on other pickups?*

I was on *Apollo 10,* and on *11* I was the first guy in the water. The *Encyclopedia Britannica* shows a picture of a helicopter, the command module, and a guy jumping. That guy is me. It says we are SEALs. But that's wrong. We were UDT Eleven.

The first guy in the water puts the sea anchor on. [The sea anchor is similar to a parachute and is deployed to drag in the water and prevent the capsule from being pushed along by the wind.] He snaps it on to a lifting lug just below the door. He looks in the door and gets a thumbs-up from the astronauts. Then he goes down and looks at the anchor, makes sure it's deployed.

Then he calls in the flotation device. Once the guy in the water calls them in, two more jump in. Now there are three guys. You run this cable around, hook it on the back side—no, you start from the back side and run it around. The bag is folded so when you bring it around each side, there is a continuous cable so it unrolls.

The third guy is down underneath there making sure it unrolls correctly. The air temperature is 105 degrees and the water temperature is about 82. You're in a full wet suit, mask, and twin 90s [air tanks]. Plus you've got a little bit of chop. You want about a foot chop. It helps rock the command module so you can get the collar around.

By the time you get it around, your arms are just so heavy. You're tired.

You pull it together, lock it, and then snap on O_2 bottles to fill it up. Then you call in the boat. They throw the boat—two boats—to you. One is a swimmer boat, one a recovery boat, for the astronauts. You fasten one on either side of the door.

The *Apollo 11* astronauts were the first men to set foot on the moon. Scientists worried that they might bring some unknown disease or

life-form back from outer space. An elaborate procedure was established in which the astronauts were decontaminated and then sealed
in an isolation chamber during the supposed incubation period of any
bugs they might have brought back. The frogmen were responsible
for the first phase of this process.

Then you call in the BIG [biological isolation garment] swimmer,
the biological decontamination swimmer. He has a Betadine solution
that he washes everything with. He washes the command module before
he opens the door. Then he opens the door, throws a bag of BIG suits
in, and closes the door.

Then the astronauts put on their suits. We trail a boat off. We're
hanging on the boat upwind. If we get downwind, we have to go into
isolation with the astronauts.

As the astronauts come out, he [the BIG swimmer] washes them
down because of this green mung from the moon.

Once they are washed down, they're sitting in their boat. The ship
takes off. We sit there for an hour while the Betadine solution works.
The ship is four miles away, just at the horizon, while you're sitting
in the water. They come back and pick up the astronauts. We uncouple
the boat they were in and sink it. Then we stab and sink our boat. Then
we get picked up.

The hookup man rides the command module until the crane comes
over the side. He hooks it up on the lifting sling. Then he comes off,
gets the Jacob's ladder, and crawls up.

Chapter 9
Unlucky Thirteen

Even the most unsuperstitious engineers and managers at the National Aeronautics and Space Administration might have been forgiven a momentary twinge of anxiety as preparations progressed toward the third manned landing on the moon in the spring of 1970.

Up to that point, the Apollo moon-landing program had gone remarkably smoothly, moving almost flawlessly from the early unmanned tests of the spacecraft to manned earth orbit. And then had come the first flight around the moon by *Apollo 8,* the test of the lunar lander by *Apollo 9* and *10,* culminating in the historic landing on the moon by two *Apollo 11* astronauts on 16 July 1969.

A second successful venture to the surface of the moon was made by *Apollo 12.*

And next would come *Apollo 13.* Unlucky thirteen? Many people consider thirteen a uniquely unlucky number. But unlike the builders of a skyscraper, who often simply leave out the "unlucky" thirteenth floor, there was no way for NASA to get around the fact that thirteen comes after twelve and before fourteen.

Instead of ignoring the superstition or trying to find a way around it, the NASA managers put up a brave front—perhaps somewhat like a small boy whistling as he passes a graveyard at night.

They scheduled the launch for 1:13 P.M. Houston time—that's 1313 the way the military keeps time. And, to aid in the recovery of the returning space capsule, they chose UDT Thirteen.

Looking back later, James A. Lovell Jr., the command pilot on *Apollo 13*, pinpointed a series of omens that perhaps should have warned of trouble ahead.

At the last minute, the command module pilot who had trained for the voyage for two years was removed from the crew because he had been exposed to German measles. His replacement, from the backup crew, had only two days of training with the other two members of the prime crew before liftoff.

There were troubles, too, with one helium tank, which seemed to be improperly insulated, and an oxygen tank, which had been installed in *Apollo 13* after it had been removed from *Apollo 11* for repairs—and had been dropped.

If anyone had misgivings, they were not enough to delay the flight. *Apollo 13* took off from the Kennedy Space Center on schedule at 1313 Houston time on 11 April 1970. About five minutes after liftoff, the crew felt a small vibration. Then one of the engines shut down two minutes early. This meant other engines had to burn longer than planned to put the spacecraft into the proper orbit around the earth.

Those seemingly minor glitches were soon forgotten as Lovell, Jack Swigert Jr., and Fred Haise Jr. broke free from earth orbit and began their journey to the moon.

At this point, the huge rocket engines that had pushed them into space had been discarded. What was left was a three-part spacecraft. The astronauts were in the command capsule, the cockpit where they expected to spend most of the voyage and where they navigated and controlled the flight. Attached to the capsule were two other units. One, called the service capsule, contained oxygen, water, propellant, and power units. The other was the lunar module, the LM, which two of the astronauts would fly down to the moon's surface—and back up again—while their companion circled the moon in the command capsule. The LM was connected to the command capsule by a tunnel through which the astronauts could crawl. Early in the flight, they crawled into the LM to see if everything was all right. It was.

For two days, they sailed uneventfully through space. To the three crew members and the ground crew monitoring its progress, *Apollo 13* seemed to be the smoothest flight yet, almost boring.

And then, fifty-five hours and fifty-five minutes into the voyage, the astronauts heard and felt a sharp bang and vibration. It was just after 7:00 P.M. on the thirteenth of April. Looking out the porthole, they could see the craft was venting a large volume of some kind of gas. It formed a cloud so bright that observers reported seeing it through a telescope from Houston—200,000 miles away.

The gas was oxygen. One of two oxygen bottles—the one that had been dropped—had exploded. The blast not only blew a hole in the side of the service module, but it also caused a leak in the other oxygen bottle. The oxygen from those two bottles was not essential to keep the astronauts breathing. They had a system that constantly cleansed and recycled the air they breathed. But without oxygen from the damaged tanks, the fuel cells that provided electrical power would go dead and the command capsule would become uninhabitable and its control systems unusable.

One immediate result of the explosion was that the crew did not have enough power to turn their small rocket engine and head back toward earth. Their only way home was to continue on, fly around the moon, and use the gravity of the moon as a kind of slingshot to hurl them back toward earth. They would have to remain in space—and try to stay alive—for four more days.

About fifteen minutes before their command module ran out of power, the astronauts crawled through the tunnel into the LM. The plan, worked out by the three crew members and a growing army of experts on the ground, was to use the LM as a lifeboat. The lunar module was equipped with oxygen, water, and batteries to supply electricity. But the LM was only designed to support two astronauts for forty-five hours—time to get from the capsule to the moon and back again safely. The crew had to find a way to stretch the supplies in the LM to keep the three of them alive for ninety hours.

They cut use of electrical power to the minimum and each of them sipped only six ounces of water a day.

But then a problem that would have been familiar to any frogman cropped up. The system for purifying the air the astronauts breathed was similar to underwater breathing rigs. The air in the capsule is drawn through a canister containing lithium hydroxide, which cleans it of carbon dioxide and returns oxygen to the capsule. The men calculated that, with the lithium hydroxide canisters in the LM, plus the canisters from the backpacks on the space suits, they could make it back to earth. But after a day and a half in the LM, a warning light indicated the carbon dioxide was rising to a dangerous level. They had not taken into account the demands placed on the system by three, rather than two, astronauts.

Fortunately, those on the ground had foreseen the problem. They told the astronauts how to build emergency scrubbers [canisters that purify the oxygen], using plastic bags, cardboard, and tape, so they could use the square canisters from the command capsule in the round openings in the LM environmental system. Without that fix, the *Apollo 13* crew would have died from breathing the exhaust from their own lungs before they could reach earth.

Confined to their lifeboat and breathing from their jury-rigged system, the astronauts flew around the moon, made a correction in their course to aim them toward the South Pacific, and headed home. As they approached earth, they jettisoned the battered service capsule— and got their first chance to see how badly damaged it was. Then they used the power of the LM to bring back to life the command module, which carried the heat shield they needed for reentry into the earth's atmosphere.

When they crawled back into the command module it was so cold and clammy that, as the power came back on, it actually rained inside. The temperature was thirty-eight degrees and, as Lovell later said, they were "as cold as frogs in a frozen pool." They knew almost exactly what it feels like to be a frogman in a SEAL delivery vehicle.

Shortly before plunging down into the atmosphere, the astronauts used the pressure in the tunnel to blow their lifeboat clear of the command module.

The landing itself was uneventful as their parachutes dropped them gently into the deep blue Pacific near Samoa at eight minutes after noon, Houston time, on 17 April.

Their splashdown was within sight of the recovery ship, the USS *Iwo Jima.* As the command capsule settled into the sea, three members of UDT Thirteen jumped from a hovering helicopter and began the now-routine process of attaching a sea anchor, surrounding the capsule with a flotation collar, and opening the hatch to welcome the astronauts back to earth.

Members of the recovery team included SN Luco W. Palma and MR3 Roger C. Banfield. After the tension of the last few days, the recovery operation was anticlimactic. In fact it was quicker and smoother than normal. Because the astronauts had not set foot on the moon, they did not have to be isolated to protect the earth from strange bugs from another heavenly body. With the help of the frogmen, they were quickly lifted from their rubber rafts and delivered by helicopter to the deck of the *Iwo Jima.*

In 1970, the frogmen were still enjoying the glory days. The odyssey of *Apollo 13* had been followed by millions of people throughout the world. President Nixon flew to Honolulu to welcome the astronauts home.

But, for the members of the underwater demolition teams, there was another reality—the war in Vietnam. It was not unusual for a frogman to bask in the glory of a spacecraft recovery and, a short time later, find himself surveying a dark beach on the Vietnamese coast or dodging booby traps and blowing Viet Cong bunkers.

On 18 September 1970, just five months after the *Apollo 13* recovery, Palma and Banfield were members of a patrol through "Indian country" near Hoi An in the northern part of South Vietnam. Although their primary assignment was beach reconnaissance, the UDT men were often called on to provide security for technicians installing sensors used to detect movement of enemy units. On this day, the danger, as it turned out, was not from armed Viet Cong, but from a well-hidden booby trap.

Hospital Corpsman 3d Class Lawrence C. Williams tripped a booby trap made from a powerful 105mm artillery shell. The explosion killed Williams and Palma, who was just behind him. Pieces of shrapnel tore into the back of Banfield, who was just in front of Williams. Banfield was a machinery repairman, but on this day he was, fortunately, acting as a radioman. The radio strapped to his back caught most of the metal, except for one piece that struck him in the lower back. Although seriously wounded, he survived.

Another UDT Thirteen member on the patrol lost an eye. In all, UDT Thirteen suffered two deaths and eight men wounded in the few months after the unit's involvement in the *Apollo 13* recovery. This was at a time when UDT Thirteen was supposed to be limited to twenty men in country, although a number of "visitors" actually swelled that number from time to time.

Even then, the bad luck that had followed *Apollo 13* seemed not to have run its course.

On 30 October 1991, the *Apollo 13* recovery ship, the USS *Iwo Jima,* had just left the port of Manama, Bahrain, after routine maintenance during Operation Desert Shield when a steam pipe in the ship's boiler room ruptured, killing ten sailors.

Frogmen
in Vietnam

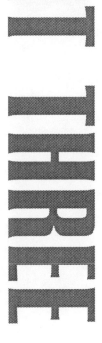
PART THREE

Chapter 10
Good Fun in North Vietnam

Jack Luksik is one of the navy's most experienced SEALs. With an education provided by the navy, he has advanced to the rank of commander. But when he became a frogman in 1966, he was a very junior enlisted man. This is his story of his adventures on the coast of North Vietnam:

I came into the teams and was assigned to UDT Eleven August 16, 1966. I was in Vietnam with both UDT Eleven and SEAL Team ONE.

When I was in UDT, there was an invasion plan—maybe invasion is the wrong word—an amphibious landing—planned north of the DMZ [the so-called demilitarized zone between North and South Vietnam]. The objective was to sweep across that little neck of North Vietnam, just north of the DMZ, turn south, and sanitize the DMZ. Because in fact the DMZ really wasn't.

We did all the appropriate recons that were necessary for an amphibious landing. We did miles and miles and miles of this beautiful white sand beach. There's a gold mine over there in resort community, Club Med–type business if the Vietnamese were interested in turning it into a capitalist enterprise. There are a couple of hundred miles of some of the finest beaches I've ever seen.

When did you do this survey?

Early to mid-1967. We were on the USS *Ogden*, LPD-5 [landing platform, dock]. It was a new ship at the time, commissioned in 1962.

An LPD can ballast down, then open the stern gate. They wouldn't ballast down for us. They'd open the stern gate at night and we'd take our IBSs [rubber boats] and paddle in and anchor them maybe a thousand yards out and then go and do what I like to call "administrative reconnaissance under combat conditions at night."

We have the two types of reconnaissance—a combat recon, which is the classic predawn recon where you go in to find obstacles and go back and blow them before a landing. And that's generally for a thousand yards or less of beach. In an administrative recon, you just check the gradient of the beach and note obstacles.

To run a recon like that, you have your swimmer line extending out from the beach, with guys every twenty-five yards to the point where you reach the three-and-a-half-fathom curve—twenty-one feet. Our classic responsibility is from the high-water line to the three-and-a-half-fathom curve for clearance of obstacles and hydrographic reconnaissance.

Myself, as the cartographer, and the platoon commander would walk a baseline on the beach, used for reference. You make an approximation of where the high-water mark is. Then you correct it to mean low water when you draw the chart.

What was your rank then?

I was an electronics technician seaman apprentice.

We put down two stakes and then we used red lens flashlights so you couldn't see the light unless you were directly in front of it. We'd shine the two flashlights out to sea and the swimmers would line themselves up.

As the cartographer, I'd run out the line real fast. Of course you can run faster than these guys can swim. We'd set up the two stakes and then basically run in a circle to see if there is anything prominent to note down for the hinterland part of the chart.

Speed was of the essence. You want to cover a couple of thousand yards at twenty-five-yard increments. That's a lot of work. We had to move fast. The swimmers swim at one speed but there is a lot of setup in moving these two posts and trying to check out and see what you can see.

The two guys on the beach were moving fast all the time. If you lag and the swimmers have to wait for you, then your swimmer line gets jagged and you start to lose accuracy. You wanted to keep the swimmers all in line, all swimming at one speed and not have them stop and wait for you. That necessitates a lot of fast moving on the beach. You don't have time to walk real slow and be tactical, as we were trained to.

That was always good fun because you never knew what you'd be running into. The fishermen, a lot of times, would sleep at their boats, just above the high-water line. Sometimes they would be armed, sometimes not. You're running around, you'd trip over a boat—you couldn't see them—and you'd wake these people up.

We didn't carry weapons—guns—simply because they were too big of a pain in the butt. The platoon commander decided that would certainly keep us from running off and doing something stupid on an individual basis. I mean, if you don't have a gun, you're not going to shoot at anybody. That didn't go over real big at the time with the platoon.

You'd trip over a boat you didn't see sitting there and fall in. A guy would be getting up. You could hear him wrestling around. You know the sound of a gun being picked up. You can tell somebody's holding a weapon. You distance yourself as fast as you can.

Did you actually stumble over people?

Oh, yes. There was no moon, heavy cloud cover, no high-tech cities around, no lights. At times, it was so dark you could barely see your hand in front of your face.

So we'd wake these people up, they'd jump up, come screaming and hollering, shooting.

Did you ever run into military units, like an infantry company?

No, we never ran into a company of NVA. But once we woke somebody up and they started hollering, we didn't stick around to see if anyone was going to come. The obvious assumption is, yes, someone is going to come. That's why the man is hollering.

Did these people you ran into shoot at you?

Sure, like I said. But frogman luck always held. It turns out anybody—not just Vietnamese—at night, or even in the daytime, people shooting into water, they shoot high initially. In the daytime, of course, they can correct their aim. They see where the rounds are landing by the splash. But at night, particularly shooting into the ocean, they have no idea.

We'd watch the tracers. It was rare that anything hit the water near you. Of course you still have the knowledge that those individuals are trying to kill you. It was good fun.

The only time I really had concern was when they would throw grenades. It would hit the water—particularly for us guys, one or two, who were right up on the beach—within throwing arm distance. We thought we were had. A grenade falls right beside you in the water and it's nothing you're going to find and pick up and throw back.

It hits the water and you know it's right around there and you figure, oh, man! The only thing you can do, the reasonable thing to do, is go toward the sea. Fortunately, they did a lot of home manufacturing of grenades. And throwing them in the water, the vast majority of times, the waterproofing on their fusing didn't work. We never had any go off. We didn't have any casualties.

Frogman luck was with us. In the event of a compromise, which that was, we would pull back into a swimmer pool off the beach, wait an hour, and then go back in the same spot being more careful not to wake these people up.

We'd do that all night and then just before dawn we'd go back to the ship and draw up the charts, hit the rack, wait until the evening, then go back and pick up where we left off.

You were actually in North Vietnam?
Yes, this was a little bit north of the DMZ.
Did you know why you were doing it?
Uh huh.
How many of you were involved?
We had a twenty-two-man platoon. It was an augmented platoon because the gradient there was shallow and you didn't have enough swimmers to do the three-and-a-half-fathom curve with one sweep. And that's the wrong place to be making multiple sweeps.

We had two guys on shore and twenty guys strung out, twenty-five yards apart, a standard flutter board line. They would measure the depth, then breath-hold, dive down, and swim a zigzag course looking for any obstacles that could hamper a landing craft.
How did they record the depth?
They had a standard swimmer slate.
Did the invasion, or landing, ever take place?
I guess General Westmoreland [Gen. William C. Westmoreland,

commander of American forces in Vietnam] decided he didn't want to do that. Like most things in Vietnam, there were a lot of political considerations.

How long did you do this?

I think the longest time out was forty-five days. Almost every night. It was great.

Overall, it was about four months of recon. That wasn't all north of the DMZ. We did recons from just north of the DMZ down to south of Da Nang. I believe after the monsoon season, the platoons that went over there would redo them from the DMZ south because everything changes with the monsoon season.

After the monsoon, we would do channel blasting off in the Cua Viet River delta. You could travel five miles to go a quarter mile, picking your way through sandbars at the mouth of that river after the monsoon season.

We'd used Mark 8 hose [an explosive charge encased in long sections of rubber hose, which can be laid in a pattern to shape the force of the explosion] and make mat weaves and blow channels so boats could resupply the marines in Hue. That was great. We had some fantastic shots.

It took a whole day's evolution to put the mats together and swim them in place and get it all set up. When it finally did go, it was well worth it.

It sounds as though you were enjoying yourself as a young seaman.

There was very little incentive to advance at that time. The lieutenant had to order me to take the seaman exam. My paycheck was about eighty bucks every two weeks. We were drawing jump and demo, which was $110 a month, which doubled our pay. The increment in pay between seaman, seaman apprentice, and third class was very little. I was having a good time. Why advance? They were going to give me this job to do anyway.

Chapter 11
Operation Jackstay

In 1966, U.S. forces—and especially the navy's frogmen—were still trying to learn how to fight a strange new kind of war in the tidal rivers, mangrove swamps, and jungles of Vietnam. Between 26 March and 7 April 1966, members of UDT and SEAL units joined for the first time with marine recon teams and regular navy and marine forces for a major combat operation.

Operation Jackstay, as it was called, was hailed at the time as a successful assault on the Viet Cong forces operating near the mouth of the Saigon River, harassing shipping trying to reach the South Vietnamese capital. Norman Olson, who later retired from the navy as a captain, was the commander of UDT Eleven at the time. This is his account of Operation Jackstay:

I had UDT Team Eleven, in Subic Bay. I had just flown out and I got to Subic and my whole goddamn team was gone.

"Where the hell are they?"

Well, they said they were on a special mission down in Vietnam.

I said, "Well goddamn it, I've got to get there."

So they flew me over there, got me in a helicopter and they dropped me onto this APD. And my whole goddamn team was on this thing.

The goddamn ship was almost capsizing from the people on board.

They had drawn in just about every rubber boat, every Boston Whaler they could find. When I flew in to this thing, I'm looking down at the ship and there must have been a hundred of these boats and stuff all around the ship. It looked like a mother duck with all these little ducklings all over the place.

I got on board. There were outboard motors completely surrounding every one of the gun tubs. People are cleaning weapons. And I'm going, holy shit, what is going on? It was about noontime. I walk in the wardroom and it was like a reunion. John Callahan, my XO [executive officer]. Bill Early is there. He's an adviser. Jim Barnes has his [SEAL] detachment. All these guys.

I say, "What the hell's happening?"

Everybody was sort of dancing around the answer. The only one I could trust, Jim Barnes, had been in country operating in the Rung Sat. So I went up to the forward troop compartment.

I said, "Jim, come on up here. Tell me what the hell is going on."

And he said, "Well, I'll tell you, as far as I'm concerned, it's so ill conceived I'm not going to participate in it."

He had the advantage. He was working for Naval Support Activity Saigon. He didn't work for the amphibious group.

He said, "I'm not going to go in with you guys."

I said, "Thanks a lot, Jim. You're the sons of bitches who have all the training and you've got all the gear and you're not going to go."

And he says, "You're absolutely right. I think it's a poor operation. We're not going to play in that game tonight."

I said, "Well, I don't have a choice."

This is when they were going to do one of the first amphibious operations in that area. I can't remember the name of it. I thought I would never forget the goddamn name.

Jackstay?

Jackstay! It was a horrible experience. We got put in—you've got to understand in those days the UDTs had no SEAL training whatsoever. The SEALs had had small-arms training and did all this land warfare stuff. The UDTs by and large didn't do that. We had no good weapons. We had some M16s. We had M1s. We had a few shotguns. We had .38-caliber revolvers.

We were supposed to be put into this river as a blocking force. Which essentially means you put us on one side of the land between the rivers. The amphibious force was to land, flush the VC out, and push 'em into us and we were supposed to take 'em out.

Jesus Christ!

So I got there and said, "Who conceived this goddamn operation?"

Well, it was too late. We were going to go.

This was a very ill conceived operation. It turned out we were all allegedly heroes as a result of it. But our whole team could have been wiped out. We weren't trained for that. The irony of this was that [another UDT officer] had been assigned to the PhibGru staff in WestPac. And he conceived this. He was something of a loose cannon.

Everybody is out there milling around on the fantail. There is going to be three or four people in each of these boats.

So I get back there and I said, "How about getting me a weapon?"

[The staff officer who planned the operation] says, "What do you want a weapon for?"

I said, "There's no way that team is going in there without me being there. I'm not trying to be a hero but I'll be goddamned if I'm going to send them into such a screwed-up operation as this and I'm not going to be there."

So he says, "Well, you're a married man."

I says, "You should have thought about that before you dreamed up this."

I had an M16. I hadn't been checked out on this thing. I'm getting checked out on the fantail. They give me a .38 [caliber pistol]. Now these .38s had been in the teams in World War II. The holster of a .38 is sewed to a pad that goes on the web belt. So I got this thing on my side.

And we go in. And when I think back on what a screwed-up operation . . . [The staff officer] is in a Mike boat in front of us. [A Mike boat is a medium landing craft, used for river operations and beach assaults.] And it's like the mother duck leading us into this river. This is about four o'clock in the afternoon.

We had this Mike boat here and all the little rubber ducklings were behind him. His master plan was, he would stand in the Mike boat and he would point and then the first boat would pull off and go into this ambush position.

This was a known VC haven and we were out there like it was another day in Coronado.

We had radios but they didn't work because the canopy, the coverage in that area, was so thick.

But he said, "Well, the plan is, one of you guys, when you get in there, will shinny up a tree and put (we had these blue and gold T-shirts) the gold on top of the canopy so if we have to bring helicopters in, we will know where all these ambush positions are."

Well, shit, this stuff is so thick you can hardly move in it, this mangrove. So anyway, he goes in and drops us all off. I'm with three or four other guys. We land, the boat springs back. We have to crawl through all this crap and we set up this position. And I'm sitting in a damn tree or whatever the hell it was. All of a sudden I hear a "plop." It's all mud on the bottom. And I look down and there is my .38 in the holster, sitting in the mud.

How the hell did that happen? It had dry-rotted, over the years it had been in storage, that sewn portion had dry-rotted. And the goddamn holster, here I am in this position and the .38 laying . . . so I struggle down. Took me about half an hour to get down there and pick the goddamn thing up. I picked up the gun, stuck it in my belt. I'm going, oh, oh, this is a bad goddamn sign.

So we were all strung out. We sat in there all goddamn night. The amphibious landing was to come in this way. We had our people in these positions all along the bank. But the VC knew we were in there. And they'd set up over here and they were firing. They had heavy machine guns. They were firing over here to try to draw fire. Now thank God, our people had sense enough not to fire back.

I think we were all scared shitless, frankly. We didn't have a clue as to what would happen. One group had four shotguns. This river was a sizeable river. However, as the night went on, the tide went out, and there was no goddamn water in this river.

And one group, Mike Troy, who was a double gold medal winner in the Japanese Olympics, swimming—he was an ensign, and he had three other guys. They had the four shotguns.

We ended up in the middle of a major exfiltration route for the VC. So the VC are shooting, trying to draw fire, and they're moving across the river. I mean, there is no water. If there is water it's probably about waist high. So Mike takes his guys and he slides them into the water and they sat in the water all night. They could have touched these people walking by them. And they let 'em get the hell through.

The next morning, the funny stories started coming out. It was bizarre. There was some shooting and I guess they killed a couple of people. We were the only ones that had any body count and I'm not sure it was valid. So this great amphibious landing that came in and flushed these people out, we were the only ones who saw a shot fired in anger.

Then, the next morning, here we are, we all got through the night, the sun is rising and [the staff officer] is in this frigging Mike boat again and he's tooling through and as he gets to each ambush site, he waves 'em on.

And here we are, we troop in behind him again and we're tooling up the river. What a time to hit us! I'm saying, my whole team could have been annihilated.

The bottom line to this is, it was horrible planning. Now we had to do it. We were obliged to do it.

When we finally got to the ship, I said, okay. I had enough gunner's mates and guys who knew enough about weapons. I said I'm going to restructure this and Jim Barnes said he was going to participate and we broke it into three or four groups. I felt reasonably qualified.

We had a marine recon group that I felt was pretty good. And out of the UDTs, I put about three groups together I felt were capable. We compiled all the weapons. We got the best weapons for them, the best mix and match that we could find.

For the next three or four days, our people went in and set up ambush sites all along the river, basically under Jim Barnes's guidance because he knew the river pretty well.

We found a weapons factory and a hospital, a rest camp. We went in there. Our mission was to blow the whole thing up, which we did. When we fired those shots, it was like being on Jell-O, the whole ground is sort of mud held together by tree limbs. When you fired these shots, the goddamn thing was just like standing on a plate of Jell-O.

Another UDT veteran recalls participating in an operation in the delta area east of Saigon in the mid-60s. He says he thinks it was Operation Jackstay but he is not sure. He tells of his experience on a night-time reconnaissance:

We did a recon on Blue Beach just before the invasion. That's where they squeezed them down on the peninsula. We did recon on one beach, made a lot of noise, let them know we were there, and then we went around and did a secret recon on another beach.

That's when [my swim buddy] got caught in a fishnet. This kid came out in this little boat to see what was wrong with his fishnet. And of course when he got out there, I was trying to help [my swim buddy] get loose as quick as possible.

And I was running out of air. And there that little boat was. So we both came up on either side of the boat and we grabbed him and pulled him down, him and the boat both, and kept him down and wrapped him in the net. By that time, [my swim buddy] got free and we went on back out. We left the kid and his boat both wrapped up in that net underwater.

Chapter 12
"Heaviest Load I've Ever Carried"

Sometimes, the UDT frogmen were assigned to carry out land combat operations very similar to those normally associated with the SEALs. Often, they were the less glamorous jobs, carrying heavy loads of powder or blowing bunkers, but still in danger of running into heavily armed Viet Cong units. One former member of a UDT team vividly recalls one such sweep:

We weren't supposed to have ammo on the plane, but we did. When we landed at Tan Son Nhut, we were loaded. They sent us out to blow bunkers along these rivers where people were getting ambushed. We went out with these Vietnamese—really, montagnards. I swear I will never do that again. They carried cigarettes in their ammo pouches. They didn't give a damn.

This was more like a SEAL than a UDT operation?

Yeah. It was a neat operation. I wanted to go out on it. Once I got out on it, I thought how stupid I was to be there. Because I was carrying powder. Everywhere I went I carried powder. That's why I wear these things [indicates hearing aid].

There were three rivers. One of the other UDT guys was on one river with a lieutenant. Another guy was on the second river and I was on the third with an army sergeant. We started out on a four-day op to sweep down the rivers, blowing bunkers. By the second day, we had lost comm with the forces on either side and we had no air support and had gotten to a point where they were going to resupply us.

That night, we were on the forks of a river. It was my twenty-fifth birthday and I remarked to the sergeant that, for my birthday, I get one kill and a drink of water.

Just before dark [the night before the resupply] boats kept coming across. First, there was one boat with one guy in it. This was about twenty-five yards away from us.

Viet Cong?

Yeah. We were out with montagnards. The army brought the montagnards down to do these sweeps. We had to keep them in check to keep from shooting the first boat. We wanted the big boat.

The sergeant had this M79 grenade launcher.

He says: "Can you shoot this thing?"

Being a cocky young frogman, I said, "I can shoot the wings off a gnat with that."

He handed it to me.

He said, "We're going to initiate the ambush on your shot."

About that time, a boat came out, turned, and went on down the stream.

He said, "The next one. There should be two people in that boat. You take the first one. I'll take the second."

When that boat came out, there was a big guy standing up, rowing the boat. There was a guy in a blue uniform sitting down behind him.

He says, "You take the guy standing up."

I took the M79 and did a John Wayne. You know, licked my thumb on the sight, then I flipped the sight down and just held it where I figured it should be and pulled the trigger. Boom. I watched the round go out, thought, oh, God, it's going so high. The M79 is just like shotgun. You break it down, put in the round—the golden apple—close it. It goes so slow. I watched it go way up to the apex. It seemed like a hundred feet above that guy. I figured, oh, man, you stupid shit. And all of a sudden that big guy that was standing up just exploded. Boom. I . . . holy shit, I hit him! Just then a mass of fire was going downrange. I handed that thing back to the sergeant.

He's impressed. He says, "You want to carry that thing?"

I said, "No, no." That was the luckiest shot in the world. I couldn't do that again in a thousand years.

That night was real scary. I put up a little Vietnamese hammock waist high, which was stupid. Because all the shooting starts at waist high. I'm laying there. I'm tired. This was the aftereffect of the ambush.

I kept thinking: If we get in a fight, I'm going to die because I'm waist high.

But I was too tired to move out of the hammock. And then my butt started getting wet. I felt out there, the river was up and I'm laying in the river.

I kept hearing babies crying and women talking. Moaning. All night.

That morning, I saw we were at a fork of the river, where two rivers came together and went on together. My hammock laid so I had a field of fire down the river. Just as it started to lighten up, a boat came down. The water was receding. There were three guys. I had my weapon across my stomach.

About that time the machine guns open up and just cut 'em down. Then it stopped. I started easing out of my hammock. I heard a guy going splash, splash. I told him to stop and there was no more splashing. When it came up light, across on the bank was this guy just mangled into the mud.

The boat we had hit earlier came floating down and was caught on a limb. We searched that boat. The guy was an NVA regular. By that time, he was just a mass of flies. The body of the guy I had hit had fallen over in the river.

We moved on to the clearing where we were supposed to get water. I noticed at the back of the clearing, about fifty to sixty yards away in the saw grass, a guy carrying an M60 machine gun. I thought the other platoon was doing a sweep.

The sergeant says, "They should be up front or alongside us."

As the helos come in, they say the woods are swarming with people. That was VC out there. So we moved on down the river at a ruddy great knot—as fast as we could go. We weren't supposed to be picked up till next day.

We met up with another group of our guys and found a cache. There was a uniform factory, a drug store, sleeping quarters, and four or five buildings, in this swamp.

A fight ensued there. I got there as the firefight was abating. We captured some women and fifteen kids and an old man. The old man had been hit in the leg and the bone was broke, sticking out. Everybody who had been shooting was gone. They got away. A kid was hit, had his forehead gone. Sometimes innocents get killed in war.

Was he dead?

Yeah, nothing but nerves jerking.

Then we made a race to the pickup point. I was carrying a backpack. We had three women, fifteen kids.

The old man, we couldn't bring him out. The one that was shot, we couldn't bring him out. We had to leave him. And we had to finish off the old man. That was my first time. It wasn't rage. I don't know whether it was fear, or what.

I had to kill him.

Why?

We couldn't take him and he was in pain. He had been shot through the leg. We didn't know whether the femoral artery was nicked, but we couldn't stop the bleeding and we had to move on. And the pig. Oh, Jesus. They had a little pigpen, like a little five-foot pen, on stilts. And this huge pig is in there. And he was hit. And he was screaming.

As they were moving out, I stayed back to take care of the old man. To show you how the mind works, I knew I was going to do it with a knife. But I took out my medical kit and I gave him morphine, the whole morphine syringe. And then I turned him around. I guess the morphine was taking effect. And that's when I stabbed him. When I did, he jumped and that scared me. And I stuck him again. I was hitting him so hard I was causing him to jump because I was scared.

And then I took off.

Why didn't you shoot him?

I don't know. I have no idea. I have no idea. That's the first time anybody's ever asked me that. I didn't think we were supposed to do that. I couldn't stand the screaming of the pig. I shot him with my .38— no, 9mm. And we moved on.

Did you have any discussion about what to do about the old man?

No. We hardly ever talked, the army sergeant and I. Well, we talked, but not about what to do.

We went on to the pickup point. We met up with the lieutenant and they had hit a boat. And they had captured a female the night before and she was hit in the arm and she died during the night sometime. They had hit the boat an hour before we had got there.

The guy was still in the boat. You couldn't tell it was human, there were so many flies. I never thought it was human anyway. We talked about who we captured and all that stuff. And then we went out to the boats.

What I was going to say earlier was, when we captured those kids and that woman, I was wearing a buttpack. And this woman had two kids, one in each arm, and neither one of them could walk. And they were crying and they were crying and all I did was go, shhh, and [snaps fingers] they stopped. She stopped 'em from crying. She was struggling, carrying both of these kids.

So I put one kid on my buttpack and tied a string around him so he wouldn't fall off in case he went to sleep and I carried him for about five klicks on my back, him sitting on my buttpack in my H-harness.

How old was he?

I couldn't tell you. Maybe a year. He was a heavy load. To tell you the truth, I've carried sixty- and seventy- and eighty-pound rucksacks. But that kid was the heaviest load I've ever carried. Because that was his grandfather I had killed.

The SEALs' War

Chapter 13
A Greek Tragedy

The story of John C. "Bubba" Brewton is an almost classic Greek tragedy. It is the story of a handsome, talented young officer destined for success in whatever field he chose. And yet, as some of his friends perceived, he suffered from a fatal flaw that eventually led to his tragic death.

Brewton served two tours in Vietnam in 1968–69 and 1969–70. In his first tour, he was assistant to Lt. Richard P. Woolard, commander of SEAL Team TWO, 3d Platoon. Also serving with him at that time was Lowell E. "Bo" Burwell, a medical corpsman. In his second tour, Brewton was assistant commander of the 10th Platoon. Serving with him at that time was another medical corpsman, Robert P. "Doc" Clark. All three vividly recall Brewton's life as a SEAL in Vietnam, and his death.

When Bo Burwell became a SEAL in 1968, he had already served two tours as a corpsman with marine force recon units in the northern area of South Vietnam. He went on to serve two tours with SEAL Team TWO in Vietnam in 1968 and 1969. When he went to Vietnam as a SEAL in 1968, he was assigned to the 3d Platoon, operating out of Nha Be. This is his story of his experiences with Woolard and Brewton:

I had already had extensive service so I joined a platoon already in country. We were at Nha Be. We worked in the Rung Sat and in Long An Province, primarily.

The Viet Cong had a significant force in the T-10 area [a particularly dangerous area in the northeastern section of the Rung Sat Special Zone]. It had all the rear service for the regiment that did attacks on Saigon and the surrounding towns. They'd do their attacks and then come back into this safe area and hide.

They were also doing like a hundred shipping attacks a month on the rivers from the South China Sea to Saigon. They were just shooting these guys up left and right. They were using mines, handheld rockets. They were using command detonated mines. And of course small arms off the banks.

We started targeting these people. We would go in there quite often. That's what we were there for. When we left they were making only three or four attacks a month. So we made quite an impact there.

That was the 3d Platoon. The officers were Lieutenant (jg) Woolard and Lieutenant (jg) Brewton. John was my squad leader.

He and Woolard were probably two of the best matched platoon commanders, because they got along so well. And they had such extraordinary leadership, I thought, under fire.

I have been in a lot of firefights, a lot of gun battles. But those two people, for leadership under fire, I haven't seen it matched. Both of them were just so cool.

Several instances come to mind. It bothered all of us that Brewton was so cool, because he would do things probably some of the rest of us wouldn't have done. I remember in firefights, while the shooting was still going on, you would look out there and see him wandering around collecting intelligence, something the enemy may have dropped. And we're taking fire at that time. It was almost like he had a certain confidence about him that nothing would ever happen to him. And therefore he—it wasn't as if he could walk on water. But if he did, he wouldn't get his feet all the way wet. He did have a great confidence. And that's one of the things you'll find with great military leaders. And we had many of them in the SEAL teams.

There was a night in particular when John Brewton was the patrol leader. We had patrolled into this place and set up on a pretty good sized road, like a logging road, up away from the swamp area. They had little hootches and hiding places back in the woods.

We had looked pretty much all night and hadn't made any contact. So we decided we'll set up an ambush. It was starting to get dawn.

So we'll just set up on this road junction—a dirt trail and this path, foot path, that came into it. There was a huge tree there. We couldn't see the tree real well in the dark but the guys put up a claymore on the side of the tree, aimed right down at the road junction.

We set an L-shaped ambush with the main force out on the road and myself and [Engineman Chief Solomon D.] Atkinson on this short leg. I was right up next to the V in the road. As soon as daylight come, you could hear the coughing and hacking, these guys getting up and having their first cigarette. They're coming out of their hiding places. There must have been two dozen of them that congregated right at this spot, where these two trails came together.

Well, it was daylight and under the rules of engagement, we had to challenge. So Lieutenant Brewton stood up and in his best Alabama accent, he *lai day*-ed—stop, come here or whatever. These guys looked around and started running in all different directions. We had the machine guns and we opened fire. My land, we were shooting, the tracers were hitting these guys, and they were going down.

And all of a sudden they fired off this claymore mine, up on the side of this tree. Well, we didn't know, and the people who put it up there didn't know, but that tree was rotted. That thing exploded! It knocked some of the warrant officer's teeth out. It knocked us down. It blew up the tree. It killed some [Viet Cong] people, too. We had two or three bodies out there.

The shooting was still going on and all of a sudden we see something bob up out there and it was Lieutenant Brewton. And he was out there checking these people, seeing what they dropped, if they dropped any weapons. The kinds of things we would collect and try to get away with. To see who had had a gunfight with us. He was a bit overconfident. But he was a wonderful person. He and Woolard were so well matched. The organization, everything just flowed so perfectly. We thought we would all be together forever. These are the type people who make you feel: I've served with the best.

One time we had gone in on an operation and, it was such a beautiful night, we had just kept on going. And by this time we were getting toward the end of our tour. I guess the animalistic senses, or the sense of well-being in combat, had overcome common sense. And fear. This particular night was such a beautiful night we had started in an operation and we just kept patrolling, patrolling.

The platoons made a brief record of each operation on what they called a "Barndance card." The Barndance card kept by SEAL Team TWO, 3d Platoon, dates this operation as the night of 10–11 October 1968. The patrol was led by Woolard, accompanied by Brewton.

It was in the same area where John Brewton got killed. This was before. This was on the '68 trip. This night, there were probably eight, nine, or ten of us. Toward the end of the tour, those who liked to go would be all these people wanting to go. And then of course you had the ones who didn't like to go and they would look for all these little excuses. They were coughing or they had an ingrown toenail.

This particular night, we had patrolled on in and we got totally out of the range of the supporting weapons from the heavy SEAL support craft. We came into this area, a great huge field, I would say probably five hundred acres. And there was a road which connected these two hamlets. You could see the lights, probably a mile distance apart.

Here went this Viet Cong riding a bicycle. He's got a woman on the bicycle and he's talking all sorts of sweet nothing. We had some Vietnamese with us and they could figure out what he was talking about.

At this point the lieutenant told us, three of us, to go up and scout this little hamlet. We could see these lights over there. So there was three of us who got up fairly close to this thing. All of a sudden we started to get a blinking light—a signal. Of course we didn't know how to answer this signal.

Two of the folks were going to stay there and observe this thing and I was going to go back. While I was on my way back, there was a confrontation with the guy coming back on the bicycle. He got shot for stopping and taking his weapon out. By that time, we had gotten together and gotten back to the group, the three of us.

This little village is starting to come to life. Of course we had nowhere to go. We just sat there. Here they were coming and you're cut off. Where are you going to go? You don't really know where to go. It happened so quickly the only thing we could do was put out some claymores and hope to catch them as they came in.

We were cut off. The village had us cut off from the trees we had come out of. You hear dogs here and you can hear people coughing here so you pretty well knew where they were. We were surrounded. Here the folks came.

Somewhere in the firefight, Lieutenant Woolard got shot in the leg and the arm. He was not far from me. I had a Stoner machine gun and I was putting out a lot of tracers. As a matter of fact, that was the last tracer I ever fired, last one I ever will shoot.

Why?

They come right back at me. Someone can see them and they can direct the fire right into you. There was a lot of those white-green things, the AK, come right back in there.

There was an initial gunfight, then they pulled back. We tried to get a Sea Wolf out to us. Well, the Sea Wolf was broke. One of them was up but they weren't supposed to fly unless both were up.

Going back to these two officers we had—the personal relationships they had made around the BOQ [bachelor officers' quarters]—this one pilot heard this on the loudspeaker in the officers' barracks, that SEALs were in trouble. He gets his crew together and says he's going out there to do something about it and here he comes.

While he was flying out, there was one of these AC-47 gunships, either Spooky or Puff. The helicopter pilot got them to come in there.

At one point he said, "If you don't hurry up and get here on station, I'm going to be on the ground with those SEALs."

They kept telling him to go on back. No, he wasn't going to go on back. As it turned out, there were something in the vicinity of three dozen Viet Cong bodies that night. Three to four dozen. Thirty-eight comes to mind.

It was quite a successful night even though having a lieutenant [Woolard] shot. He got medevaced to the army 3d Field Hospital. Some of us went up there to see him. They'd already sewed up his legs and sewed his arm up. But during this whole fight, getting back to the fight itself, nobody even knew he was wounded until he had everything secure. And at that time he got over to me to put a bandage on him.

Whenever we went to the 3d Field Hospital to see about him, he said he was ready to go back to the unit. We dressed him up and brought him back. It wasn't against his will. We just put his clothes on him and took him back. We had a jeep. That night, he was aching to go again. This is only a couple or three days since when he was hit.

He said to organize some kind of operation where he didn't have to get out and wade in the mud. So we did this. [The platoon's Barndance card dates this operation as occurring on the night of 21 October 1968—

ten days after Woolard had been wounded.] We had our light SEAL support boat that rode real low in the water—real low profile. The motor was pump driven. You could idle that thing down to where you couldn't hear anything. The only thing you heard was the sweep of the Bendix radar.

This night, we were trying to catch these people moving supplies. We had four boats [destroyed] and thirteen kills that night. We had our boat completely loaded down with weapons and stuff we had taken out of these sampans. We had a terrible lot of equipment.

As we came back through the area where we had had our last shootout, we noticed a little blip on the radar screen. The lieutenant [Woolard] and myself, we were sitting up on the bow. I had a Stoner machine gun. He had a Starlight Scope. He would spot things. We would pop a flare and shoot them.

Up on the bow there it was even quieter than down in the boat. We heard a noise. The lieutenant turned around and gave the boat captain [indicates a hand signal to speed up]. Let's get out of here.

He turned sideways.

Someone turned on a spotlight. It was just miscommunication. At that time we took a couple of B-40 rockets.

We had six out of nine in the boat that was wounded. One guy, it blew him out of the boat into the water. He swam and got back on. He had a machine gun around his neck. I guess you can do a lot of things when that adrenaline gets going. He got back on the boat. It was just lucky it stunned the boat driver enough so he didn't just gun it.

Of course I had a couple of little chunks of stuff in my head—about the only place they could hit me without hurting. It stunned everybody, this huge explosion right on top of you. I jumped up. I got my machine gun. The concussion had blowed the belt out of it. I jumped and I grabbed the M60. The guy who was manning that got gut shot. And it wouldn't shoot. We had the Mark 20 Honeywell [grenade launcher] amidships. This thing, the belt of ammunition had blown right through it and tore off some of the grenades. They were lying right there.

Finally I found a shotgun and began shooting it into the bank. And the other guy started shooting. By that time we had people recovering and started getting out of there. And that's when we started doing the first aid.

One fellow we nearly lost that night. He had a certain amount of intestine hanging out. You just get in and do the best bandaging job you can do in those conditions, with a small penlight in your mouth. He kept getting fainter and fainter. His blood pressure was going down. Finally we got a serum albumin in him. His spleen was hit and he had internal bleeding.

Another fellow I assume is an admiral today, Jay Prout. [He is RAdm. James Gregory Prout.] He was the boat officer, in charge of the boat support unit. He was hit in the throat. Just barely missed his trachea and the big arteries there.

Of course the boat had a couple of dozen holes blowed into it. We limped to a South Vietnamese outpost. We had a medevac coming in and the rest of us would bring the boat back. And when we had all these people off, Mr. Woolard came over to me. And good lord, half of his shoulder was laying down on his back. It took close to 135–140 stitches to sew it up. You never knew it. He went right on directing operations. He's making sure everything is taken care of before you knew anything was wrong. Here he is, these bandages are not even dirty from a couple of nights before, and we've got him shot up and tore up again. He was a pretty extraordinary person.

Woolard, now a captain assigned to the Pentagon, looked over the Barndance card for the night of 21 October 1968. His memory of the night differs somewhat from that of Burwell. While Burwell says he doesn't recall Brewton being on that operation, the Barndance card lists him among those present. This is Woolard's recollection:

I remember this night. I got a Purple Heart this night. I was already wounded at this stage. I had been shot in the arm and leg a week or so before this, so I was not patrolling [on foot]. This was not a hard op. If you wanted an easy op, you just jump in the boat. You could man the organic weapons of the boat. We were in a light SEAL support craft, an LSSC. There were four pintels you could put grenade launchers or an M60 or whatever.

We were in the T-10 area. Nobody would go there but the VC. It was an area that nobody had really operated in. It was a bad area. The ships were taking a lot of fire.

There was a bunch of us in the boat. We spotted a sampan. They couldn't see us. We could see them on the Starlight Scope. We could hear them but they couldn't hear us. The LSSC at slow speed was a very quiet boat, with underwater exhaust. A good boat. If it was coming toward you at slow speed you wouldn't hear it until it was very close, ten to twenty meters away. At high speed, of course, you could hear it and if it was going away from you, you could hear it.

So we saw these guys one hundred or so meters away. This time of night, where they were, they had to be bad guys. So we started intercepting their course with our course. They made it to the bank before we did. We fired them up and killed a bunch of them.

We got their weapons and everything and we felt pretty good. This happened early in the night so we figured, let's stay in for a while. We went to another place further in the T-10 we thought might produce some action from our intelligence reports. We set an ambush there in the boat. This is just a boat sitting in the water where it cannot be seen from anywhere except right near where it was. You don't silhouette yourself out in the middle of the river. You pull off on the side someplace.

Actually Brewton was in charge of this op. I was the guest patroller that night. Due to the wound in my leg, I couldn't patrol. I would occasionally go out with the other squad to see how Lieutenant (jg) Brewton was doing—Lieutenant (jg) Woolard supervising Lieutenant (jg) Brewton. We waited there for a few hours and then we decided to go on down very quietly past the area of the first hit to see if any of the bad guys had turned up to investigate what had happened to their comrades in our first ambush.

We went past that spot and we didn't see anything. We were heading downriver and this is pretty vivid in my mind. Myself and Brewton were sitting in the front of the LSSC with our back against the windscreen. Right down behind us in the cockpit was the driver and my boat detachment commander, a lieutenant by the name of Jay Prout, now RAdm. James Gregory Prout.

Jay was in charge of the boats. He was senior to me but he did what I wanted because he was in support. He ran one or two LSSCs and the big Mike boat. Inside also were five or seven guys, SEALs from my platoon manning the weapons.

We were tooling downstream and all of a sudden I got this baaaad feeling.

I said, "Bubba, I think we better get out of here."

He said, "Yeah."

The boat was going downstream and we were closest to the right bank, maybe twenty meters away. I was sitting on the starboard [right] side of the boat, Brewton was sitting on the port side. Our backs were against the windscreen. Down behind us, as I said, was Prout on the radio and giving orders to his coxswain.

The other SEALs were behind us. So, I got the bad feeling. We agreed to get out of there. I turned.

Bubba turned around and said to Jay, "Jay, let's get out of here!"

The coxswain eased up the throttle a little bit. I said, "No!"

I turned to Jay and I said, "Jay, floor it! Let's get out of here right now!"

And so we did and the boat surged forward for about five yards and came to pretty much a halt. The reason for that was, there had been a lot of artillery firing upstream from us and a lot of broken branches had fallen in the water and this Jacuzzi pump [propelling the boat] had sucked up some leaves and stuff and it had to be cleared. The intake had been clogged.

And right around then we heard this big bang and I looked down. Maybe I heard something, but it was below the conscious level of hearing. I heard something on my right. All of a sudden a rocket round went off from the riverbank about twenty meters from us. And it hit in the water between us and the bank of the river. A B-40 or an RPG-7 going off at night when your night vision is really in there is an impressive sight.

I remember hearing this loud noise and seeing this thing coming toward us. And when it hit the water, it was this big red-orange flash going into the water and it went right down into the water. I felt a little tugging at my shoulder. At that time we were trying to get the boat to go faster. So I turned to my right. I was carrying a shotgun. I emptied the shotgun in the direction where the RPG had come from. And after hearing the RPG go off, the shotgun, which is normally a pretty loud weapon, sounded like a kid's popgun.

That was the only return fire. The blast of this thing had kind of knocked everybody overboard and had blown the belt out of the feeder tray of the M60s. All the guys in the boat were in kind of disarray. One guy, [ADJ3 Alvin F.] McCoy, he was on the M60, took a piece of shrapnel right in the gut. A couple of guys were almost blown out of the boat, just kind of hanging on the back of the boat.

We kept slowly going downstream but we were still in the ambush zone. They fired another round. At the time, I thought it went over us. I heard the initial bang of the thing but I didn't hear when it went off. So I thought it was a dud or it had gone over us. And then we were gone. We went on downstream. We got everybody accounted for, we called in some helicopters to strafe the place where the shots had come from.

Then I said to Burwell, who was a corpsman, I said, "Hey, Bo, take a look at my shoulder, I think something might have happened to me."

He said, "Yeah, boss, I think something happened to you. I think we better get you out of here."

We pulled into a little place and they medevaced me. I got my shoulder all ripped up by a piece of RPG where the RPG had hit the water and a piece had flown up into the boat. It tore my jacket all to pieces and I've got a scar on my shoulder this long from it. But I didn't feel it at the time.

I was in the 3d Field Hospital and the guys came up to visit me. And I said, "Whatever happened to the second round? Was it a dud?"

And they said, "No, boss, you've got to come back and take a look at the boat when you get back."

What happened was, the second RPG had hit the boat about four inches above the waterline, directly amidship and it hadn't gone off. We would have all been wiped out if that had gone off. That boat was armored, but it was light armor, ceramic armor. It would have just killed everybody. You would have written off a SEAL squad and a boat.

I reckon the VC or the NVA or whatever they were were in such a rush they forgot to take out the safety pin when they fired at us.

The standing joke between myself and Brewton really got solidified. The first time I'd gotten shot up was a week or so before this. On that op, if I hadn't been where I was, Brewton would have been hit. If the bullets hadn't gotten me, they would have gotten Brewton. And on this one, where the first RPG came from, if it hadn't hit my shoulder—I was like this, looking over my right shoulder. If it hadn't hit me here, Brewton, who was sitting on my left looking at the trajectory of that RPG fragment after it hit the water—it would have hit him right in the head. It would have taken his head off.

He just laughed about that and I just laughed about it, too, because we were both alive and more or less well.

I used to say, "Hey, Bubba, you've been lucky so far but when you get back to the States and I'm not there to protect you, a safe's going to fall on you. Or you're going to get hit by a truck or something like that."

And he'd just give me that big old Alabama grin and he'd just laugh about it.

My joke with Bubba was about him getting wounded if I wasn't there. My serious problem with Bubba was that Bubba made an assumption that would turn out to be fatal: that he would always make contact on his terms.

I said, "Hey, Bubba, we're not the only people who do the ambushing. We could get unlucky. They could nail us one of these times."

He said, "Nah, it'll never happen."

I noticed that he had a tendency after setting an ambush at night or doing his patrol, when it came time to extract, he would be kind of casual about it, to be brutally honest about it. He would assume that having been in that area and knowing what was going on around him, that there could not be anybody there that he did not know of. And so he was free to just walk on out and basically administratively go to the helo LZ [landing zone] or whatever.

I said, "Hey, Bubba, this is bad tactics."

Bubba was one of these guys you couldn't tell him anything. He was from Mobile, Alabama, and went to the University of Alabama. He was a cross-country runner. He had been a cheerleader down there.

He was a great guy. He was big. He was tough. He was good looking, brave, smart, had lots of initiative. He was just a great guy. He was my Ranger buddy. I loved this man. But he had this . . . I couldn't get it through his head that this was bad tactics.

Woolard, Brewton, and Burwell finished their tour with the 3d Platoon in December 1968. In the fall of 1969, they were all back in Vietnam. Woolard was commander of the 3d Platoon in the Camau area at the southern tip of Vietnam. Burwell returned with Woolard for his fourth tour in Vietnam as medical corpsman. Brewton could have remained in Little Creek and waited for the opportunity to return to Vietnam as a platoon commander. Instead, he chose to return sooner as assistant to Lt. A. Y. Bryson, commander of the 10th Platoon. He was again operating out of Nha Be in the delta region between Saigon and the South China Sea. Woolard continues his account:

What happened on his second tour was he was out on what I think was a platoon-sized patrol and they ended up in a base camp after having set up all night in an area. They were moving toward their extraction point in the morning and walked into a base camp and got shot up. This happened Thanksgiving Day, 1969, and he died of wounds 11 January 1970. That's the short version.

A slightly longer version is: This happened in the T-10 area near Nha Be where he had been on his first tour. So he was back there with Bryson working out of Nha Be again. I was down at Camau, 150–200 miles away. I would occasionally get up to Nha Be.

I remember the day before Brewton got wounded, one of the other platoon commanders—at that time there were three SEAL Team TWO platoons located in Nha Be—a friend of mine named Doug Ellis, said, "Hey Rick, glad you're here. You know Bubba. We've got to talk to him about going up to 3d Field [hospital in Saigon] and getting some medical attention because he's got some sort of infection in his body. He's got this boil on his nose and it hasn't gone away. He's got an ulcerated leg from where a hot shell casing burned him during a boat ambush a couple of weeks before and that's not getting any better. We've got to get him to go get some medical attention."

I went and talked to Bubba. As I said before, Brewton is one of these guys you couldn't tell him anything if he didn't want to hear it. We tried to talk him into it, going up to the 3d Field Hospital.

He said, "Hey, look, I'm two-thirds of the way through my tour. I'm going to go back, I'm going to marry Cheryl. I'm going to get out of the navy soon. I mean, it's almost over. I don't have time for that. I'll do it later on. I'm not going to bother."

He wouldn't reconsider. That was the night before Thanksgiving. Thanksgiving Day, he got up in the morning early. I saw him leaving. I guess it was the night before. I saw him leaving. That's the last time I ever saw him when he was in decent shape.

In 1969, Robert P. Clark was thirty-four years old, an E-6 and the senior enlisted man in the 10th Platoon of SEAL Team TWO. He was also the platoon's medical corpsman. The other SEALs called him Doc. He had been through the navy's most advanced schools for medical corpsmen and had served for four years with marine units at sea before becoming a frogman. But never, in his long career as a corpsman, had he actually treated a wounded man in combat—until the afternoon of 24 November 1969. This is Clark's account of the day John Brewton was fatally wounded:

I was on the operation the day John was shot. John had a staph infection in his nose. We said he shouldn't be out operating. But John was one of these guys who wanted to be out operating all the time. He was a good young operator. He just wouldn't stay out of that dirty, muddy crap.

We were operating in the Rung Sat Special Zone. It seems like the whole platoon was there that day. Usually I operated with my squad. Usually Brewton was with the other squad. So this was a joint operation.

We had been on an op where we had been given some intelligence. We set up an ambush. Nothing happened and basically we were extracting from the ambush when we walked into what was probably a Viet Cong base camp. We were going through water anywhere from knee deep to thigh deep and the next thing we know the shooting started. They were shooting from an enclosed bunker and just kind of spraying the area.

Not only did Brewton get shot, but Bob Christopher [EN2 Robert D. Christopher], one of our machine gunners, who I believe was on point at the time, was shot through the head and some of his fingers were blown off. He was also shot through the thigh.

Because I was the medic in the platoon, I was on rear security. We were leaving the ambush point, all going in a line. We had found an old abandoned sampan, looked it over. We got a little further and that's when the action started.

When the firing started, I was behind. Everybody has a field of fire. Everybody went their own way.

The next thing I remember hearing is, "Hey, Doc, get up here!"

I charged through everybody to get up . . . That's when I found Christopher facedown, shot. Brewton is over here to the right. He might have been shot first.

I got to Christopher. I thought he was dead. I found him lying facedown in the water. He had returned fire until he had taken all of these wounds. I thought he was dead. I heard him gasp.

I turned him over. I got another corpsman who was on the op with us to come over and keep him afloat basically laying in water until I could get the serum albumin, which I carried in a little pouch on my back. I got an IV started in him. I got people to come up to return fire. We were taking fire at this time too.

I got [Lt.] A. Y. Bryson, who was the officer in charge, to call in a medevac.

I got a dressing on his head. I think the bullet went in and came around and came out his jaw. I used to carry an ace bandage and what I did was I took the ace bandage and wrapped the fingers that were just kind of hanging there. I wrapped them in ace bandages.

Then I noticed a lot of red, which was blood, down in his lower extremities. I didn't even know he was shot in the leg. It was the femoral artery. I saw he was bleeding real bad. So I real quick got a tourniquet on that to stop it and then put a pressure dressing on that.

Brewton was hit, too. We had another chief hospital corpsman on this op with us, from another platoon. I'm not even sure why he was on this op with us. His name was [HMC Erasmo] Riojas. He was— I guess he just went out in the field to go out. While I was working with Christopher, he was working with Brewton.

I was so involved with Christopher, just to keep him alive, to keep his head above water. And of course the rest of the squad was returning fire. There was a pretty good firefight there for a while.

It's funny. Once I started treating Christopher—I know there were two guys, one on each side of me. A guy named [SH2 James J.] Folman was on one side. I think [AO2 Thomas H.] Tom Keith was on the other side. They were suppressing fire. To tell you the truth, I don't remember hearing anything. It was going on all this time. There were people in the bunker. They were shooting at us and we were shooting at them. I just don't remember any of that. I shut it out. I had a job to do and that was to save this guy's life.

Up to this time had you had experience in combat as a medic?

Not in a combat situation. This was actually my first time I had to do anything like that.

Did you have to move?

Actually, they came right down through the canopy to get us. I thought moving Christopher, anyone, we might kill 'em. I don't remember whether it was a medevac or a Sea Wolf that came down and got us out.

Were you under fire during the medevac?

No. We had suppressed all the fire so they could come down and get us out.

I remember I rode the helo back. My officer in charge told me, when we put the guys in the helicopter, Bryson said, "Doc, you go with them to make sure they're all right."

Christopher, because of the serum albumin I'd given him, he was starting to come around. He was having a lot of pain and he didn't know where he was. He didn't know what was going on. I couldn't give him any morphine because of his head wound. I was basically just trying to keep him quiet and hold him down until we got to Saigon.

You flew right to the hospital?

I don't remember whether we went directly to Saigon or one of those MASH-like units on the outside. They ended up at the hospital in Saigon.

Our base wasn't that far from Saigon. We could go in on a daily basis to see how they were doing.

What was the quality of medical care?

The hospital in Saigon seemed almost like a hospital here in the States. We felt once we could get them to a hospital, they had the best chance they could. It was getting them from that environment. A lot of times when you were operating and you had a casualty, you had to call for a medevac and the medevac had to get there and they had to come in and pick up the wounded and take them out. Well, of course it takes time. In this case, from the time they were shot, it was probably a good hour from the time we actually took fire until we got them to a hospital.

Did Christopher survive?

Yes. I saw him at one of our UDT/SEAL reunions a while back.

But Brewton died?

Once John got shot, he's lying in all this dirty, muddy water. We saved his life and got him to the hospital. They put him on these massive doses of antibiotics. But it was an almost irreversible kind of thing. He wasn't getting better and then his kidneys shut down. Eventually, he just died. I think it was the infection from the wounds plus the staph infection he already had.

Woolard visited Brewton a number of times in the hospital. His account continues:

They initially misdiagnosed him. They thought he had malaria in one hospital and then they sent him to 3d Field Hospital. I can tell you my impression of 3d Field Hospital. I had to have myself kidnapped from there by my platoon. I just wasn't getting good treatment.

They thought he had malaria and then—he had been shot three or four times, more times than they thought he had, as it turned out. They ended up having to take off part of his leg, and then they had to take it off higher, and finally they took it off up here [indicating near the hip].

When they did that, they found out he had another bullet lodged in him they didn't even know about. He just got worse and worse and finally died. Every time we got up to see him he looked worse. If they had x-rayed him thoroughly and found that other bullet, that was the source of the infection. He had something else [infection] on top of that that he had had earlier.

His fiancée came over. Admiral Elmo R. Zumwalt Jr. was commander, naval forces Vietnam. He took good care of Cheryl Kurit, who was Brewton's fiancée, put her up in his personal trailer. When it became apparent he was going to die, she came over and his father as well. Zumwalt took really good care of them. He personally presented him with his Purple Heart in the hospital.

After Admiral Zumwalt became chief of naval operations, he changed the name of an FF-1086 [class fast frigate] from whatever it was going to be to Brewton in honor of Bubba.

Burwell also visited Brewton in the hospital. His account continues:

We went up to the hospital to see him. My understanding was John had some kind of a staph infection and when his body got weakened by the wound, the staph spread more quickly. I knew he had some very bad infection. In fact, the day we went to see him, the day before he died, you'd have to get real close to him and talk to him. His hearing was just about gone. And his breath was almost like urine. His kidneys had just about quit functioning. John was quite a man.

Years later, I was in Alameda when a ship came to bring the bones of the unknown, that they were going to put in Arlington. Right across

from the vessel I was working on at Alameda Naval Air Station, sometime in the night, in slipped the ship that was carrying these remains.
And it was the USS *Brewton*.

The next morning, I was going to go aboard that ship and say, "Hey,
this guy right here was my squad leader."

So I got my dress uniform because I wanted to look the part. And
lo and behold, when I went down there, the ship had already slipped
away. It was like John, you know, slipping in and then gone again during
the night.

Chapter 14
A Narrow Escape

On the night of 13 March 1968, Lt. Robert W. Petersen and members of his 7th Platoon of SEAL Team TWO left My Tho in the South Vietnamese delta in two boats. Their goal was to patrol through an area where intelligence reports indicated a prisoner of war camp might be hidden under the cover of triple canopy jungle.

What happened that night demonstrates how quickly a small unit of SEALs can get into deep trouble when they stumble onto a much larger force. It also demonstrates how SEALs, relying on training and teamwork, can extricate themselves from such a desperate situation while inflicting heavy casualties on the enemy.

About 2200 hours, they left the boat, worked their way through thick underbrush bordering the stream, spread out, and began patrolling across a dry rice paddy toward the jungle, visible in the moonlight about a mile in from the river.

As they approached the tree line, Petersen took half the platoon and moved off to the right. Lieutenant Ronald E. Yeaw, the assistant platoon commander, took the remaining members of the platoon, an oversized squad of six SEALs and three Vietnamese. The plan was for the two squads to patrol away from each other until they were about fifteen hundred yards apart and then move into the jungle to see what was there. Yeaw describes the operation:

We walked forty-five minutes or so along the edge of the tree line. We saw what looked like firing pits: little spider holes at ground level in the underbrush. We got what we thought was sufficient separation and headed in, very slowly. We weren't going any more than one hundred yards every half hour or so, sweeping back and forth, walking very slowly.

Then we saw a hootch here and another large rectangular hootch over here. This is probably 0300. It's double, triple canopy with pretty thick underbrush. We're peering from behind the bushes. We can see two distinct structures. It looked pretty much like a POW camp, not that I'd been to one.

Three SEALs went in this door [indicating the larger structure]. Two SEALs—myself and [ICC Robert T. "Eagle Bob"] Gallagher—and the interpreter went in this hut [indicating the smaller structure]. We kept one SEAL back here on rear security with a couple of Vietnamese.

Gallagher and I push the door aside. There's a bed there, bed there, bed here, and bed here. Four beds.

I go in, to my right. I have my pistol and a red lens flashlight. Once we get in, we kind of hesitate, kind of pause. We haven't been heard, haven't been seen. You want to keep surprise as long as you can, only break it when you know what you're going to do and how you're going to do it.

Once inside, it got darker. Right here are AK-47s [automatic rifles] leaning against the side of the hootch. I showed them to Gallagher. We knew we were in a bad guy's house. These four beds had mosquito nets. If they're going to keep prisoners, they're not going to keep them with mosquito nets.

What I did, I had the red lens flashlight and the pistol. Went to this bed, lifted the mosquito net, saw the two Vietnamese people, and shot them. There were eight people. Two in each bed. Gallagher was shooting there [to Yeaw's left] with his M16. I heard shooting next door—automatic weapons.

I turned. Gallagher had shot people here [on the left]. I turned to start firing on these other people. The next thing, somebody bumps into me. We wakened them up and they wanted to get out of there. So somebody bumped into me. I beat him on the head with my pistol and fired. But I saw somebody run out the door.

There was more firing going on. Gallagher was doing some more firing. I ran across. There was another opening. I stood in the doorway, one foot in the hootch. By this time I had put my pistol away and had my AR-15 [rifle] back out. I was looking to see if I could see anybody running away.

I couldn't see anybody. What catches my eye is a flash of light right about in the center of the hootch. I remember it like yesterday. I saw a light, heard an explosion, and the smell of gunpowder. A fragmentation grenade went off right in the center of the hootch. Gallagher was yelling he'd been hit.

I knew something had happened in here but I wasn't sure what it was. I thought a grenade had gone off but I wasn't sure. There wasn't any panic. Everything was quiet and calm, no problem. I felt a little slight pain in the center of my back. I was more concerned with where this person was who had left.

I took a step to go back inside the compound. Next thing I knew I was chest deep in water. There was this canal. I was down here in the goddamn canal. What had happened is, I passed out. I had taken a step with my left foot. I've got grenade wounds in my left foot, thigh, back. What hurt me the most, something went right through my ankle. I had been pretty well stitched up the left side. But it was the foot that caused the problem. I had taken a step with that foot and just passed out.

I had no idea I had a problem. None. Absolutely none. I remember turning to go back in the hootch and then I'm in the water.

I'm at the bank here. One of these guys comes over, looks at me, says, "What the hell you doing down there?" I don't know. I crawl out, no problem. Crawl up, get up on my knees. I go to stand up and fall down. I have no idea what the problem is. I'm getting pissed now. I get on my knees, go to stand up, get about halfway up, and fall down. Hook Tuure comes over. He's got a bullet someplace but he can walk.

He says, "Let me help you."

I say, "All I know is I can't stand up. I don't think I'm hit but I can't stand up."

He grabs my arm, puts my arm around his neck. One of the nicks [from the grenade] was right in my armpit. When he picked that arm up, I thought the whole world was coming out of my arm. It took a razor thin wound and just opened it up.

It hurt to the point I pulled my arm back.

I said, "Hook, I don't know what's wrong. Go find Gallagher [the senior petty officer] and tell him he's got it. I'll get myself out of here. I don't need any help."

We were starting to get organized. By this time, the patrol was ready to move out. I'm still trying to stand up. We have everybody accounted for. There was a lot of firing from other aspects of the tree line. The VC were reconning by fire. There were rifles going off all around us, hoping we would return fire. Mike Boynton had something in his back but he could walk. He carried the interpreter, who was badly hurt. Mike got the Silver Star for this.

Gallagher was hurt on the right side but he could walk. I could not support myself on both feet so I used my weapon as a crutch. I told Gallagher to get us out of here but I don't need any help. What followed was half an hour or forty-five minutes of getting us about five hundred meters out through this dense jungle. By this time, it was 4 or 4:15 A.M. and the sun would soon be coming up. The object was to get out and set up a helo landing zone. There was a lot of firing going on.

Before we hit this hootch, I called Lieutenant Petersen, who had the other squad. He said they hadn't found anything and were moving out to their helicopter landing zone. So while we're doing our thing, his squad is moving toward their helo LZ. The goal is to be out before sunrise.

The spot report filed after the operation says Petersen's squad encountered and silently killed two VC. It continues:

Heard many voices to east. Evaded north being followed by approx fifty VC. Set perimeter. . . . Called for Sea Wolf cover and slick extraction. Engaged approx twenty VC approaching from east. . . . Extracted by slick following Sea Wolf strike.

We moved through the underbrush without talking, without firing, in good order. We got to the clearing. There was a hootch there. The point man went out and cleared the hootch. We set up in the hootch. The VC hadn't seen us but there was a lot of firing.

We later figured a 550- to 600-man main force reinforced battalion had stopped in this area for the night. I think we hit a main sleeping area.

With Yeaw hobbling along using his rifle as a crutch, Gallagher, who had also been wounded by the grenade, took charge of the withdrawal and found a site for the helicopters to land. While Yeaw and Tuure worked the radios, Gallagher organized the tiny defense force to protect the landing zone. For his performance that day, he was awarded the highest navy award, the Navy Cross.

The other SEALs were picking off guys as they were running up to get us. We killed fifteen or sixteen ourselves. We were set up inside this hootch. Hook Tuure, the radioman, couldn't get the boats to tell them we were ready for extraction. The radio wouldn't work. The VC were still firing but didn't know where we were. It seemed like ten or fifteen minutes before we established radio contact with the boats on the river. We relayed them the situation and they called for helo support. Gave them the sitrep: five wounded, need immediate medevac and gunship support.

I took a morphine shot because I was starting to get some pain every time I stepped on this foot. Not a lot of pain. Then the helicopters came, probably fifteen or twenty minutes later. It was light by that time. The gunships shot up the tree line, about one hundred yards away. Two helos took the other squad. The VC were shooting at the helos. The helos were shooting back.

The army medevac said, "I ain't coming down to pick you up; there's too much firing."

The Sea Wolf [navy helicopter] told the medevac: We'll provide you with cover. But you're going down there. You either land your helicopter or we're going to shoot you down.

That's close to what he said. I didn't hear that firsthand.

There was a lot of shooting. The VC were beginning to get their act together. I made contact with the medevac. He said to throw a flare.

By this time the VC could see us. We took a few rounds, but not many. I'm not sure how bad it was. If they're shooting at you, you can't tell they're shooting at you. Unless you get hit. You can't hear very much except the sound of the helicopters.

The medevac says, "Okay, we're going to come down but we're only going to send one bird."

So shit, they only send one helicopter for nine people. Normally the helos only take six. But I figured, we've got three Vietnamese. They count less than half the weight of an American SEAL.

The bottom line is, the helicopter settled down. We got the interpreter on, the other guys scrambled on, I scrambled on, in front between the pilot and copilot. We had two other guys. They were returning fire, they were firing back out. And then the helicopter lifts off, gets about a foot off the ground. I tell him to set the bird back down. We don't have everybody. It takes a while to get nine guys into a one-sided helicopter.

He set the helicopter down, finally, got it back down. The other two guys jumped on. The helicopter takes off. And man, the max RPM light is flashing and the helicopter is shuddering. I mean, it's one of these, "I think I can, I think I can. Thump, thump, thump." It finally started picking up. Meanwhile the helicopters were shooting pretty close. The door gunner from the other medevac bird is making passes with his M60.

We landed at Dong Tam, the army medevac facility. They put me on a stretcher and we went into the building. I sat up on the bed. This nurse is asking me questions, like what is your name and what is your blood type. Meanwhile somebody starts cutting off my boot. He cuts away my boot. Last thing I can remember is looking over and seeing more blood than I ever—you know, he took that boot out, the sock was totally red. Boom, I passed out. Just fell over and woke up the next morning.

Reconstructing it, what had happened, near as we can tell, is somebody from one of the beds or someone we hadn't seen went out the door. I remember standing there at the door and looking down. Right outside the door there was an aboveground bunker. The person who went out the door, best we can figure, went in the bunker, grabbed a grenade, just pulled the pin, and kind of threw it inside the center of the hootch.

That would explain where the grenade came from and why I couldn't see anybody outside. There was a canal next to it, with a bank going down. I had taken a step, passed out, and somehow rolled into the water. Hitting the water had wakened me up. But I have absolutely no memory of how I got from here down there.

Petersen got together with some SEALs and led an army company into this area later and found two-hundred-plus bunkers that had been recently lived in. From other information, we estimated between 550 and 600 people. We basically got in without them seeing us—and back out. Between our nine-man group and seven or eight in the other patrol, we got somewhere between thirty and thirty-six by body count, another twenty-plus killed by SEALs probable, and unknown number killed by helos.

We figured they took somewhat of a hit that night. We think the helos did a lot more damage than we'll ever know. You don't fire 2.75-inch rockets—fifteen or twenty of them—into an area like that without doing some damage.

With a small unit like that, you can go from being very mobile and very good to being very immobile and very vulnerable.

I know there were five [out of nine] of us bleeding, some of us hurt pretty bad. I was hurt pretty bad. Tuure had taken one or two in the leg. I'd say we were in serious trouble.

When you sit back and reflect, you say, we were lucky to get out of there. Well luck had nothing to do with it. It was total ability and total skill, discipline and total reliance on the other person. It was a result of having been in very difficult situations in the past, whether in training or in actual operations. Everybody pulled together and did their part, didn't become a part of the problem if they didn't have to be. As much as they could, they became part of the solution. I wasn't going to become part of the problem in getting out of there and I could become part of the solution in directing fire and that kind of stuff.

Gallagher was hospitalized in Vietnam and returned home with the platoon a few weeks later. Yeaw was evacuated to Tokyo and then to the Philadelphia Naval Hospital.

I was in Philadelphia about a month. Mentally, that was the worst part. Once the cast came off, I would go down to do physical therapy a couple times a week. I was doing physical therapy with guys who were missing legs, missing arms. You'd sit there with a guy who had half his leg missing, or whole leg, or a leg and an arm. I had all my parts. All I needed was to get my muscle back in shape and I'm looking over at this guy and he's exercising his stump.

It was early July by the time I got back to the team, still on crutches. I got back in shape and was back in Vietnam in February '69. There were other ops, but nowhere near as uptight or with as good results as we got that night.

Chapter 15
First Blood for Squad 2-Bravo

The action on the night of 13 March 1967 was a routine ambush, virtually indistinguishable from the thousands of others the SEALs ran in Vietnam. Depending on the source, reports say as few as one and as many as three Vietnamese were killed. None of the six Americans in SEAL Team TWO, 2d Platoon, Squad 2-Bravo, was injured.

And yet the events of that night have become among the most controversial in the more than thirty years the SEALs have been in existence.

The basic facts are undisputed: the squad led by then-Ens. Richard Marcinko left its base near Can Tho in a new, heavily armored LCM-8, or Mike boat. They went ashore in an area along the Bassac River known to be a transit point for the Viet Cong. It was their first land combat operation and they were eager to make contact. They set up an ambush, fired upon a sampan, killing its occupant, or occupants, and were picked up about ten minutes later by a small STAB—SEAL team assault boat—which took them to the larger boat.

The SEALs then went to the aid of a South Vietnamese outpost under attack by the Viet Cong and, firing from offshore, helped prevent it from being overrun.

Shortly after the operation, Marcinko accused another officer, then-Lt. Larry Bailey, of failing to support his squad when it got in trouble—

in effect charging Bailey with cowardice. The two men had a heated exchange, although their accounts differ on where and when it took place.

The incident probably would have faded away if Marcinko had not revived his charges against Bailey in a book, *Rogue Warrior,* published in 1992.

In 1980, Marcinko founded the antiterrorist SEAL Team SIX. He later set up a unit called Red Cell to test security at naval installations. In 1990, he was accused and convicted of conspiracy, bribery, conflict of interest, and making false claims against the government and served more than a year in a federal prison. It was while he was in prison that he wrote his controversial best-selling biography.

In his book, Marcinko says he initiated the ambush when "one Vietnamese in black pajamas, no hat, no visible gun; an Asian gondolier," came toward the hidden Americans. They all let loose with thirty-round magazines. The Stoner machine gunner fired 150 rounds. Whoever was in the sampan was blown to bits. All the SEALs found in the boat was a small cloth pouch and a watch.

Then, Marcinko says, the water around him started kicking up and one of his men shouted, "Automatic fire . . ." Another man [ICC Robert T. Gallagher], he says, reported, "They're coming from the back side, Mr. Rick." Marcinko says he radioed for help but got no answer.

For eight or ten minutes, he says, they took fire until a STAB showed up. "We moved down the bank, shouting for covering fire as we slithered, ducked, and rolled our way through the jungle underbrush, as VC bullets sliced the leaves just over our heads or dug divots too close for comfort as we scrambled toward the STAB."

Bailey, Marcinko says, had gone off in the larger Mike boat chasing a sampan instead of backing up the squad when it got in trouble. When he and his squad boarded the Mike boat, Marcinko says he confronted Bailey, grabbing him by the shirt, and banging him against the bulkhead until Bailey slumped to a sitting position and remained there with his eyes unfocused.

Of those who were on the scene that night, only one, James "Patches" Watson, now manager of the UDT/SEAL Museum in Fort Pierce, Florida, gives an account closely paralleling that of Marcinko. In *Point Man,* his memoirs, published about a year after Marcinko's book, Watson says there were three men, rather than one, in the sampan they ambushed. He does not recall the furious firefight reported by Marcinko. Instead, he says the only fire they received seemed to be one man firing sporadically from the far bank. He agrees with Marcinko that they could not raise the support vessels on the radio.

He, too, reports that "the lieutenant"—he does not use Bailey's name—was off in the larger patrol boat chasing sampans. Watson also says he caused the destruction of a rubber boat when he threw an incendiary grenade that landed on the hidden boat.

What really happened that night?

Bailey, who has since retired from the navy as a captain, gives a quite different account of what occurred. This is his recollection of the night of 13 March, related in an interview at his home near Mt. Vernon, Virginia:

Fred Kochey [another SEAL officer] had to go to Dong Tam so I volunteered to take his place that night. I wanted to be where the action was and this was a prime river crossing area.

I took the STAB as an extra boat with the Mike boat. It was briefed that we would use the STAB to intercept radar contacts.

As I recall, we put Marcinko's squad ashore out of the STAB. Some of them remember going ashore in rubber boats. I don't remember that, although it could be the case.

Then the Mike boat and the STAB went downriver a mile or mile and a half and anchored, with the STAB tied alongside the Mike boat. All of us are in the Mike boat. All of a sudden somebody draws attention to a blip on the screen. It looks like a ship. We got excited about the VC having a boat that big. But it was going upriver, instead of across.

I jumped into the STAB with Bill Bruhmuller and the coxswain, Ron Fox [GMG1 Ronald G. Fox]. We chased this contact about two miles up the river. In so doing, we went past Marcinko's ambush point. By the time we had caught the boat, we had gone maybe five hundred yards past Marcinko's position. Still, we were a mile or so closer to Marcinko's position than if we had stayed at the Mike boat. In no way was Marcinko's situation jeopardized. His primary support was the Mike boat anyway.

We pulled alongside this radar contact. It turned out to be this little Vietnamese minidestroyer, an old French coastal patrol craft. We pulled alongside. Every gun was trained on us. An American who was aboard told me later that they were about to blow us out of the water. But they decided we were too fast, going the wrong direction. Happily, they did not shoot.

We radioed the Mike boat and started idling back down the river, going south or southeast. Just as we got abreast of Marcinko's position, then's when all the chtt-chtt-chtt, chtt-chtt, boom, boom started. We couldn't have been more than five hundred meters from his actual ambush site when that happened.

So I got on the radio to the Mike boat and talked to Sam Braly [Lt. Sam W. Braly, the skipper of the Mike boat].

I told Sam, "I'll stick around up here. You go ahead and weigh anchor and get under way. I'll pick Marcinko up in the STAB because there are only three of us in it."

We wait for five minutes or so and there's no contact with Marcinko. I call back to the Mike boat and ask Sam if he heard anything. He had not, so we waited for the emergency extraction signal, which was a little blue-green pencil flare. You carry it in your pocket just like a pen. You pop it and it sends a little tiny flare up 150 feet or so, visible for miles. If you'd lost radio contact for any reason, you popped the pencil flare. That was the extraction signal.

We didn't get any kind of signal, no radio contact, no nothing. So then we start trying to call Marcinko, both the Mike boat and I. And neither of us could reach him. We tried different frequencies. The Mike boat and I were talking back and forth all the time and we were getting worried.

Finally, Braly said, "What are you going to do, Larry?"

I said, "I'm going to go in and get him."

Braly said later he thought we were absolutely bonkers for going in there in the dark. He had to vector us in by radar. We couldn't even see the shoreline. We had three idiots on the STAB, three stooges. You had the coxswain who had no weapon. You had Bill Bruhmuller and me. We had a couple of AR-15s [an early version of the M16 rifle] and maybe a couple of magazines of ammo.

With our hearts in our throats, we beached the STAB. Bruhmuller and I jumped ashore, leaving Fox alone in the boat.

Is Fox a SEAL?

Fox was a SEAL. He retired as a lieutenant.

Bruhmuller and I go in, fifteen or twenty meters, not far, just stumbling around. As they used to say, going toward the sound of the cannon.

We didn't know if our guys were okay and they had shot up a lot of ammo or whether the VC had got them. There was a lot of firepower expended in just a few seconds. Flares, willy peter [white phosphorous] grenades exploding. Tracers. There was too much fire for what ultimately turned out to be two or three killed.

With our hearts in our throats, literally, we went ashore, moved twenty meters in. I came face to face with Jim Watson.

He says, "Mr. B. What are you doing here?"

I said, "We didn't have any radio contact with you guys."

How did you know it was Watson in the dark?

They were talking. We heard them coming.

He says, "Hey, Mr. B. Look at my war trophies."

He held up a plastic bag. I recall a couple packs of Vietnamese cigarettes. He told me later there was also a watch.

Then here come the other guys and they ask: What are you guys doing here?

So we loaded them all on the STAB. They said [in Marcinko's and Watson's books] that there were sailors joyriding on the STAB. The STABs were piloted by our guys. There were only three of us, all SEALs, on the STAB. We loaded them all in the STAB. On the way out, Marcinko asked why we came in. I told him we couldn't make radio contact. Later, I asked his radioman, who was Joe Camp [RM2 Joseph H. Camp], what happened to the radio, did it get wet or something.

He said, "Oh, no. In the excitement, I forgot to turn the radio back on."

Joe's dead now. Missing in Nicaragua.

We put them back on the Mike boat and start steaming north toward Can Tho.

Marcinko says we got radio indications a Vietnamese outpost was under attack. Absolutely not true.

We came around a real sharp bend, around Checkpoint Juliet. There was a mud fort, like a *Beau Geste* fort. Literally, just as we came around the bend, our wits were blown because the VC picked that moment to open up an attack on this fort.

Lieutenant Braly consulted with me and Marcinko about what we should do. The decision was made, collectively, as best we could, without any radio contact with the Vietnamese in the fort and without any language ability either: we should try to pick out the VC and help relieve the siege of the fort.

You could see shadowy VC figures running back and forth. We popped some flares. We were able to bring some pretty good weapons fire to bear. We were only fifty meters away from the perimeter fence. We started hosing them down with everything we had. I was using an AR-15. We had .50 caliber, .30 caliber, grenade launchers, and a 106mm recoilless rifle firing from the pilot house. We probably made two, three, four firing runs. We'd go by the fort, make a 180-degree turn. Go by the fort, boom, boom, boom, all the time keeping it illuminated.

Those poor VC. I almost felt sorry for them. They must not have had a clue what was going on. We must have expended several thousand rounds of ammunition before the firing stopped, the VC withdrew, and we steamed away.

One thing Marcinko has in his book has a basis in fact. He says I was manning a machine gun and he and someone else were in the STAB and were being rained on by hot brass from the machine gun. Actually, it was Bruhmuller on the .50. I was moving around, directing fire, shooting with my AR-15.

It was prudent to get the STAB loose from the Mike boat. Jim Watson, and I think Bob Gallagher—it was a pretty heroic thing they did—jumped down into the STAB.

They went out in the river, just two or three of them, and they started their own firing runs. Marcinko and his boys went back separately in the STAB after the incident was over.

Not one word was spoken in anger between Dick Marcinko and me, all through the night, until the afternoon of the next day.

We got in at two or three o'clock in the morning. Normally, we'd do the Barndance card and then the next morning do the spot rep [spot report, a more detailed account sent to higher headquarters].

The first indication I had that Marcinko was less than pleased with my performance came the next morning, when Chief J. P. Tollison came to my quarters and asked about the accusations Marcinko was making against me at the base club.

I had no idea what the chief was talking about. Upon learning that Marcinko was telling everyone who would listen that I had left him in an unsupported position during his ambush operation, I went to Lt. Jake Rhinebolt, the Detachment Alpha officer-in-charge, and asked him to investigate. He did this and determined that Marcinko's accusations were false and that I had acted properly throughout the evening.

One of the most serious questions that has been raised about Marcinko's account was whether his squad was ever in danger from heavy enemy fire.

Gallagher, one of the most experienced men with the squad that night, says he was not aware of any. This is his account of what happened, as set out in a statement written at Bailey's request:

I was the last man in the ambush line and closest to the Bassac River. Approximately one and one-half to two hours later the ambush was triggered. I did not see or hear the enemy; however, I did cover my area of the kill zone with fire. After about thirty or forty seconds the firing died down. The squad was doing a lot of talking and was very excited.

At this point, a sampan drifted by me into a shallow area. I walked out to the sampan; it was empty except for some cigarettes and a watch. At this time firing broke out and a grenade exploded in the water about seven yards from me. Looking around, I observed several members of the squad firing wildly. I did not detect any incoming fire and concluded that the grenade in the water was most likely one of ours. I then waded ashore and assisted in getting the squad organized into a perimeter. During this period several members of the squad continued to fire out of control.

Extraction took place approximately ten minutes after the ambush was triggered. We were picked up by the STAB with Lt. Bailey, Fox, and Bruhmuller aboard. . . . I was the last man to board the STAB. Extraction was uneventful. . . .

COMMENTS: I remember the above operation vividly, and the account contained in the book *Rogue Warrior* is not accurate. Specifically, I do not believe that Bravo Squad came under enemy fire at any time during the canal ambush operation, and it is absolutely untrue that I stated there were VC coming up on our rear. It is also untrue that the Mike boat went upriver chasing a sampan, or that Lt. Bailey left us exposed to enemy fire. As a matter of fact, I recall Lt. Bailey being aboard the STAB which picked us up ten minutes after the ambush was initiated. We were under no fire at all during the extraction.

I can categorically state that there was no confrontation between Ensign Marcinko and Lt. Bailey on the Mike boat. . . . If there had been, I, as Ensign Marcinko's second-in-command, would have observed it or, at the very least, been told about it. Besides, it would have been out of character for Ensign Marcinko to confront Lt. Bailey in such a manner, as he was two ranks junior to Lt. Bailey, and for Lt. Bailey to have allowed it to happen without defending himself.

Ronald J. Rodger, another member of the patrol who later retired as a lieutenant, gave a similar account in a letter to Bailey:

I don't remember the exact dates, but I recall being with my squad (2B) on an ambush operation on an island in the Bassac River shortly before we went to My Tho from Can Tho. We opened up on a sampan navigating in a canal in a free-fire area during curfew hours and killed two or three Viet Cong. After the ambush the squad sort of wandered around before we were picked up. I remember that there were a couple of tracer rounds that flew way over our heads from some unknown source, but I don't believe that anyone ever fired at us. The next thing I remember is that a STAB, a small, fast SEAL support boat, landed on the beach and picked up the squad. I remember that Ron Fox was coxswain of the STAB and that Bill Bruhmuller and Lt. Larry Bailey jumped out of the boat and came in to see what was happening with us, since they had been unable to establish radio contact with us. We met them a few yards from the riverbank and returned with them to the STAB, which then carried us to a Mike boat out in the Bassac.

I believe this operation was our first land operation and the only one in which Squad 2B made contact with the VC the entire time we were in Can Tho, as we only conducted a couple of land patrols before we went to My Tho.

Bruhmuller, a veteran SEAL who now lives in Panama City, Florida, was in the STAB that extracted Marcinko's squad that night. His account, provided in an interview, closely corresponds to that given by Bailey, with one exception. While Bailey and Gallagher say there were only three men in the STAB, Bruhmuller recalls one other SEAL, MM1 Kenneth C. Robinson, as being with them. Bailey has since contacted Robinson, who told him he was going to go in the STAB but remained in the Mike boat because the other three left so quickly. This is Bruhmuller's recollection of the events of that night:

Dick had taken his squad in. We were supposed to support them. The Mike boat got an alert on the river that something was moving. They dispatched the STAB we were in. We went down to check it out. It turned out to be a Vietnamese military vessel. So we turned around to come back and as we were coming back to our location, to the Mike boat, firing started. We didn't know what was going on because we couldn't raise them on the radio.

We really had no idea of what was going on although I don't re-call any foreign weapons fire. You can tell the difference between an M16 and an AK-47. When we heard the initial burst of fire, I don't recall any foreign weapons fire at all.

Bailey decided, hey, one thing we better do is we're going in to that beach and find out, did these guys all get waxed or . . . We better get in there and provide them some support.

Larry Bailey was very responsive to the reactions that were going on. I thought the action Bailey took was dangerous enough in itself because we didn't know whether these guys had run into a major element and gotten killed or what the deal was. Even if it had happened that way, we don't leave our own people behind. We were going to go in there and try to do something for them.

So, Bailey and I, we jumped off the boat and started in. I think Ron Fox and Robbie Robinson stayed in the boat. They manned the helm, and the M60. And Bailey and I jumped out of the boat to go see if we could support these guys. Yeah, Bailey was right there. No doubt about it.

You didn't know what you were going to get into when you got off the boat?

Had no idea. We could have run into an ambush ourselves. Our whole objective was to go in and find these guys, see if they were all right or lend some sort of help or assistance to them.

We jumped off the boat, went in a little bit, waited a few seconds to see if we could hear anything and then we heard these guys coming back to the river our way. They were fairly noisy, noisier than you would be if you were trying to get out of an area without somebody hearing you. I guess it was obvious to them that all activity had stopped and they were moving out to the river.

They weren't all pumped up about having hit a major target or anything like that. There was no discussion I heard of Bailey leaving Marcinko or what have you. I don't know why that came out that way. Personally I think there were some ill feelings between the two officers. But as far as Larry being chicken or anything like that, that's not true. As far as Marcinko doing his job, he did his job. What occurred between the two later on, I just don't know. I didn't see any of this picking him up and dropping him. It's not a good career move. An ensign just doesn't grab a lieutenant and slap him around, I don't care how mad you get—not in front of witnesses, anyway.

Watson gives a similar account. Both he and Marcinko say they were stranded there and you didn't come get them.

That's a damned bald-faced lie because we damn sure did. I shouldn't say lie. But we certainly did. We responded to it immediately. They were not let go. If anything, they did the wrong thing by turning their radios off. I think they stated that later on, that they did turn their radios off.

Wasn't it common to turn the radio off so it wouldn't make some sound and give away your position?

You can turn the squelch on that thing down so no one can hear anything, but at least you have it on. If you're my radioman and you get killed and I'm trying to holler for help and I can't because you've got that thing turned off and I can't because I don't even realize that radio's off? You know, I'm liable to get waxed because of some stupid thing. I don't think it's a good thing to turn that radio off.

A lot of what happened down there was dumb luck. We had two platoons, four squads. I was with a platoon and our first night we got a hit. It was dumb luck. We stumbled into this thing. It wasn't by design. We picked a place out on the river where we thought the VC would be and we sure enough got a hit. We hit a major crossing of people. They had to bring PBRs [patrol boat, river] in to get us out of there.

The other squad from our platoon got a hit. And then Marcinko's group got a hit. And Larry Bailey went out a couple of times and didn't encounter anything. It was dumb luck. You heard something going on down the river, so you try to insert and hope you can find some activity.

There was no intelligence. The intelligence we used to get from the army was as much as six months old. We'd go down to intelligence headquarters and get reports. They'd say there was a small contingent of armed VC. We'd go in and we're liable to find there's a damn battalion in there. That taught us right off the bat we can't rely on this intelligence. We decided we had to make our own intelligence. We'd flip a coin, let's go here. Flip a coin, go there.

We reacted mostly to the reports of the PBR forces. All the sections of the river were given names—Juliet, Foxtrot, that kind of thing. If they received heavy fire or saw a lot of activity, that was a pretty good indicator something was going on down there. We'd go down and try to interdict some of that kind of stuff.

That thing with Larry Bailey, when we were coming up off that op [after picking up Marcinko's squad], it was just dumb luck. There was a Vietnamese outpost just being overrun. We just happened to be going by. With the .50 calibers, you could just fire right across this field. It was beautiful. You couldn't ask for a better field of fire. We illuminated the area. You could see this outpost was trying to defend itself. You could see all these little guys running toward the outpost. You could see who were the good guys and the bad guys.

I got on one of the .50 calibers. The STAB is right alongside. We were just steaming up the river and the boat was tied alongside.

Someone said, "Get that STAB out of there."

So I think Gallagher and a couple of guys jumped down into the boat and were going to move it. I can remember Jim Watson bitching. I was right over that STAB. And there were a couple of VC up on the bank firing down at them and I was firing at these guys up on the bank.

These guys in the boat were bitching: "Goddamn it, you stop fooling with that gun . . ." because all this hot brass was falling down on their head. But they didn't realize what was going on. These guys were shooting at them.

We were able to eliminate a lot of the aggressors. If I recall, Larry Bailey was later presented a VC flag for the support we gave that outpost. But it was just dumb luck.

That whole situation really upsets me—the implication of SEALs not supporting each other because that's just not true. I'll tell any one of them to their face: We were there to support you.

Marcinko served time in prison and he has made these controversial statements in his book. Do SEALs still accept him?

Oh, absolutely, I would follow Dick Marcinko anywhere. The entire enlisted community backs him, which tells you he was a good commanding officer and took care of his people. It is only a small contingent of the officer community that may have reservations about Marcinko.

One thing I can tell you about Marcinko. He always did his job. He always communicated with his enlisted people. He'd listen to them. And he made his own decisions based on their recommendations. He was very good about that. He always took care of his people. I don't recall Marcinko ever leaving any of his people out on a limb.

Do people feel he disgraced the SEALs?

If anything upsets the people, it's the fact that SEALs were put in that limelight. All of a sudden there are stories in the *Navy Times* about the SEALs. I think that's what they resent. It's not Dick Marcinko. It got into the public eye. That's what hurt. He's writing books now. Good luck to him. But I don't want to see any slanderous things said about the teams. There was just too much togetherness to see us torn apart.

What was your reaction when you read what Marcinko said about that operation on March 13?

I was shocked when I read it. I told Marcinko, "That's not the way it happened." He says, "Well, that's the way I remember it." I said, "Nah, nah, nah." I hate to see it hurt two good friends.

In another statement prepared at Bailey's request, Braly, then a lieutenant in charge of the Mike boat, says that when automatic weapons fire from the ambush broke out, he was in radio contact with Bailey in the STAB and attempted to contact Bravo Squad. He continues:

By the time the LCM was under way Lt. Bailey had closed virtually to the extraction point. I proceeded there also at best speed (eight knots). Enroute, I gave Lt. Bailey a few corrective radar vectors, and when he beached the STAB, I stopped the LCM to avoid congestion in the extraction area. We were roughly 1/2 mile away.

There was no visible weapons activity on [the island], nor had there been since the initial flurry. I was concerned, and apprehensive, about Lt. Bailey's decision to approach the ambush site on foot, and with absolutely no information regarding conditions at that site. I suppose I rationalized that he had the required knowledge, training, and skills. Today, in retrospect, I think he must have been either completely insane, or possessed by an absolutely irresistible death wish.

Once the extraction had been effected, I vectored the STAB to the LCM and everyone boarded. There was a brief and confusing "reunion," with everyone wanting to tell his story and congratulate everyone else. Spirits among Bravo Squad were very high. To my knowledge, there was no confrontation between Ens. Marcinko and Lt. Bailey, certainly not in the vicinity of the pilot house. Had a confrontation such as is described on page 87 of *Rogue Warrior* occurred elsewhere on the boat, my crew would certainly have informed me.

Henry J. "Jake" Rhinebolt, who retired as a lieutenant commander and now lives in Maine, recalled his investigation of the incident in a letter to Bailey:

As a result of my informal investigation, I concluded that, since this was Ensign Marcinko's first land combat operation, he became excited and confused, which somehow led him to try to fault Lieutenant Bailey. It was also my conclusion that Lieutenant Bailey acted properly in all he undertook that night.

Having read Mr. Marcinko's book, *Rogue Warrior,* I am distressed that he would bring up the same false charges he made in 1967 and even elaborate on them. Regarding his account of his assault on Lieutenant Bailey on the LCM-8, I unequivocally state that such an event never took place. If it had, I would have heard about it officially and unofficially the next day, as an event of that nature would not have gone unreported to me. That an ensign would, before witnesses, assault an officer two pay grades higher than he is, would be a very uncommon occurrence.

In a letter to Bailey, Robert A. Gormly, who led another squad nearby as part of the 13 March operation, recalled a confrontation between Bailey and Marcinko the following day. Now a retired captain living in Chula Vista, California, Gormly wrote:

You, Dick, Jake Rhinebolt (not absolutely sure he was present), Jess Tollison, and I were sitting in one of our rooms at the PBR base in Binh Thuy when you and Dick got into a heated discussion concerning your nonsupport of him on a recently conducted operation. I believe he called you a coward or words to that effect, for not being quick enough to extract him after his squad had gotten involved in a firefight. I recall you challenging him to step outside to fight and him declining the invitation.

It seems to me the entire incident was over in a matter of minutes and at the time we all sort of laughed it off, since there was some disagreement as to whether Dick's squad had ever taken hostile fire. It was early in our deployment and none of us were "combat hardened"—some were seeing VC behind every mangrove tree.

That is as best as I remember the incident. It was a long time ago and only a small vignette compared to what was to come.

Chapter 16
The Bullfrog

Commander James Eugene "Gene" Wardrobe, the product of a broken home with a tough childhood in Sacramento and Dallas, joined the navy when he was eighteen years old, with only a ninth grade education. He became a frogman two years later and almost immediately was sent to Vietnam to chart the coastline.

Years later, having advanced through the enlisted ranks, received an education from the navy, and earned a commission, Wardrobe was surprised one day to find himself the Bullfrog—the longest-serving SEAL on active duty.

During his service as a SEAL in Vietnam, Wardrobe became deeply concerned about a subject many SEALs are reluctant to discuss openly: indiscriminate killing.

In two lengthy interviews at the Naval Special Warfare Command headquarters in Coronado, Wardrobe openly talked about this sensitive subject, his attempt to change things—and the surprising outcome of his efforts.

Wardrobe is of stocky build with a shock of sandy hair and blue eyes. His round face is evidence of a tendency toward overweight. He speaks slowly, deliberately, dredging up some painful memories, beginning with his first Vietnam tour with SEAL Team ONE, Mike Platoon, operating out of Nha Be in the Rung Sat Special Zone in 1968:

My commanding officer was stupid. He was also brave beyond belief. He would go anywhere, completely without any intelligence. But he never planned his ops carefully. As a result, it caused us to have a number of problems, and a lot of casualties. Frankly we didn't have a whole lot of understanding about what he or higher authorities wanted us to do. We had been trained to conduct static ambushes in the Rung Sat, but after one month we were transferred to another area to do ops in entirely different terrain—rice paddies and tree-line areas.

So this [officer] took us on an op one night. I asked him where we were going.

He said, "We're going to this village." He pointed on the map to a village two klicks in from the river.

He said, "I've heard reports they're in that area. Don't worry, we'll find some VC in there and we'll ambush them."

The PBRs took us to the insertion point and we patrolled to this village. Shortly after we arrived, this young couple walked out in the moonlight, got into a little sampan, and were about to go somewhere when he shot 'em. The whole platoon opened up, too. I didn't fire. I was the grenadier.

At his order, we took off at a run to go back to the river. On the way, we received fire from VC that were running parallel, firing at us from the tree lines. That's when I started putting out rounds from my grenade launcher.

Later, when we got back to the base, [the officer] wanted to know why I hadn't fired. And I told him. I asked him, "How do you know those people were VC? They weren't armed."

He said they were violating curfew, but that was not the point: I should have fired to ensure platoon discipline.

I told him I didn't come over here to murder people. I wasn't going to fire at unarmed people.

That's the kind of leadership I was stuck with on this trip. I was a newly promoted first class petty officer. There were four of us who were first class petty officers in this platoon.

The next disaster after that op was the death of our senior leading petty officer, BM1 Walter Pope. We were in an armored LCPL [landing craft, personnel, light]. Pope always cleaned his weapon immaculately.

But what happened, there was a pin in his Stoner [light machine gun] that held the sear down in the weapon. He had cleaned his weapon so many times that the little detent wire had fallen out and he had not noticed it missing.

As the boat proceeded to our insertion point, Pope's squad was up inside the forward compartment. My squad was back aft on the stern.

The vibration from the boat caused Pope's Stoner to vibrate. The pin fell out of the cocked weapon and it started firing rounds into the ceiling. Bullets were ricocheting, wounding Frank Toms and others in his squad.

Pope stood up and pulled the muzzle of the machine gun into his stomach to protect his buddies. He took a total of forty-three rounds. It was the most heroic thing I ever saw. This [officer] nominated him for a Bronze Star medal—posthumous. I couldn't believe it. Somehow I thought the navy could have said more, done more to recognize his sacrifice.

About two weeks later [the officer] had another idea. While we were in Nha Be, two SEALs had come up with an idea called underway insertion. We would ride the patrol boats up the rivers close to the bank. The boats don't break their engine RPM. You get off and the VC don't know you got off because the boats never slow or stop their engines.

On this op, we were going to snatch an alleged high-ranking VCI [Viet Cong infrastructure, a person in the Viet Cong organization]. Well, this [officer] kept the boat in the middle of the river instead of in the shadows and the shallower sides of the river. A sentry saw us out there and fired warning shots. Lights went on in hootches along the bank.

[The officer] gave the order, "Get in the water!"

I said, "Didn't you hear the warning shots?" His reply was to shove me off the boat with his boot. Everybody got in trouble on the swim in to the bank because we were so heavily loaded and we didn't have enough flotation and we hadn't rehearsed this procedure well. It was a good three-hundred-yard swim. We were really exposed.

The correct concept was, you would step off the back of the PBR and, at best, you would be in waist-deep water.

This just proved once more, this officer was stupid. He had made us get off the boat in the middle of the river. This was supposed to be a clandestine maneuver, but there were warning shots and other indications we had been detected. They knew we were there.

I've always been a strong swimmer. I saw a man go under and heard a cry for help from our radioman, who said Skinner Devine [SFP2 David

E. Devine] had just gone under. I dumped my gear and swam to the radioman. I dove down to try to rescue Devine and thought I had him. But guess who I rescued? It was the officer. I found him at about twenty feet down. I learned later that he was trying to rescue Devine and in the process had gotten himself in trouble. Devine drowned and his body was recovered the next day.

When it became apparent that people were in trouble, I sort of took charge of the op. I told the radioman to pop an emergency extraction flare to get the boats back. We weren't going on any snatch that night. The next day, I wrote a report of the incident to the detachment officer in charge. I wanted [the officer] brought up on charges. The detachment officer in charge told me there wasn't much we could do. He handed the report back to me. I still have it in my scrapbook.

I got into a big argument with this [officer] about how bad his ops were becoming. I told him we had to rehearse, that we had to have better intel. We really got into a terrible argument. He sent me up to where SEAL Team TWO SEALs were operating out of My Tho. He said, "Go up there, take a day off, cool off."

He was planning another op. I begged him to slow down. Both Pope and Devine were first class petty officers. There were only two first class E-6 petty officers left, myself and another guy named Donny Patrick. I went to My Tho for the day. I was supposed to come back that night on the PBR. But the boat broke down and didn't make the run so I spent the night on the PBR.

I was lying there on the PBR and I turned the boat's radios to the frequencies I knew. And this [officer] went out on that op anyway without me. The next day I learned the following story.

They were going up the river to the insertion point, again out in the middle of the river, and again there were some warning shots.

The officer had missed the designated insertion point. He ordered the boat turned around and went back despite the fact they heard warning shots. They inserted against a bank at low tide and the VC were waiting there. One of the VC had an M79 grenade launcher. When the boat hit the bank, he fired the grenade, which blew Donny Patrick in half and wounded everybody else on the boat. From the description I heard, it was a massacre. [Both platoon officers] were medevaced and subsequently medically discharged from the navy with 100 percent disabilities.

Everybody else in the boat was wounded, the whole platoon. I had heard it all on the radio. Heard them screaming for help, for gunfire support. That really traumatized me. Of late, I've been diagnosed with PTSD—post traumatic stress disorder. This tragic comedy of errors bothers me a lot. I still have nightmares.

When I got back to the detachment the next morning, I got a call from CTF-116, our ultimate boss. He wanted to know the status of the platoon.

I said, "I don't know how to tell you this, but I'm the only one standing up. The only one that can walk." So SEAL Team ONE sent us two new officers and some replacements. And when everybody healed, the new officers tried to improve morale and to get us to go out and do some more ops. These officers were better. They were certainly better planners.

There was a real dilemma in the teams at this time. We knew the VC traveled either the left or right side of a river. They always had their weapons pointed in the direction of the closest bank. In some cases, they even had pins pulled on grenades and they would toss them toward the bank if they heard a noise, at the same time rolling themselves and their sampans over into the water. If they heard anything or if you *lai day*-ed them, you were going to get a grenade tossed into your ambush site. But the rules of engagement said that you had to *lai day* them. You had to give them a chance. Or you had to be fired at before you could fire. The one exception was in the free-fire zones. If they were out there, we were told, we could shoot 'em.

Knowing all this, a lot of SEAL officers and petty officers said: If they're out there, that's their tough luck. They shouldn't be there. I'm going to shoot 'em.

Halfway through the platoon's tour in Vietnam, it was moved from the mangrove swamps of the Rung Sat Special Zone to an area of open rice paddies near the Ham Long River, in the delta. SEALs in another platoon took them on several break-in patrols in the new area.

We would patrol in, sit there all night. We were coming from the rivers as far as two thousand yards inland. We really felt vulnerable because we had not trained for this environment of tree lines and rice paddies and we had no intelligence.

One night the officer and an automatic weapons guy from the other platoon gave us a break-in patrol. We patrolled in to a suspected VC area and set an ambush. An old woman came walking down the path. [This automatic weapons guy] just killed her for no reason. Just shot her full of holes. I remember stopping and looking at her and we started to run and then the whole world came after us. I said, "What happened?" This guy said it was a mistake. And the officer defended him. We had heard about this guy. And he was a psychopathic killer.

That [killing of the old woman] added to my commitment, if you will. Here's my first break-in op and here's this lunatic, this psychopath. We asked him later, "You guys are supposed to break us in. We could see that was a woman. You're supposed to be a seasoned gun." This guy killed for love of killing.

The officer said, "If you get in a firefight, he's the kind of guy you want to have. He's fearless."

I was always against that. I always argued against indiscriminate killing.

Later, much later, a year later. We were back in the States. We were all mustered one day at lunchtime out here in the grinder [mustering area at the SEAL compound in Coronado]. And a young lady was brought by the CO. She came down the line and she picked this guy out. He had raped her during lunch up here on the beach. They sent the guy to prison.

The new officers were aggressive and we started running ops again. We were contacted by a Green Beret who was an adviser to fifty ruff puffs [Vietnamese regional force soldiers] operating out of Cho Lach.

He told us there was a tax collector operating right here [near the village] and he had a twenty-five-man security force. The problem was that the market was over here [on the main river]. The people from this town couldn't get their goods to market past this tax collector and his twenty-five men. He also was a pretty evil guy. He even took young women and girls and turned them over to his men to rape. The Green Beret had had several firefights with them but couldn't whip their ass. So nobody knew how to take this guy on.

My wife was expecting a baby and I kiddingly told these two new officers that I could figure out a way to get this guy. To get the morale up from the previous devastation, they put it out to the whole platoon:

whoever can figure out how to kill this tax collector will get two weeks R&R anywhere in the world.

I submitted my plan and my plan won. And what we did was, we rented two good-sized junks from the town and had them put large amounts of vegetables and fruit on board, loaded them up like we were going to market. And we had a squad in each one of these junks, hidden. I was on the lead junk and I was sitting back on the stern and I would give the signal to fire. I did not want to fool around with this guy. I said I would initiate when I saw this tax collector. When he came out, I would initiate with a LAAW [light antiarmor weapon] rocket and that would be the signal to fire.

Also, I had coordinated with the Sea Wolves, four gunships, to be orbiting about two miles away, out of audible range. I had briefed them where this twenty-five-man security force was. I also had coordinated with the river patrol to have four PBRs with mortars standing by down the river. And I had also briefed them where the twenty-five-man force was. On the night before it was to happen, the Green Beret, we had him take his fifty popular forces and go up there and come around from behind and set up an ambush directly across from where the tax collector operated on the canal. So we had fifty backup reinforcements on the opposite bank.

The plan was to go up this Cho Lach canal, connecting the Ham Long and the Mekong Rivers. When I saw the tax collector, I would initiate a LAAW rocket. Our junks would ferry these fifty popular forces over here. We'd land them and put out a skirmish line perpendicular to the river and when we made contact with this twenty-five-man security force we would have the helicopters come in and strafe 'em and we'd have the riverboats mortar them, too. And if that didn't take this guy out, I didn't know what would.

I was an E-6 and I planned that whole op. It went off like a movie. We got up there and we were all dressed up in black pajamas. We had the conical straw hats on our heads. This tax collector came out with two bodyguards. He was leaning up against a tree smoking a cigarette, with his rifle cradled in his arms. He waved us to come over to be taxed. When I got perpendicular to him, I pushed the hat back. I had the LAAW rocket sitting right on my shoulder. He was about forty meters away. I hit him with the rocket in the chest. He disintegrated. [In SEAL legend, the rocket also vaporized a large amount of money being carried by the tax collector. But Wardrobe says he has no idea whether the man was carrying any money.]

My guys in the lead boat jumped up with M60 machine guns and shot the two bodyguards. And the plan went into effect.

We ferried the fifty ruff puffs over, got 'em out in their skirmish line. They advanced on the coconut grove where the twenty-five-man security force was. We got in a hell of a firefight. I called the helicopter gunships in. The boats came in as planned and fired their mortars. We killed them all. And that night the town, the liberated town, threw a huge feast for us. The mayor came and publicly thanked me and our whole platoon. It was one of the better ops. I was an enlisted man. They gave me a little authority and I went nuts.

I have always loved planning. I saw so many officers that weren't very good at organization and didn't plan their ops carefully. I'm a perfectionist. That's the quality of the operation I saw us able to do rather than just walk around and shoot people that may or may not be VC. I couldn't understand how people could live with themselves. The tax collector and his security force were concrete enemy. Not only was the tax collector a VC, but he was evil. He needed killing. And I got to go home two weeks early, for my daughter's birth.

Chapter 17
More VC than You'll Ever Want

Even though Wardrobe finished his first tour in Vietnam with a satisfyingly successful operation, he returned to Coronado deeply troubled by his perceptions of the failure of leadership by some SEAL officers and, even more, by what he had seen as indiscriminate killing. He continues his account:

I had formed my own code of what was right and wrong, even though I only had a ninth grade education. I wanted out. I wanted to get out of the navy. I was unhappy with the government of the U.S. The country was taking tremendous casualties, but we weren't winning the war.

I told my commanding officer, Capt. Dave Schaible, I was going to be a California highway patrolman. "Uncle Dave" convinced me I had the potential to become a warrant officer. If I would reenlist and be a SEAL instructor, he said he would do everything to make me a warrant officer. He also pointed out that the salary was much better than that of a highway patrolman.

So I stayed in and became an instructor in SEAL basic. They still had SEAL basic indoctrination then. I became sort of the Don Quixote of SEAL Team ONE. During my classes, I told people that they did not have to kill indiscriminately, that our boys in a SEAL team—we were so well trained that we had so much advantage, with the night, our stealth, the element of surprise. The average SEAL got a year to a year and a half of training before he ever deployed to Vietnam.

131

I told them, "You are in fact, in reality, the baddest in the valley. You are the baddest guy in there. If you're hiding on a trail and these guys come by there and there's only one or two of them, why do you have to shoot 'em? A guy alive is much more valuable than a guy dead."

They had rewards for getting various levels of Viet Cong infrastructure—VCI. I asked, "Well, how do we know whether someone was high ranking or not when he's dead and the Vietnamese who had fingered him are gone with his money?" I was told, "Wardrobe, shut up." I was tired of being told to shut up. Where was the truth? I felt like a vigilante instead of a professional. It bothered me bad. I didn't want any part of it.

Two new officers had been working up to go to Vietnam, but had had a few problems getting along with their chief. They were Lt. Sandy Prouty, Naval Academy graduate, and Ens. Roger Clapp. Both were good officers.

I had them come to my house for breakfast. I said, "Here's the ground rules. If I go over with you, we're going to collect intelligence. We're going to operate on hard intel. We're going to pride ourselves on the quality and detail of our briefings to our enlisted men. We're going to make every effort possible to bring everybody home. And most of all, there will be no indiscriminate killing. If you guys can't handle that, I don't want any part of it."

I refused to go back over there until these officers and I reached an agreement that we weren't going to have any indiscriminate killing, even if we were in a free-fire zone. They accepted my terms so I went with them on that second trip.

The commander of naval forces in Vietnam assigned us at a coast guard base near Vung Tau [on the coast east of Saigon]. It was the R&R center for all the Americans and, reportedly, all the VC. Right on the beach. The war machine over there by then had declared that area— all mangrove, part of the Rung Sat Special Zone—a free-fire zone.

The platoon we relieved had reported high-to-moderate body counts. I did some snooping around and found that platoon was one of those platoons that had made the conscious decision that if there were people in that free-fire zone, they shot them.

In the next month, we went on thirty-one operations. We never fired a shot because I wouldn't allow it. Every night, I would look through the Starlight Scope or the binoculars. I would make a decision.

We had a lot of young guys and they were anxious for their first taste of blood, if you will. So I had a lot of morale problems begin to develop because they wanted to get into a good fight. So one night, to prove my point, we saw nothing. So we shot up the water in front of us and did what we called a false extraction, called the boats like we had hit something, made a lot of noise, lot of shooting, had the boats pretend they had extracted us, and then they left.

We remained behind. And sure enough, it worked. Here came four sampans. We were trying to get these guys the fight they wanted. I looked through the binoculars and talked it over with a Vietnamese SEAL. And we came to the conclusion they were civilians again. That they were just fishermen. So we *lai day*-ed 'em, to come over where we were or we'd blow them out of the water. And I showed this to my men. In the lead boat there was an old man and a young boy. They both had their ID cards. And I showed my men. I told this old man to point to the day it was issued, on this card. And the guy pointed to his name. The guy couldn't even read.

So I said, "See what I mean? These guys have ID cards, we drop leaflets, the propaganda helicopters go over with their loudspeakers. These people can't read. Look at their nets."

They had little quantities of fish. Some of the more paranoid guys argued, well, they're going to give those fish to the VC. So what? I showed 'em. Look at their faces. These are real human beings. You want to kill these guys? Look at the boy's face. And that helped.

On our first thirty-one operations, we never fired a shot. And on every one of those ops we could have killed a lot of people. But in my estimation, all these curfew violators in these free-fire zones were nothing more than fishermen trying to stay alive.

So Prouty and Clapp, realizing that if this continued, we'd have a mutiny, went to Saigon and saw Admiral Zumwalt's staff and begged for a reassignment to a hot area. The reassignment they gave us was Seafloat. There were more VC down there than you'll ever want. They said, you want action? It was as far south as you can go in the Camau peninsula.

On our first operation we were surrounded by two companies of VC. We were almost killed.

That first op was a real rude awakening. We went after a medical cache. We went in by helicopter, not quite a whole platoon. More like ten guys. We found the cache. We had picked up a couple of VC suspects. We were trying to get out of the area. We started receiving a lot of heavy fire and the helicopter gunships above said there were two companies and they were encircling us and we were in a lot of trouble.

We had known there was a local company. But not that another company had come down from the U Minh forest. A helo—a slick [a transport helicopter rather than a gunship]—came in to get us out. But the helo couldn't lift off with the prisoners and a whole cargo net of medical supplies, tons of it. So I jumped out of the helo and Prouty jumped out. The radioman jumped out. And an automatic weapons guy.

Four of us remained behind. The helicopter lifted off. We were in a real jam.

Lieutenant Prouty asked, "What do you think?"

I said, "I think we are in big trouble."

We were getting a lot of fire but they couldn't see us because we were in a high, grassy area. And then—I never saw anything like it— a dark storm moved in. It started raining, torrentially. Visibility became almost zero. It was like God was protecting us. We were out of smoke, we were almost out of bullets. I was getting low on grenades.

[Lieutenant Ted] Grabowski had been listening to all this back at Seafloat. Even before we realized we were in trouble, Grabowski is a smart guy and had sensed we were in more trouble than we realized. Grabowski had scrambled Black Ponies [OV-10 Bronco fixed-wing planes] out of Binh Thuy. He also had coordinated with the Vietnamese Air Force for two old Sabre jets. We got Black Ponies. They came in and dropped their loads. The Sea Wolves made six hot turnarounds. They completely gassed and loaded ordnance six times. That's how fierce that battle was. And finally the Sabre jets came in dropping five-hundred-pound bombs on these guys and it still didn't slow them down.

Prouty asked me, "What do you think we ought to do?"

I said, "Looks like we're going to have to sneak out of here and run for the river and try to E&E [escape and evade] down the river."

Prouty was back on the radio talking to the Sea Wolf pilot.

The pilot said, "I'm out of bullets, we can't see you anymore. The storm's bad. We're taking heavy fire. I'm almost out of gas. I'm going to have to leave you guys. I'm sorry but it looks that way."

Prouty says, "Okay, no problem, we'll be okay."

There was something in Prouty's voice. This guy said to Prouty, "Sandy, is that you?"

He said, "Yeah, it's me. Sandy Prouty, Naval Academy, class of . . ." whatever. And the Sea Wolf pilot—they were buddies. And the Sea Wolf pilot said, "I'm not leaving one of my classmates behind."

So instead of leaving, he dumped all his ordnance.

He said, "I think I've got a pretty good idea where you are. I'm going to punch through the cloud and hope I don't run into a coconut tree. I'll give it one last chance to see if I can get you guys out."

And I'll tell you, it was as if God guided this ship through the cloud because he punched through and he was like thirty feet from us. And bullets were flying and hitting the helicopter. He took rounds right through the rotor housing, but it didn't stop him.

Finally, he lifted off. I was the last one to get in. I was standing on the skids. We heard bullets whinging all around us, but not one of us got hit. It was some kind of miracle. The VC must have been really angry.

Everybody had been crowded around radios in the whole area and they were listening to this operation go down. And there had been silence after they heard the pilot saying, "I'm coming in to get you, Sandy."

Well, when I got in the helicopter, the first thing I did was, I put the helmet on—I was really elated and happy to be alive—and I said to the pilot, "Sir, would you like me to suck your dick now or when we get back to Seafloat?"

What I didn't know is that everyone was listening. Word had spread all through the Camau peninsula: There's a real good SEAL op going on. They told me later. There was this awful silence. No one knew if we were captured or what. And the next thing they hear is Wardrobe making that obscene remark. Everyone laughed, cheered, and popped cans of beer.

That bird was out of gas, on empty. The big red "master caution" light was on but somehow he got high enough so when the engine stopped, we could autorotate down in the middle of a rice paddy about eight miles away—far enough away so they didn't have time to come and get us. The pilot called on the radio to have support helos bring us some gas. They came and dropped fifty-gallon drums. We siphoned it into the helicopter and it brought us back.

Yeah, we had asked to go to an area where there was more action and real VC and they gave it to us.

Chapter 18
"My Worst Disaster"

Wardrobe continues his account of his second tour of duty with SEAL Team ONE, Mike Platoon, operating out of Seafloat in the Camau peninsula in Vietnam:

We had problems sometimes with army pilots inserting us with helicopters. Most were warrant officers. There were two kinds of army helo pilots. There were idiots that would take any chance whatsoever or they were complete cowards and they would land you a hundred yards from where you wanted to go, hoping not to take any fire. There never seemed to be any in between. Ha! They were either real cowboys or really reluctant warriors.

There was another tax collector, who had been confiscating sampans from the local populace and selling them to villages in other areas. We had heard there would be this big meeting of four or five district VCI with a province level chief to turn over the monthly funds. We knew where they were meeting. I wanted to hit the guy. But I needed to find a pilot who was gutsy enough to take me right into the enemy compound, no matter what. Right to the meeting. Not land me a hundred yards away in a rice paddy. Because I wanted to jump out of the helicopter, bust in the door, and clean these guys out.

One morning over breakfast I was complaining to a fellow SEAL friend, Frank Flynn. He was advisor to a Kit Carson outfit [scout units made up of former Viet Cong]. I didn't know there was an army captain helicopter pilot sitting behind having breakfast. He had overheard my remarks.

He said, "I'm you're man. I'm fearless."

I said, "Yeah, you're either a hot dog or you're a phony."

He said, "I am very good at what I do."

I said, "Okay, I want to get these people real bad so I'll give you a try."

I showed the guy on the map where the VC meeting place was. He wanted to do a high visual recon, flying the flight path of the daily mail helo so the VC wouldn't be alerted and suspicious. I said okay. He checked it out and told me he could do it.

The target was a big building—a hootch but bigger than usual. It had a bunker in the back. I told him I wanted him to hover the helo over the left rear corner so we could jump out from the skids. That would give us fields of fire so we wouldn't be shooting ourselves.

He said, "No problem."

I said, "It's pretty tight getting in there. You've got a lot of coconut trees surrounding the hootch."

"No problem."

Lieutenant Prouty, the Mike Platoon commander, put Wardrobe in charge of the operation even though he was an enlisted man. "He encouraged the enlisted men to run missions, if you could prove you were capable, to develop a sense of responsibility," Wardrobe says. "He never once during this mission interfered with me. To his credit. He was a hell of a fine officer."

I told everybody in the platoon it was going to be a hairy op. It was voluntary. I didn't want anybody to go that didn't think they could cut it. I got ten volunteers. I briefed it. We had a real good plan. We loaded up and took off.

This army pilot was flying treetop level and damn if he didn't miss it!

He flew right over the top of the hootch. I yelled at him. He banked real hard, back around. They were alerted. When he came back around we were hanging on inside for dear life. The g forces were bad—worse than a roller coaster—when he turned that thing. When he came in for another approach, I was crouched between the two pilots. I saw two VC run out of the hootch and they were shooting back at us. He flared the helo just above the corner of the house where he was supposed to be. But when the bullets started hitting the helo, he adjusted so the helo was in fact over the middle of the roof. He flared the helo to protect himself from the bullets with the underbelly of the helicopter.

But what he forgot about, the bozo—you can say that in your book, that I called him a bozo—was the rear rotor. The tail went into a coconut tree and the rotor disintegrated.

Just before that happened, I had yelled for everybody to get out. Everybody jumped out and slid down this big roof to the ground. They formed their defense perimeter just like we briefed. Hearing that tail rotor go into that coconut tree, I got a sickening feeling. I remember the pilot yelling at me, "Get out!"

Just as I jumped out on the roof, the skid on the helicopter broke the main beam of the hootch's roof and I fell upside down through the roof, landing on the back of my neck. I would have broken my neck but I had a can of serum albumin taped to my H-harness. It smashed the can. The impact from the fall knocked me unconscious and the whole roof fell on me.

Here I am in this room full of VC and the roof falls in on us. My officer, Prouty, and the radioman, Decker, also fell through the roof. The radioman would have been killed except for the radio. Not only did the roof fall on us, but the helicopter lifted up into the air, the rotors disintegrated, and then it flipped over and landed on top of us, bursting into flames. The door gunner jumped out and he saw my arm sticking out of the rubble and he dug me out. He got Decker and Prouty out too.

Everybody was all cut up and bruised. Prouty had a dislocated shoulder. We all struggled to get away from this burning helicopter that was going to explode any minute. Bullets were cooking off, rounds, rockets, everything was exploding. It's a miracle we weren't all killed.

Finally we got out to the perimeter just as the helicopter blew up. What we didn't know was that most of the Viet Cong had gone into that bunker. When the helicopter blew up, I never saw anything like it.

I did a head count and I was missing Doc, my corpsman, HM1 Richard Wolfe. I asked for volunteers to go back to the hootch to look for him. I had two volunteers, a guy named Farmer [AO2 Lance G. Farmer], another guy named Crumbo [PH3 Kim H. Crumbo], and they came with me. They were both automatic weapons men. We walked back to the bunker and I noticed the bunker had been cut in half. The whole top of it was gone. And inside all these Viet Cong were fried, crispy critters. Just bodies in there. Piled on top of each other. When the helicopter exploded, it had cut that thing in half, killing everybody inside.

And then about ten feet away, I saw movement, and I went into the bush and drug a wounded VC out of the bush. I drug him with me. He was all banged up, bleeding, and everything. Crumbo and Farmer found Doc. Doc was lying right where he was supposed to be. I shoved the VC prisoner over to Crumbo.

Doc was a great man. Real aggressive. You could always count on him to do everything just like you'd briefed him. And that's what got him killed. He was exactly where he was supposed to be except when the helicopter broke up, those damn blades had cut the top of his head off.

I didn't know what to do. I saw the top of Doc's head and I put it back on his head and I put a bandage around his chin to hold it. The kid, Crumbo, freaked out when he saw that and he grabbed that prisoner and he stuck his Stoner machine gun in his mouth and said, "You rotten son of a bitch, die!"

I yelled at him and said, "Don't! You'll regret it."

I got right in his face and I said, "Kim, don't do this. You'll regret it. He's just a soldier, doing his job."

And he stood there for the longest time with the barrel stuck in that Viet Cong's mouth. That guy's eyes were shut as tight as you can shut 'em. Crumbo, still crying for Doc, pulled the gun out and he didn't kill him.

I tied this bandanna around Doc's head. When I picked him up all his brains fell out all over my feet.

We didn't know what to do. The VC were moving in on us again. We got the word from the Sea Wolf pilots: another main force was coming. We were determined not to leave Doc Wolfe behind. We were trying to carry Wolfe, but he was a big man, over two hundred pounds. He was six foot something. It is awful hard when you're trying to carry a dead guy. We were having an awful time, not like in the movies. We jumped into dugouts and headed out into the river.

But the Sea Wolf pilots told us the VC were moving ahead of us and were going to ambush us upriver. They ordered us to get back to the crash site. They said they were going to send another helicopter to get us. They thought they could get us out before the main force got there. So we set up a defense perimeter.

While waiting, I think that was the closest I ever came to losing it. For a second there, I felt like just dropping my weapon. Like a kid. I wanted to go home. Just quit. It was dreamlike. I felt for a second like I left my body. I wanted to just tune out. Disappear. Beam me aboard, Scotty. It only lasted a few seconds. And in that moment, I knew the value of BUD/S [basic underwater demolition/SEAL training] and Hell Week and the mud and all the harassment. An ordinary guy would quit. A SEAL can't quit. Those guys were really whipped, still looking to me for leadership. We were still in a jam. The VC were coming. Lieutenant Prouty, with his banged up shoulder, never interfered with my leadership.

Finally, they sent us a helo and lifted us out before the main force got there. And we were a mess. Everybody was banged up, cut up, bruised, battered, shaken pretty bad.

I guess that was my worst disaster. That was really rough to lose a great man like Doc.

Chapter 19
The Sting

Wardrobe's obsession with efforts to avoid killing innocent people took an unexpected turn. He tells what happened:

We went up into this no-man's area where the boats always got ambushed. And the chaplain, for some reason, wanted to come along that night. I was really anxious that night. I had been careful up to then, avoiding accidentally shooting fishermen who were curfew violators. But this area had a terrible reputation. It was a 100 percent free-fire zone. Every time we went up there we knew we were going to get into it. So I had a little different attitude.

We inserted in a French graveyard right where the river had a Y. Right in the middle of the little peninsula was the graveyard. We set up a static ambush right there among the grave markers. No sooner had we got set up than the boats ran into a sampan with two armed Viet Cong and took them prisoner. They broke radio silence and asked me what to do.

I said, "Shut up and get out of the area."

We sat there for about an hour and the next thing I know I heard this loud noise and here comes an ocean-going junk to our right. It was full of supplies. It was bigger than your average Vietnamese boat. It had a high stern area and had a tiller and was heavily laden. It had a big outboard engine.

It was three or four o'clock in the morning. I couldn't see the guy at the tiller clearly but I thought he was armed. I shot him. As soon as I opened up, the whole platoon opened up. We got no return fire at all. We ran out into the river and grabbed the boat but we couldn't find the body. When we checked out the boat, we found a frightened old woman who had apparently been sleeping down in the bilges, and that's what had saved her.

My interpreter said she said we had just killed her husband and they were just farmers and they were bringing the food to market and the reason they violated the curfew is they were trying to avoid tax collectors.

I was devastated. I thought that I had had the power in me. All these years, I had been trying to be so humane, so discretionary, to keep from doing that. And my worst nightmare had finally come true. I thought that I had killed an innocent person. Unintentionally, of course, but it bothered me real bad.

I would not go out on any operations. For the next two or three weeks I would not do anything. I gave this woman, out of guilt, all my money. I got my men and I made them patch her boat. I ordered them to overhaul the engines.

Lieutenant Prouty didn't know what to do.

He said, "You've got to get over this. I've got to have my old Gene back."

I told him I was never going to fight in this stupid war again and all I cared about was this woman. I waited on her, brought her breakfast, lunch, and dinner.

Everybody on Seafloat came up to me and said, "What you've done is really noble but you've got to get over your grief."

I said, "I want volunteers. When I get her boat repaired, I'm going to take her back up to the graveyard."

They said, "You can't go there in broad daylight."

I said, "I know. I want volunteers."

I couldn't believe what happened next. The Swift boat navy guys, they were so proud of what we were doing for this old woman, they volunteered, with two boats. So we towed her boat. We had big fifty-pound sacks of rice. We had taken up a collection. She had hundreds of American dollars. She had food, everything. She was a rich woman.

And we towed her back to that French graveyard where we had

ambushed her and her husband and let her go. I even gave her a chart. She said she knew how to get home from there. She sailed off crying. I was crying, waving good-bye.

As she went away, the other boat was holding off to the right, right where the ambush had taken place. In this area, we experienced extreme tidal ranges. No one had been up there since two weeks before. The tides were known to take a body out and then bring the body back in. And there was the body. The other boat crew noticed it floating in the water. So they hauled it alongside. It turned out the guy was an NVA adviser. They pulled the documents out of his pocket.

They called over on the radio and they said, "Hey, Wardrobe. We just found her old man. Guess what?"

This guy was an NVA adviser and they were taking that food to a sapper team we eventually hit. They were taking them their food rations.

And she's sailing away, with all our money and all the riches we bestowed on her.

The officer in charge of the other boat said, "You want to go get her?"

I told them, "No, let her go. That's the biggest con I've ever had." I call it "the sting." That woman played that role for two weeks to the hilt. She never confessed they were VC.

Besides, I grew from that experience, real internal growth. As soon as we found that body, in the NVA uniform, with the documents, it felt like a hundred-pound weight had been taken off my shoulder. I felt liberated. I had not killed an innocent man.

Chapter 20
Like a Shooting Gallery

Jack Luksik, who had surveyed the beaches of Vietnam as a UDT frogman, became a SEAL in 1967. This is his account of his introduction to ground combat in the southern part of Vietnam:

In 1967, some selected people were drafted into the [SEAL] teams from UDT. That didn't ride very well with some of the guys in the teams. But I volunteered to go and it worked out fine.

I was in SEAL Team ONE in the Rung Sat Special Zone trying to keep the Viet Cong from sinking ships. This was from November or December 1967 through May 1968.

We had very little of the restrictions that were later put on. We had a lot of flexibility. But that particular platoon was a hard luck platoon. On our third patrol, Frank Antoine, who was the point man, had just relieved Lenny Scott, who was our other point man. They had just switched off.

We were strung out probably a hundred yards in the brush—a full platoon. This is in the daytime.

Frank stood up. Him and two LDNN [Vietnamese SEALs] scouts were dropped.

We had patrolled into, unknowingly, a base camp. But the platoon commander probably didn't realize we were in the middle of a base camp. Right then he brought up the rest of the platoon. It probably would have been more prudent to grab the dead bodies and back out. What he did was pull the platoon right up into the center of this place.

He pulled the platoon into the kill zone and basically took two or three more casualties. Nobody else got killed. We were taking fire from about 360 degrees. They probably shot as many of their own as they did of us. We were right in the center. In a way, it was kind of nice. We could attack from any direction.

One comical thing. Lenny Scott, the other point man, had gotten into the prone position.

He hollered, "Goddamnit!"

He had gotten shot in the ass. Later, we figured the round had probably bounced off something else before it hit him. It went into the cheek of his butt but it was kind of funny. In retrospect, even he got a chuckle out of it.

My radio got shot. I was very fortunate. I had a collapsible canteen on top of the radio. The round hit the canteen and then the radio and knocked me on my face. I had this hot liquid pouring over my head and I couldn't see. It ran down into my eyes. I knew I'd been hit. I'd just got knocked down. Son of a gun, I must be shot in the head because I don't feel any pain.

We were told in combat med, if you get hit in the head, you're not going to feel any pain. So I thought, oh, jeez! So I had to take time out from the firefight and I'm trying to figure out . . . feeling over my head and it dawned on me, aha. It's my canteen. Hey, I'm not shot. That's great. I was a happy dude.

Fortunately, everybody saved my place and I got up and picked up the fight.

We had a Sea Wolf fire team for gunfire support and cover. They were on thirty-minute call. They got into the air out of Nha Be pretty quick. Basically, they pulled our butt out of the fire.

They laid an excellent base of fire around us while we called up two slicks. We had moved from where we were, which was really a dense thicket, into more of a clearing. After the Sea Wolf fire team had laid down this great base of fire, we set up an LZ [landing zone], a hot LZ.

The first slick came in. We McGuire-rigged out the two dead scouts and Antoine. [A McGuire rig is an emergency procedure in which one or more persons are attached to a line dangling from a helicopter and transported while hanging below the craft.] I don't know whether that helo dropped the McGuire rig and came back or whether it was two other slicks. Then we jumped on board. The two birds took off. We had everybody.

The radioman is the last guy in, even though my radio was out. I was hanging on the skids—standing on the skids, not quite inside the bird. It took off and we were taking a lot of fire. We're flying and I'm looking at the instrument panel of the helo and all I'm seeing is red lights. The guy had all kinds of problems but he nursed it into Nha Be.

Both those birds had taken so many rounds that they decided to just strip them for parts and junk the air frames. I felt we were very fortunate. Certainly Frank Antoine wasn't fortunate, but I thought frogman luck did us well, considering what we stepped into. We came out smelling like a rose.

There was a lot of criticism of the platoon commander that he shouldn't have brought the whole platoon up. But hindsight is always twenty-twenty.

How many people were in the base camp?

From the volume of fire we were taking, there must have been thirty or forty people around. They undoubtedly had heard us coming through the dense vegetation leading up to that spot.

What did you expect when you were going there?

We had no intel to indicate there was a base camp there. The purpose of the patrol—we had a predawn insertion—was supposed to be a daylight movement through space where nobody was supposed to be, moving out to a stream junction and setting up an ambush site for the following night.

Just prior to Tet, we worked with [Lt. Richard] Marcinko's platoon in Binh Thuy.

We were patrolling through a banana plantation and came upon a bunker. We were getting fire from the bunker. The banana trees are situated on mounds. So we took cover behind a mound, basically line abreast behind the mound. We were exchanging shots with the bunker.

We sent out a flanker, our grenadier. He was flanking to the right, coming around, getting on top of the bunker, and he was going to toss in a couple of grenades.

Could you see your flanker?

Oh, yeah, we could easily see. He was out of view of the door of the bunker. We were watching his progress, keeping the people in the bunker busy until he got over there.

Well, just as he was getting on top of the bunker, this kid Roy Keith, for whatever reason, decided to make a one-man attack, right up the middle. And the whole platoon, pretty much in unison, told him to get down. But he jumped up, headed straight for the hole, the entrance, at the back of this bunker.

And right about that time, the occupants of the bunker decided it probably wasn't a healthy place to be. Three or four of them exited. But before the first Viet Cong had gotten out of the bunker itself and before our flanker had gotten in place to throw a grenade, Keith came within about five foot of the door of the bunker.

The first guy out had an AK on full automatic and damn near cut Keith in half, killed him on the spot. And then, the first guy came out. Our flanker, he had an M79 grenade launcher with canister rounds and nicely took off the guy's head. Before he could reload, the other two or three came out and took off.

It was like being at a shooting gallery. We were all on line behind this mound and these guys come tearing off across the front of it and we just nailed them. That was very clean.

I have no explanation as to whatever possessed Keith to take off and run like that.

That was our tenth or twelfth op in country. That, coupled with what happened on our third patrol, morale wasn't as high as it could have been.

What happened to your platoon during Tet?

We got sucked into perimeter defense of the base there at Binh Thuy. Tet came and went and nothing happened around us. But we were ready. Then we went back to Nha Be and for the rest of the six months ran our ops and did it correctly and nobody got hurt.

Was the rest of your tour pretty quiet?

Well, there were no engagements that we didn't win. It's been my experience, and I think you'll find most people at the time aren't particularly concerned about being afraid because you're too busy doing your job. You can get scared later, at that point in life when you realize your own mortality. I didn't see anybody who showed any outside signs of fear in combat. I think fear is part of it but I guess that's the difference between being a professional and being a coward. If you're a professional, you do your job and you do it well.

How good were the enemy soldiers?

The Viet Cong didn't grow up with a good diet. One of the consequences is a lot of them tended to be nearsighted. They didn't get proper corrective lenses. Consequently, they are lousy shots. A lot of their people were conscripts and not quite as dedicated as they might have been.

But their leadership, considering the very difficult conditions they ran their operations from, did an excellent job.

Chapter 21
"Everything Is Written Down"

Most SEALs have great confidence in their own abilities and the abilities of their comrades, working together, to make things come out all right. But many of them have a feeling that blind fate often has a powerful role to play as well. Jack Macione is convinced that a couple of his experiences are proof of the role fate plays on the battlefield:

Let me tell you a profound story. This is awesome. I really believe everything is written down and all we do is play the script.

I was relieving Jake Rhinebolt as OINC [Lt. Henry J. Rhinebolt, officer in charge of the SEAL contingent in Vietnam]. This must have been July 1967. We had flown over in a DC-6, a four-engine, lumbering, monstrous airplane. We had been in the air for something like eighteen hours. I think we had made a couple of hours' stop in Hawaii.

We got to Tan Son Nhut, the door opens, there was Jake at the bottom of the ramp, stairs, whatever they had.

They all call me Blackjack.

He says, "Hey, come on, Blackjack. Jump in the jeep. I'm going to go down to brief General Westmoreland."

So I said, "Great." I turned to the chief and said, "Take over."

I jumped in Jake's jeep and down we went to MACV [Military Assistance Command Vietnam] headquarters. We come into this darkened war room. All the charts and the lights. God, there he was, General Westmoreland. I really admired him. So I sat in back and Jake briefed him up.

It was this: that we had some intel that a Viet Cong, a North Vietnam courier, a high-ranking infrastructure courier, had been walking south for the last three months or whatever it was. It was a long time. And somewhere in this vast thousands and thousands of square miles of jungle we were going in to get him.

After the brief, Jake says, "You want to go?"

I said, "Yeah, I want to go. But come on, Jake, you gotta be shitting me. This guy is walking south. He could be anywhere in a couple thousand square miles of jungle. And we're going to find him?"

He says, "Well, we got some good intel. He's supposed to be here tomorrow night."

"Jake, we could pass in the jungle ten feet apart."

"Well, we're going to go in. You want to go?"

"Shit yes, I want to go."

I didn't have anything. So I borrowed some guy's weapon and some grenades and ammunition and black face and bam, off we went down the river.

The plan was to make an insertion, rubber boat, into this area called the—I think it was some secret zone. No friendlies had been in there in twenty years. So we go in like two or three in the morning, two rubber boats, get on the beach.

The plan is that one squad is going to cross over the inner waterway. We're on the South China Sea. You get on land and walk a few yards and there'll be an inner waterway they put the boats on. We're going to move up to this hootch, three–four hundred yards.

We split the squad. I'm tail end Charlie. As we're weaving along this path, all of a sudden the whole squad stops in midstream. Like a caterpillar stopping. All stopped at once.

I happened to be right on the edge of the embankment on the South China Sea. Coming by in a sampan are four guys with AK-47s. I could have reached out and touched any one of them. We didn't make a sound. They were talking Vietnamese. We knew it was probably a bodyguard or it could have been the guy, but probably not.

No sooner had they just cleared me and I hear a noise behind us. So I look back—it's three o'clock in the morning. I grab [HM1 Paul

T.] Schwartz, the corpsman. He had the shotgun. I pushed him down on one knee right where I was. I look back and I see these shapes coming. The reason I can see them is there is a water inlet. I can see the silhouettes against that bright water.

We're supposed to make contact with our other squad by radio, but they never contacted. So we figure the radio's out. But now they're walking in behind us. And I'm pissed because it's dangerous. So the first thoughts I'm having is chewing somebody's ass out.

Anyway, here come the shapes. Right in front of me is a branch. As he ducks under the branch, I see this conical hat. I know I've got Viet Cong.

The guy comes up, bumps right into me. So I push him over and tell him in Vietnamese to get his hands up. He brings his rifle around, but he's close to me. He shoots but the rifle is up against the side of my head. I push him off. I hear Schwartz pumping off the shotgun. Cachung! Cachung! Cachung!

I'm deadly from the hip. As a kid I'd gone night after night after night shooting rats at the dump. I'm deadly from the hip. When I went through a pop-up target course, I never aimed. I just shot from the hip and I was always four-oh. [Perfect. The highest numerical grade on navy evaluations is 4.0.] Always. So I let off a round. Well, I know I hit the guy because it flips him over a bush into the South China Sea.

There's a lot of shit going on. Shooting going on. Dark. We had full tracers on our guns at night. So I run over to the bank and I see this black head going downstream. The water is going pretty fast. The tide. And I say, "Is there anybody in the water? Any of my men in the water?" In English.

No answer.

Peewee Nealy [ENC Richard C. Nealy], the little bantamweight, says, "Shoot the son of a bitch!"

So I shoot, hit the guy, and the head disappears.

The shit has hit the fan. I jump in the water. I'm going to cover the waterside flank to make sure we don't get our own flank from someone coming around.

I lay my grenades up on the bank. I'm in the water. I'm kind of watching the waterside. There was a lot of shooting and all of a sudden it gets quiet.

I stayed there for about two hours. Not a sound, nobody moving. Suddenly, underwater, it feels like somebody grabs me. I turn around and see a knapsack floating.

I pull up on it and on the end of the knapsack is this guy I had shot two hours earlier. The tide had taken him out to sea, turned him around, and brought him right back to me. The bullet had hit him, almost micrometer measurement, right between the eyes. Had blown his head off from behind his ears back. His brain was hanging out by the spinal nerve and the fish were eating it.

I pull him up on the bank and look in that knapsack. It was the guy we were looking for.

He had the locations of six major arms caches. It took trucks to load.

He had the names of over one hundred Viet Cong agents working for the U.S. and the South Vietnamese government in Saigon. He had a lot of stuff. He was the guy we were looking for.

Can you imagine? Was that written down, or what? I had just come twelve thousand miles, didn't have anything to wear or put on. I go down the river, and it's the guy we're looking for. And if he'd been one foot either way in the jungle we never would have seen him. If we'd been fifteen seconds one way or the other we wouldn't have run into each other.

It was one of the greatest intel finds of the war, up to that time, and probably of the whole war. I was so naive, let me tell you. He had forty thousand dollars in American in that knapsack. I kept four hundred of it for a beer party. Some naval intel guy is still laughing about that, 'cause I'm sure he took it home with him.

Chapter 22
Blowing Bunkers

Jack Macione recalls another event that convinced him not to ignore the role of fate:

This is another profound one.

We got asked to clear out this area. The Viet Cong had built big mud igloos. They looked like igloos. The rivers of course were the highways. So in this real bad area they would shoot at the boats and then jump in the igloo. They had killed several people. So the area commander asked us to go in and clean it out.

It wasn't our job. It was the 9th Division's job. The army. But, you know, we do anything. Whores. This is the day I get three Purple Hearts. No it wasn't. That happened later.

We each took forty pounds of high explosives in haversacks. In socks, with a short fuse, a thirty-second fuse. Each of us was carrying twenty socks. So we were blowing these bunkers.

What we would do is, we would holler "allee allee outs in free" and throw it into the bunker. Up to that time I had been a demolitionist seven or eight years. And I had never had a misfire. A misfire is when the cap goes off but the main charge doesn't. It's not uncommon to have a misfire. There are very few people who can get by their time in the team without having a misfire. But I'd never had a misfire. It was kind of a little pride thing.

So we were going along, throwing two-pound socks. Let me tell you the power of a two-pound sock. It is maybe two and a half pounds, about as big as a carton of cigarettes—a carton of regulars. If you cut off a piece of C-4 [the explosive] about half the size of a pack of cigarettes, you could split a railroad rail. With a two-pound sock you could take out the walls of a building.

You have a fuse puller. You pull the fuse and it spits fire into it and lights it. About thirty seconds. So we go along pulling the fuses, hollering "allee allee outs in free." If nobody comes out, we throw it in. [The fuse puller is attached to a length of timed safety fuse, which is cut into thirty-second lengths, the number of lengths depending on how long the operator wants to delay the explosion. The safety fuse burns down until it reaches a cap, which it ignites, causing the C-4 explosive to go off.]

I had blown maybe eight or ten bunkers. We walk by this one bunker, holler allee etc. Nothing. Nobody comes out. I throw it in. We start walking away. I hear—"clap"—a misfire. The cap goes off but the charge doesn't. It's the only misfire I'd had up to that point. Incidentally, its the only misfire I ever had.

I say to Peewee [Richard Nealy]: "I'm going to go in that bunker and get the explosive. Because the Viet Cong would get it and make booby traps."

So I start crawling in this tunnel. Pitch-black. I'm sure from the inside I'm silhouetted against the light. I get about halfway in that tunnel and grab ahold of somebody's hand.

Man! I did the four-minute mile on my knees backward. I didn't have a weapon or anything.

So I yell in there. A woman comes out with a six-month-old baby, both of them completely unharmed.

My only misfire!

We asked what the hell she was doing, why she didn't come out. The Viet Cong told her—they called us the Sea Tiger—the Viet Cong told her we would eat her baby. So she found it quite unusual that we gave her some food and sent her on her way.

Chapter 23
"Something's Happened to Mike"

Mike Bennett, who participated in three *Apollo* astronaut recoveries, later served in Vietnam. He, too, became convinced that fate explains some of the strange things that happen in combat:

Speaking of funny things. I can't remember when it was, but we were still on Seafloat. We were going to try to open the channels between two main rivers so the boats could get up and down there to get to both rivers.

And as we would go upriver, we would find these stakes stuck in the river. The Vietnamese would take these bamboo poles in their little tub boats. They would stick these bamboo poles in the mud and shake 'em. And we couldn't pull them out with a Mike boat. We'd wrap lines around and try to pull 'em out with a Mike-8 and we could not pull 'em out. So we'd blow 'em.

What were they there for?

To stop our boats from going up the river.

So we'd put Mark 8 hose in there and blow 'em. So we got up to one of these stops. We got out, alongside the river. We did a sweep around the river, looking. Didn't find anything, so they told me to go back down to the boat, bring the boat up so we could blow this thing.

I said okay. So I'm looking for booby traps and stuff. And I hit something with my leg and I looked down and there's a piece of monofilament line wrapped around a stick about that big. And the stick looked like it had just been whittled. Like somebody had just whittled it. And my heart started pounding. And I thought, holy shit.

I turned around and looked, right back there. There was a grenade sticking out of a Schlitz beer can. This baby right there. [Pats can sitting on his desk.] And I said, "Grenade!"

And of course everyone went down. But me. My mind's telling my body to get down and my body's telling my mind, I'm not moving. I'm not moving. And I couldn't get it to move for anything.

And Roger Sick says, "Where? Where?"

And I'm pointing at it. And he came around and he took a safety pin out of a tri-bandage and he stuck it in that hole and just as he stuck it in the hole, the pin fell out. I've got it right there. It was an instantaneous fuse.

Yeah, I tripped that booby trap and it did not go. It wasn't my time. I found out later, talking to my mother . . . All of us kids, for her birthday, my dad bought the ring and each one of us kids bought their own birthstone for her ring.

She was working at the hospital back home the same day I tripped that grenade. And she looked down at the ring and my stone was missing. And through our correspondence we found it was the same day.

My mother said she felt in her heart, in her soul, that something was wrong and that made her look at that ring. The stone was missing. My aquamarine stone was gone. She says, "Something's happened to Mike."

And about twenty minutes later one of the guys tripped a grenade just like that and it blew the back of his head off. He survived but of course he had to learn how to walk and talk all over again. We medevaced him out.

We went on upriver and we were blowing . . . We were loading these little creeks trying to open up another river. And it seemed like the more explosive we put in the little river, the bigger dam would appear. Because when the explosion occurred, it would boil the mud up and completely dam off the river instead of blowing it deeper.

We used forty-pound cratering charges. We loaded the river with fifteen links of Mark 8 hose, interlaced with forty-pound cratering charges. We had it all set up where the cratering charges would go off. Since we were making these new dams, we figured out that we'd set the cratering charges with forty pounds in the middle, twenty pounds at the ends. Those charges would go first and then the links of Mark 8 hose would go and blow the mud out of the way.

So I guess we had about a thousand pounds of explosive loaded. And we went off downstream and we were getting ready to blow it. And this beautiful white stork came flipping in. I guess his wingspan must have been six feet. He come swooping in, real slowly. And he landed in this tree. Just about the time it was "fire in the hole."

He landed and he fluffed himself. And Whooofff! That thing went up and it just covered him.

And I thought, "Oh, man, we just disintegrated that dude."

When all the wash came back down and the smoke cleared, he was still up in that tree. Squawk! Squawk! Squawk! I thought, holy cow, and he shook himself off and he jumped and he fell out of the tree and he walked around the bank and finally he just took off. We screwed up his whole day.

We never did get anything opened up. That was the biggest dam we blew, that day. And as we were going back, we had forty links of Mark 8 hose. We had twenty forty-pound cratering charges in that boat. And we were on that boat. Usually it's the one in the middle. We had a monitor in front but we didn't have anyone behind us. And we were tracking downriver again, going home.

I was up by the coxswain and—no, as we were coming down the river a sampan was coming up. And the boat slid and it just mashed that sampan. People stepped out on the bank with all their goodies and stuff. It just tore that sampan up, sunk it right there.

I told him [the coxswain], "Charlie's going to get you big-time for this. You just ruined one of his sampans."

And the coxswain says, "I'm not scared of anybody. Who gives a shit?"

I says, "Man, Charlie's going to get you. I don't want to ride this boat. You just jinxed the boat. Charlie's gonna get you."

We made it down the river, down around the next corner and kaboom, we got hit. Charlie hit us twice. He hit us with a B-40 in the bar armor and the Styrofoam. [Boats were protected by metal armor, backed up by Styrofoam to absorb the energy of a shell.] The second one put a four- by six-foot hole in the engine room. And the coxswain turned the boat hard astarboard, both engines full ahead and put her up on the bank. And of course we jumped off, set a perimeter, shot up the banks.

The monitor lit off and sprayed the bank with fire. Nothing. We went over and found the hole where he was in, found the launch tube. He had tied bamboo poles together and had eleven flashlight batteries taped together. And he was touching the wires to the ends of the batteries to set those things off. The bamboo pole holds it as a launch tube. Just roll up the fins and stick it in there with the head of it out. If he had fired those things as quick as he fired them, four seconds earlier, he would have hit the well deck and we wouldn't have been here because of all that powder we had in there.

In Vietnam, when you got off the plane in Tan Son Nhut, it was pucker factor. It wasn't til you got on that plane and landed in Hawaii that you . . . [a sigh of relief].

Our homecomings weren't that great. We usually landed at North Island [the naval base in San Diego Bay], loaded up the trucks, and came down the beach, back toward the team area [at Coronado] and that's when we got this great welcome home.

They knew we were coming back from Vietnam. As we came down by the beach, we were looking at the honeys and they'd see all our combat gear and stuff. They'd throw beer bottles at us and holler at us. It wasn't any welcome home. But we got used to it. That's what they paid us extra for. It was definitely party time once we got home.

Chapter 24
"I Don't Want You Operating . . ."

In the fall of 1970, Lt. Thomas Hawkins, commander of the seventh platoon of SEAL Team TWO, and another officer were ordered to the far north of South Vietnam to consider operating in that part of the country.

He and members of his platoon were based at that time in Nha Be, east of Saigon, by then a quiet backwater of the war. They wanted to move deep into the delta south of Saigon where the Viet Cong were much more active. But higher authorities wanted to dispatch them to the northernmost portion of the country—the area known as I Corps—to attempt to stop enemy mining of the Cua Viet River.

"We looked the place over and decided that was the worst place you could send a SEAL platoon," Hawkins recalls. Hawkins describes what occurred next, setting the stage for a frustrating assignment as the U.S. sought to turn over the fighting to the Vietnamese:

By the time we got back to Da Nang and subsequently to Saigon, a ferryboat had been blown up on the Cua Viet River. The Chief of Naval Operations of the South Vietnamese navy was in a helicopter over the river when the boat hit a mine and blew up right in front of his eyes. I was told he had a relative on that ferry. The South Vietnamese army didn't have the resources to stop the mining.

We were told, "Hey, you're going up there whether you like it or not." My platoon got sent up.

We moved into temporary spaces in Frogville, the UDT base in Da Nang. We were given a target: a large and complex series of bunkers over on an island. We decided to have a go at it. We were really eager to do something because we hadn't really done all that much. We spent most of our time planning to do stuff rather than actually doing stuff because we were being moved around country so much.

We got aerial photographs of this thing and it was one of the most intriguing photographs I've ever seen. It looked like a two- or three-story bunker. We did a pretty good job of planning this op. This thing was beside a canal that came in off the main river. We planned to go in in typical SEAL fashion—walking up the canal.

The real problem is, we didn't have any real boat support. In order to insert, we had to use Vietnamese navy boats and there was always a communications problem and always an organizational problem.

The truth of the matter is, we liked to operate at night and those guys didn't want to get their boats out there at night.

The first night we went to do this op, we got inserted at the wrong spot. As soon as we realized these Vietnamese navy guys had put us off on the wrong spot, we came under intense .50-caliber fire. Tracers were flying everywhere. We were compromised, really compromised.

We got on the radio and pleaded for these boats to come back in and get us. Of course, they weren't going to come back while this .50 caliber was coming in there. We ended up with the whole platoon just getting into the water and lying down.

The funniest thing, when we got pinned down, guys were yelling and I was lying there, trying to get my bearings and figure out what to do. These bullets are snipping all around. It was recon by fire, which we found out later.

It goes through my mind that my big ass is sticking up in the air and I'd better do something before I get hit in the rear end. And I did. I rolled over and I'm looking up like this and I see the tracers flying over me.

And I went, "Holy shit! They're going to shoot my nose off." So I rolled back over.

We backed the whole platoon into the water and we sat there for a considerable amount of time until we can get boats back in to pick us up. Well, it ends up, the guys shooting at us were Koreans. The ROK [Republic of Korea] guys were trigger happy. There had been a lot of sapper attacks going on, which was why they wanted us to go in and kind of disrupt this VC stronghold. The Koreans were shooting at us from their base over on the other side of the water. They must have thought we were the sappers.

We decided the op had not been compromised. If we could get to our proper insertion point, we still had a great probability of running this operation.

Our aim was to insert into the mouth of the canal and walk the canal, clear up to the bunker complex. That was our plan, very simple.

We inserted. My point man found two or three booby traps. So it wasn't that they hadn't anticipated someone coming in this way, but the booby traps had been there for a long time and they were really old. I guess they never went down and refreshed the booby traps.

When we got up in there and found those booby traps, we were moving so slow. After we found the first booby traps, our time schedule was way off. One of the guys found this really well traveled path. We stopped the squad, sent a guy up to see what was up there.

He came back and said, "You've got to see this." So we took the whole squad up in there. It was a bunker complex. It was totally empty. We went inside. There were mattresses with sheets, pillowcases. This place was decked out with all the comforts of home.

We decided we were never going to make it to the big bunker and that we probably never would make it in a single night. We decided this was not an achievable objective. We left a whole bunch of literature scattered around this bunker. We had picked them up as a joke. The psyops guys, I guess, were putting them out. It was a piece of paper with a big eyeball on it. It said something in Vietnamese akin to: "We are watching you. No matter where you go or what you do, we are watching you."

We exfiltrated that night and went to sleep on the beach. Then the boats took us back to the Vietnamese navy base the next day. We decided going through the canal was not the best way. And any other way would not be good without a guide. I came back and wrote up my report. Basically I said we had a mission that didn't bear fruit.

In his Barndance card reporting on that night's mission, Hawkins wrote: "Patrolling inside canals into known highly booby trapped areas seems to be an excellent method and unexpected by the enemy."

The next day or the day after, somebody decided they would take an EOD [explosive ordnance demolition] team and blow these bunkers away. Just fly in in broad daylight. I remember hearing that the team that went in got a couple of people killed and a helicopter shot down.

We were the first SEAL platoon that had been in I Corps for a long time. The army, everybody, felt it was strange we operated at night.

I went to set up one op. I had gone to the army TOC [tactical operations center] to clear the AO [area of operations] and try to get air support and try to set up an op like I had set them up in the delta.

They are all giving me every reason in the world why I can't do things. Most of it had to do with the fact that we're Vietnamese-izing and nobody fights and we don't want you guys up here, particularly out at night, stirring things up.

I'm talking to this major who's setting up the gunship support. And we're up at the map. In the navy, when a senior officer walks into the room, they say, "Attention on deck!" and everybody snaps to.

I wasn't used to the army. Well, somebody said, "attention." They didn't say, "ATTENTION!" This guy walks up to the map and he's got one star. The navy never had one-star flag officers; they go to two stars. I'd never seen one star except on the collar of a chief petty officer. My first response to him was, "Hi, Chief."

I was introduced to him. I quickly found out he was a general officer. I was introduced as "Lieutenant Hawkins, he's with the SEAL platoon."

This guy looks at me and says, "I want to see you in my quarters right now!"

Everybody's giving me these blank stares. He did an about-face and went crashing out the door and back to his office. This major escorted me over to his office. Typical army. Nicely painted hut, little white painted rocks. Nicely appointed. Not like Vietnam. More like Fort Bragg [North Carolina]. Had a gorgeous Vietnamese secretary.

He's standing, holding the door, waiting for me to come in. The major walks me up to the door and when I walk in, the general closes the door in the major's face.

And he points a finger at me and he says, "I've heard about you assholes. You're assassins and I don't want you operating in my area."

I'm a lieutenant that's trying to set up a combat mission. He gives me this story about things are quiet up here and we're not stirring anything up. We're basically not operating. We're Vietnam-izing.

I went, "Aye aye sir, thank you very much." I went back to the TOC and said, "What'll I do?"

I basically told this major, "That's my grid. I'm going to be in there tonight. If I need help, I'll be calling you."

But I found out, in I Corps, I had to clear four AOs and never tell anyone which I'd be in. I had to clear with the Koreans, the Australians, the Vietnamese, and the U.S. Army.

I cleared all four and all had plausible missions. I got zero cooperation from the army. Zero from the Vietnamese navy. We made very fast friends with the Australians. We drank hard in off-hours and quickly gained a reputation for being inseparable. They were manning firebases and they had guys sneaking up on them almost every night. We were dying to go outside the perimeter and play with these guys.

We just wanted anything to do. But the army would not approve us operating with the Australians. We were basically stuck in a spot where nobody wanted to operate anymore. Me and my platoon were getting real, real, real frustrated. We really did want to operate and we kept running into these barriers.

The Vietnamese people were not used to friendly forces operating at night so they would routinely violate the curfew.

One night we were patrolling along the beach. A grandfather and his grandson were up there. They had violated curfew. They were out on the beach, basically a free-fire zone. When we ran into them, we just opened up on them.

We ended up shooting this kid, maybe eight, nine, ten years old, and he had a sucking chest wound. My corpsman was taking pretty good care of him. We couldn't get air cover. I called for medevac. They wanted to know whether it was American or Vietnamese.

I said, "It doesn't make a shit. I want the bird. It doesn't matter. We've got an injured kid up here."

They didn't want to fly. Down in the delta, we had the navy Sea Wolves. They were a very dedicated, brave bunch of men. It was almost a hand and glove thing when we operated with these guys. We used to use a capped strobe light to show the Sea Wolves where we were. We'd use a white flash or an IR [infrared] cap or different color cap. And the Sea Wolves could pick that out of a triple canopy. Up there on an open beach, these army pilots kept swearing they could not see the strobe light.

We finally got the kid on a medevac and the corpsman flew out with him and we got him to the province hospital. I went down the next day to see the kid and see his parents. They were crying and I didn't know what to say to them. I just simply told them I was sorry it happened but they were up there in violation of the curfew and they should not do that and they should tell the rest of the villagers.

We knew after we shot the kid that they were not bad guys. I lost some sleep over it that night. But my guys were alive. We did the right thing.

Chapter 25
They Called It Bright Light

As American involvement in the war in Vietnam wound down in the early 1970s, a few SEALs remained behind, acting as advisers to the Vietnamese. For most of them, it was a frustrating period. But one thing made it all seem worthwhile: the possibility of rescuing Americans believed to be held prisoner by the Viet Cong.

A number of operations—under the code name Bright Light— were run in various parts of Vietnam in response to reports that American prisoners had been spotted. On several occasions, the SEALs came tantalizingly close. They received reports of large men—presumably American prisoners—being moved just ahead of them. They even saw footprints that could have been made by Americans. Several raids resulted in the release of South Vietnamese. But American prisoners—if they were there—remained always just beyond the reach of the rescuers.

Tony Thomas, who was a medical corpsman with SEAL Team ONE, tells of one of the last of the Bright Light operations:

In 1972, I was in SEAL Team ONE attached to MACSOG—the Military Assistance Command Studies and Observation Group—up in Da Nang. We had army, navy, air force, marines. By that time, things were winding down.

Earlier, SEALs from both the East and West Coasts had been there and they had run some excellent operations—really kicked some butt.

When I was there, they were primarily Vietnamese operations.

I had the ammo bunker. All of our weapons were AK-47. We had 82mm mortars. The U.S.'s are 81s. It was all the other guys' munitions and weapons. When I operated with them, I operated in khakis, pith helmet—NVA.

These [South Vietnamese] operating teams would come to me with a requisition for ammo.

"Oh, we're going to go kill many VC tonight."

"That's good, Chief. What do you need?"

"Oh, ten thousand rounds of AK. Five cases of hand grenades."

"Yeah, you are really going after some bad guys."

"Oh, yeah! One hundred pounds of C-4."

"No problem."

They loaded it all in a truck and out it would go.

I'd see them the next day and ask, "How did the operation go?"

"No operation. We go tonight. Had to cancel last night."

"What happened?"

"One of the guys got sick. Going to go tonight."

"That's good."

"We need five thousand rounds of AK, four cases of hand grenades . . ."

"Wait a minute. What did you do with all the stuff I gave you?"

"Oh, we practiced."

"Wait a minute. Hold it. I didn't come in on the noon balloon."

I went to the officer in charge and told him, "We're going to get shot with our own ammo. This is what I gave them and they didn't go anyplace."

"Well, give it to them."

"Wait a minute, commander. You're not understanding me. They didn't go anyplace. They didn't go to the range. They didn't take the boats out. Where did the stuff go to?"

"Don't worry about it. Just give it to them."

"Commander, you're screwed up. You're going to get Americans killed. I want no part of it. Here's my key to the bunker. I want out of this one."

Were you Americans operating at all then?
I operated with the [South Vietnamese] sea commandos. The last op I was on we went after an American POW all the way down in III Corps, down in central Vietnam.

We inserted with twenty Vietnamese, one Vietnamese lieutenant commander, a U.S. Marine captain, a marine gunnery sergeant, and me.

To give you an idea of the mentality. The marine gunnery sergeant—we had two other staff sergeants begging to go, but they said they were going to take me because I'm a corpsman.

"We're going to take Billy Flores because he's a Mexican."

"What?"

"Yeah, the guy we're going after is of Mexican ancestry. Because of the strain he's been under and everything, he may have reverted back to his native language."

"What?"

Even so, it was a good op. We took the boats in off an LST, landed and then we walked in probably three klicks—three thousand meters. And then we were spotted. We were spotted by scouts or whatever. We saw them. We saw them and they saw us. There were three of them. It was mangrove swamp.

You couldn't see very far?
Not a long ways, no.

All the Vietnamese, with the exception of the lieutenant commander—he was from Hanoi; he was about my size—he, the marine captain, and I were dressed up as NVA. We were too big to be Vietnamese. The gunnery sergeant and all of the Vietnamese were all dressed up in black pajamas.

If we were spotted, the story was, we were survivors off a junk bringing weapons from the north. It almost worked. The three that saw us—we didn't know, but one went after the forty-man reaction force. The other two were trailing us. We snatched them up. We set an ambush and jumped them.

We said, "We're really sorry, we didn't know who you were. We thought you were a rice farmer who was going to turn us in to the Americans."

They said, "We weren't sure. We saw the khakis and we didn't know if you were north, south, what you were."

"Oh no, we're off this junk out here."

"Well, that's good because our forty guys are on the way and they'll help us unload the junk."

We had a small problem here.

One thing that the people setting up this op did do for us—after making us take the Mexican . . . They did set up everything that would fly in III Corps and IV Corps. They were at our beck and call. They were sitting on the runway.

They had a battalion of Vietnamese marines ready to come in and give us a hand. We didn't call them because black pajamas are black pajamas and we did not want friendly forces coming to our aid, thank you very much.

We even had naval gunfire. I hate to tell stories on the marines, but . . .

We had walked in three thousand meters. We didn't know where we were. We had a helo above us. We'd ask, "Where are we?" He'd put us back on track. By the time we got spotted and got into a firefight with this reaction force, we had no idea where we were.

I'm telling this marine, who's got the radio, "Have you called for extraction?"

"Well, no, not yet."

"I think it might be a good idea because I think they know we're here."

"Well, yeah, but naval gunfire wants to work out."

I said, "What? What did you say?"

He said, "Yeah, there's a destroyer out there and they want to give us a hand."

I said, "Captain, we don't know where we are! Where are you going to have them throw these shells?"

He said, "Well, I'll take care of that."

About that time—we're on a canal, maybe ten foot wide. We look down, you can see them crossing this canal. They're trying to encircle us. I take a couple of the Vietnamese and say, "Let's go back here a little ways."

So we set up a rear guard. We did good. We caught 'em.

And then I hear this, way out somewhere, this boom. He's not kidding. He's really calling in the gunfire.

Did it come very close?

No. It was somewhere in Vietnam, or maybe Laos. They fired two or three and said, that's enough.

When the firefight started, I grabbed some of the Vietnamese and we started hacking out a landing zone. I'm standing out in the middle of this thing.

You know, if you have a pipe, and you can see the daylight completely through the pipe, you figure, gee they must be aiming that pipe at me.

I'm looking up and here comes one of these OV-10s—the Black Ponies?

And I'm looking and I said, "Oh, Lord, I can see through his rocket pod. Hey, Gunny, I think we're in a heap of trouble!"

I know he was looking right down my throat. There isn't any doubt in my mind. The gunny and I are just watching. We figure we're going to eat one of these things.

The gunny is telling me—I had just bright blond hair—he kept saying, "Take off your hat! Take off your hat!"

I knocked the pith helmet off and this pilot just jogged the stick and then he let them loose and they went on the back side of us.

That's as close as I ever want to come.

How could you see through the rocket pod?

They had been making runs. There was no rocket in that one I was looking through.

Did you get out of there all right?

We didn't have any injuries. We know we killed five and we gave the air credit for, I think, seven. As we loaded on the helos, you could see bodies. We know we got five.

Were you under fire as you extracted?

No, we had a lot of air support. Cobras. Black Ponies. We were throwing diversion out the doors. We learned in UDT and SEALs: If you're lifting out of a hot LZ, throw some lead out there. That made the army pilot and copilot nervous. They told us to cease fire. We said, "You fly the bird. We'll do the shooting."

What about the POW you were going after?

The trailer we snapped up, we asked him where their camp was. He said they'd moved the camp. The Vietnamese were getting a lot out of this guy without threats or anything. He said they kept moving the camp. And he said they had moved their prisoners a long time ago.

This all happened in late January, early February 1972. By March, I was home.

Chapter 26
A Taste for Ears

From their earliest days in World War II, the navy's frogmen have surrounded much of what they do—at times, even their very existence—with secrecy. This has led to constant tension between the press, intrigued by the mystery surrounding the SEALs and UDT, and the men themselves, whose very lives often depend on stealth.

Command Master Chief Hershel Davis, a veteran of Vietnam, where the conflict between the press and the SEALs was most pronounced, says: "The warrior caste and the journalist caste will never be soul mates. If you talk to a journalist, you have violated a sacred trust."

Perhaps part of the tension came, too, from the fiendish sense of humor of men like Blackjack Macione, who tells of an elaborate sting he pulled on a reporter and of another humorous incident years earlier:

The press in Vietnam? They were dangerous. They would sensationalize things that didn't need to be sensationalized.

There was this one New York smart-ass. Cocky. I don't remember his name. He had given us the name "the assassins."

He started bugging me, thought he was clever. What he wanted to see was our collection of Viet Cong ears.

I could tell you right now we didn't collect ears. We were professional. It's just a slight difference of fate that you're not lying there and someone else is. We did not maim or mutilate any bodies. We didn't cut anybody's ears off.

But this guy wanted to see our ears. So I told everybody, "I'm going to get this son of a bitch."

So for weeks, I would deny we ever had 'em. And then I'd give him a little clue. I'd say, "If I had 'em and showed 'em to you, you'd probably do a story."

He'd say, "No, no."

There'd be days or weeks I'd just taunt him some more.

So finally I let him convince me I should show him the ears. One night I set up a meeting and made him promise this was off the record.

Finally I meet him in the bar on the base. That day I had gone down and bought a big box of dried apricots. So I strung a bunch of them up on a piece of fish line. I took one big one and put it in my wallet.

So we meet in the bar and I taunt him for three hours until he's salivating. I let the string of "ears" just peek out of my pocket. In the darkness you're not sure what you're seeing. I let him see them.

Then I said, "The big one, I've got right here in my wallet."

It's dark and it looks like an ear.

He says, "Ah hah! It took me three months but I've got you guys now. That's awful! It is debasing!"

He's going to expose us.

I says, "Awful? As a matter of fact, they're pretty darn good."

And I take the big one from my wallet and I start chewing on it.

I'm sure he tossed his cookies.

I'm sure he wrote about it but I never saw the story.

Macione recalls a much earlier incident:

During the Cuban crisis, we had this kiss-your-ass-good-bye mission. We were going to parachute into Havana. First, we were going to destroy the ships at the pier and then hold the power station.

There were something like seventeen of us going in and something like 250,000 Cuban troops. So it's like they didn't have a chance. The only thing that kept you sane was you knew you were the only guy of the seventeen who was going to survive alive.

This was a one-way trip. We made out our last will and testament and strapped on another grenade.

We had bought these twenty-foot trimaran runabouts. The idea was we were going to parachute in with these things. We were going to run into the harbor with bazookas and shoot the ships. Well, it was hard enough just hanging on without firing a frickin' bazooka.

As luck would have it, we never had to go in. I'm sure we would all have been killed.

Rudy Boesch was manning the quarterdeck. [Lieutenant] Roy Boehm was the CO. We're all standing around in this kiss-your-ass-good-bye mode, ready to go.

[President] Jack Kennedy was calling the team several times a day. Personally. Checking to see if we have everything we need.

Well, Rudy is fielding the calls coming in. So Rudy has to take a leak. So he grabs Kelly. Kelly was a seaman apprentice. Dumber than dirt. No common sense.

So Rudy says, "Watch the phone a minute. I've got to go take a leak."

The moment he leaves, the phone rings. Kelly doesn't know from shit.

This voice says, "This is President Kennedy. I'd like to talk to Captain Boehm."

Kelly says, "Well this is Flash Gordon on the dark side of the moon. The captain's not in."

And he hangs up.

Rudy comes back, says, "By the way, Kelly, the president may be calling."

Kelly says, "I think he just called."

The president calls right back, Rudy takes the call. The president was laughing his ass off.

Rudy had Kelly paint the warehouse with a toothbrush. Literally.

Chapter 27
"Vous les Américains Sont Pires que les Français"

From January 1974 until April 1975, William G. "Chip" Beck served as an adviser with the Cambodian army as it fought a desperate battle against the Khmer Rouge rebels. Beck, trained by the navy as an expert in explosive ordnance demolition, is not a SEAL, but he has worked closely with SEALs in a number of overseas assignments. In the mid-70s, he was a navy lieutenant reporting to the U.S. Embassy in the Cambodian capital of Phnom Penh. Beck is now an artist with studios in Arlington, Virginia. This is his story of the heroic defense of one small city and the eventual collapse of the Cambodian resistance:

I was an adviser to the 11th Cambodian Brigade at the time. I was the only American in Kompong Thom, this little town in central Cambodia.

There were two other foreigners there—a Norwegian doctor and a French priest who had been a chaplain in the French foreign legion. He had been there twenty-eight years and spoke Cambodian like a native. We used to call his congregation "the Christian Soldiers." After he said Mass, he would go out and show them how to put up a machine-gun emplacement with effective cross fire.

I had responsibility for an area between Kompong Thom and Siem Reap, where Angkor Wat is. I used to travel back and forth in that whole northern area.

I started out based in Siem Reap but I was so impressed by the quality of the officers and what they were doing with the men in Kompong Thom that I went back to the embassy and told them they needed a full-timer down there with the 11th Cambodian Brigade. They agreed.

The provincial governor was also a general whose name was Teap Ben. He was the political provincial adviser and senior military person. The man in charge of most of the combat forces was Col. Khy Hak, probably one of the two military geniuses I have met in my life. The guy didn't go to school until he was eleven years old and ended up completing the national military academy at age eighteen at the top of his class.

Khy Hak had studied everything from Napoleon to Mao Tse Tung. In his library, I found these huge books on the Napoleonic battles. There were maps where he had drawn in red and blue where the troops had gone and where they had made their mistakes. He could think in strategic terms. He could send massive troop units out but also have his men infiltrate into the Khmer Rouge as guerrillas. He could fight as a guerrilla or a major tactician.

When the war started, these two guys were at Siem Reap, a little outpost. They were maybe a major and a captain at the time. That became one of the few places where, when the North Vietnamese and the Khmer Rouge started running over Cambodia, they didn't get very far. They were not guys who sat in their offices and worried about their next corruption deal. They would go out and fight with the troops.

Khy Hak got wounded, for the first time in his life, during the battle for Angkor Wat. Instead of being evacuated, he had his men put him on a door and carry him into battle while he was still bleeding. It was an incredible battle because Khy Hak has a sense of history. He didn't want to use heavy artillery to take out the North Vietnamese because he was afraid of destroying the historic ruins of Angkor Wat. So he had his men go in and fight hand to hand, tactical, down and dirty.

Kompong Thom had been overrun and almost taken by the Khmer Rouge in 1973, the year before I got there, and when they sent Teap Ben and Khy Hak, literally, the Khmer Rouge were in downtown Kompong Thom. The helicopter flew these two guys in, wouldn't even land, as the troops were fighting to get back into the city. Literally, they retook the city house by house.

By the time I got there, the Khmer Rouge were still surrounding the town and attacking it, if not every day, every week. I was just so impressed by what was going on I decided to make my own headquarters there. The longer I stayed and saw what they were doing, the more impressed I got.

At one point in the dry season, Khy Hak had had enough of being surrounded by the Khmer Rouge and he said he was going to take back the territory beyond the town perimeter. We tried to get some equipment, some trucks and other stuff, from Phnom Penh to haul his troops but the corruption was such that none of that stuff was ever forthcoming.

Khy Hak decided he and his brigade, under cover of darkness, would walk out of Kompong Thom along Highway 5 and wreak havoc among the Khmer Rouge. And they did. In the course of three days they walked a hundred miles and they brought back 10,000 people from among the Cambodian population. By the time a month and a half was finished, they had brought back 45,000 people from the communist zone, brought them back into a little town that previously had only 15,000 people in it.

When Khy Hak went out there, he didn't force the people to come back at gunpoint. He would get up on a tree stump or a chair and talk to the villagers.

He told them, "Look, there's corruption in the government, there's corruption in the army. But if you come back I will try to protect you. The Khmer Rouge will try to stop you from going. I will help you get back. Once you reach safety in Kompong Thom, they will try to attack us and kill you. I will try to protect you. It's going to be hard to feed you. You will have to grow your own crops. We can't count on anybody but ourselves. But you know what it's like out here under the communists. Choose. Make your choice."

And they made their choice, by the thousands.

I flew out in a chopper after the operation got going and I couldn't believe my eyes. The Cambodian plain in central Cambodia is pretty dry, almost like areas of Kansas in some places. It's very flat terrain, very dry, very good farmland, not infested with jungle or anything.

As the chopper was coming in to where Khy Hak's field position was, I could see for seven miles a string of humanity stretching out over the horizon. It was an incredible sight. People were walking in single file, many with ox carts. People had all their belongings stuffed in these carts.

In some places you could see the wagons circled up where they had been attacked by the Khmer Rouge, almost like the old Wild West.

Khy Hak's brigade was providing flanking protection and rescuing more and more people. At one point, when I got on the ground, we were pursuing this one group of villagers who were still hostages and prisoners. The leading Cambodian troops caught up with the Khmer Rouge and frightened them off.

We were coming through this one clearing into a somewhat jungly area. All the foliage and vegetation was falling down. We didn't know what was coming toward us. It turned out it was women, children, men. This one man was carrying his six-week-old son in his arms. He had a boy sitting on his shoulders. He had a girl strapped to his back and all of his belongings. He was looking over his shoulder, afraid the Khmer Rouge were still behind him.

And this old woman came running up to us. She saw me, being the only foreigner there. She grabbed me, thinking I had something to do with it and started hugging my feet. Khy Hak told me she was thanking us for rescuing them.

I stayed out there with the troops for three days. I really wasn't supposed to but Khy Hak challenged me, "How do you know I won't lie to you? Or someone will ask you if I'm lying. See for yourself. You can tell them the truth." So I stayed there.

Three days later, when I went back, a chopper picked me up. As we were flying back, a Cambodian captain mentioned there was a Khmer Rouge battalion headquarters down below us. So the Cambodians I was with wanted to see what was down there. We flew down. There were two choppers. They used one chopper as bait to try to draw fire. The chopper I was in flew about a hundred feet above the ground, in a circular formation, to provide covering fire as needed.

Then we switched places and the chopper I was on went in to be the bait. This guy jumped out of the bushes and started firing at us. We learned later from the refugees that this was the Khmer Rouge battalion commander. The clearing was surrounded by about fifty Khmer Rouge soldiers. They were scared to death the chopper would tear them apart. And this commander jumped out, screaming and shouting at his men to shoot us.

What they didn't know was the .50 caliber on the chopper I was on suddenly jammed. They got one round off and the thing didn't work. I was sitting there with this guy shooting at us. I had asked the embassy to send me up a Swedish K and some rounds. Just before I got on the chopper, my Cambodian assistant threw it up to me. As we're flying off and I start to put the magazines in, they had sent me Uzi clips for the Swedish K. All I had was a 9mm pistol.

But we had captured some AKs. When this guy jumped out of the bush, the only thing I could do, I picked up one of the AKs and started shooting back. So I got in this gunfight with this Khmer Rouge battalion commander. Meanwhile, one of the Cambodian officers with me was yelling, "Don't kill him! Don't kill him!" They wanted to capture him for questioning.

I said, "I'm just trying to shoot him."

I aimed for his legs. The chopper was three feet off the ground, a semimoving platform. I finally got him in the legs and he went down, sort of crawling for the bushes. I had the choice of going in after him. But something told me that wasn't a good idea. Later we learned from the refugees there were all these other people—something like fifty Khmer Rouge—surrounding us, so it's a good thing I didn't go after him.

As Khy Hak had predicted, the more refugees we got into the town, the more of a political embarrassment it was for the Khmer Rouge. They intensified the pressure on Kompong Thom in March and April of 1974.

We were trying to build housing and shelter before the rainy season. We asked for rice to feed the people but AID [U.S. Agency for International Development] sent some minuscule amount of rice, maybe a couple of tons.

Khy Hak led another operation out into an area where the Khmer Rouge had been stockpiling rice they had taken from the farmers. One night, I got a radio call from Khy Hak. He says, "I need some wagons, some carts. Send about fifty out."

I went to Teap Ben and told him we needed these carts because they had discovered this rice and thought they had a major cache. The word spread among the refugees. Instead of getting fifty ox carts, five hundred ox carts gathered and went out in a single file, in this huge wagon train. I was sending out rice bags and taking photographs.

As the last ox cart went out, I hopped on the back and rode through the night ten miles out into Khmer Rouge territory and joined Khy Hak in the morning. They had something like a thousand tons of rice. Some was in silos. They would punch a hole in the bottom of the silo and the rice would pour out like water. They would back the ox carts up, just like little mice on a cartoon show, fill up one, he would pull out and the next would pull in.

As we were pulling out, some mortar rounds started falling. Khy Hak got on the radio—the Khmer Rouge had the same radios we had— and issued a challenge: "This is Col. Khy Hak. Here is my precise position. I will wait here for one hour. There is no need for you to shoot at unarmed civilians who can't defend themselves. If you want to fight somebody, fight me. I will wait. If you are not here in an hour, I figure you are too afraid to do it."

They didn't come.

Teap Ben and Khy Hak had a project to divert part of the river that went by Kompong Thom and flood vast areas of the terrain for rice crops. They built a tremendous berm or wall around the southern portion. This was not only a means of survival—long-range survival—but it would also provide a natural barrier to ground attack.

First, you had to plow up the ground to get it ready for planting. It was during this period, when part of it was getting plowed up, that the Khmer Rouge launched a two-regiment attack. This was April of 1974.

How big was a Khmer Rouge regiment?

Khmer Rouge regiments were 1,000 to 1,500 men. So they had roughly between 2,500 to 3,000 fresh troops, in addition to what had been around Kompong Thom all along. These were troops that had overrun a couple of cities to the south. They had captured some American artillery pieces from the Cambodian army.

How many defenders were there?

The 11th Brigade had just under 2,000 men. They didn't use them in the actual defense. They were holding them in reserve in case the Khmer Rouge broke through. They were on the northern part of the city near the old airport. There were about 500 soldiers, in the 10th Brigade, under Teap Ben. They became the major frontline defenders. They also incorporated as many refugees as they could and they became citizen soldiers. The refugees also worked building defenses.

As the Khmer Rouge attacked, they would have a battalion on line and they would build spider holes. The next night that battalion would move back. A fresh battalion would crawl up a little bit further, dig spider holes, attack, and fire. They were trying to come as close as they could to the final perimeter. Defenses were out about two miles from the city. There were daily battles and fights and they were growing more intense each day.

Teap Ben had two of his own helicopter crews. I asked what altitude they were flying at. He said they were flying about three thousand feet. That's out of range of small-arms fire and we hadn't any reports they had antiaircraft at the time.

I flew out with them. It was just an incredible sight. I could see spider holes and I estimated there were about four hundred people down below. All four hundred of them started shooting at the chopper I was in.

Sure enough, we flew out at three thousand feet. But then the pilot went down to about ten feet above the ground. He made eleven passes along the front lines. I had not been expecting this. We were like the duck in an arcade shooting gallery.

I could literally see the faces of the Khmer Rouge as they were shooting at us. Thank God they were poor shots because they were not leading us properly. I was shooting back at them with a grenade launcher.

The pilots each had reinforced steel plates welded into the cockpit to deflect shells. I had open air between me and the Khmer Rouge. We finally went back up. Then we discovered the Khmer Rouge had brought in some 12.7mm machine guns, equivalent to the .50 cal. Somebody shooting that got a little more accurate and hit our chopper pretty heavily. I was kind of worried I'd end up like a friend of mine who had been shot from down below up through the rear end. I was sitting on my helmet, not that that would have helped much.

One round hit a hard point in the chopper—a couple of them, actually—and sent a bunch of shrapnel through the passenger compartment. The guy next to me got hit in the head. I got hit in the back and the arm. Fortunately, when the round broke apart it lost some of the velocity. It was just kind of minor shrapnel. Stung like a bee and bled a little bit. But it didn't incapacitate either one of us. The pilots, with their armor, came out of it just fine.

Finally, we ran out of fuel and we had to go back.

Why were they doing this low-level flying?

They were strafing the enemy and providing morale for the troops—the Cambodian ground troops. On one side you would see the defenders just cheering like mad because this chopper was flying back and forth getting shot at and shooting back at the enemy. The enemy was all pissed off. There was probably not more than two hundred or three hundred feet between the lines at that point. We were the center of attention and I didn't really want to be that. We finally ran out of fuel, which pleased me. We landed at an LZ near the general's house, got picked up by a jeep, and went back to the compound.

As we walked through the gate into the compound, the first artillery round fired from the captured American guns landed in the compound.

I was walking between these two pilots. One pilot got his head blown off and the other got a big chunk of shrapnel through his leg and I came off unscathed. These guys had escaped all that fire in the chopper and thought they were safe and as we were walking in, it blew them apart.

After we took care of them, we went inside. The Khmer Rouge must have had a forward observer someplace. They were shooting at the general's house. We could hear them on the artillery net. I used to be an artillery FO [forward observer] myself in Vietnam. I didn't understand the Khmer language but I could understand the cadence, hear the guns go off in the distance when the guy gave the command to shoot. You would wait five or six seconds and the round lands.

Teap Ben said they were adjusting fire and shooting at his house. I said I'd better go back to my house and make a call and report back to Phnom Penh.

He said, "No, sit here and have a cognac with me."

I said, "No, General, I better get back over to my house."

He said, "No, *mon ami,* stay and have a cognac."

I said, "General, why do you want me to stay? I've got to get back and make my report to Phnom Penh."

He said, "They've decided to stop shooting at my house. They've decided to start shooting at the American's house. Since you're the only American in the city, that's you."

I said, "Give me a cognac."

Then they started shooting at my house. They obviously had people in town who knew where I lived.

The next morning, I was writing up some reports. I had a field telephone that linked my house to the general's house. My houseboy and his wife were cleaning the upstairs. I picked up the phone and the general was telling me in French, *"Allez en bas"*—go downstairs.

I didn't even ask why. I just scooped up these two little kids, called to their parents to run with me. We all hid under this concrete part under the stairs. And we heard these shells come whistling in. They missed my house but unfortunately landed near the bridge and killed about eleven people. They were trying to get me directly.

I think it was about two days later, I woke up in the morning and the entire town was abandoned. I couldn't see anybody.

I went over to the general's headquarters. There was only a lone operator there. He told me the general had gotten up and driven out to the final outpost that was under attack. The fighting had concentrated down to this lone outpost. Teap Ben had driven down across the plains. I got him on the radio and he said, yeah, they were there fighting. You could hear the shooting in the background.

So I asked if the road was open. He said it was open so I said I'd be down. He neglected to tell me that, although the road was open, it was surrounded on both sides by combatants. The road kind of circled around the southern part of the city. It was about four miles. As I went along I passed some checkpoints and saw some officers I knew. I picked these guys up. I had about four or five people riding in the jeep with me.

As you approach the outpost, there was this huge berm he had built as part of the dike system. It wasn't flooded yet but it was the only way you could get down there. On one side of the dike were the friendly troops and on the other side were the Khmer Rouge.

There were dead bodies lying on top of the dike. I couldn't go around them. I could only drive over some of them. In order to get into the outpost I literally had to drive through the front lines of the Khmer Rouge. I was going as fast as that jeep would go. The Khmer Rouge didn't see us until we were actually past them. They started shooting and there were artillery explosions. We called ahead on the radio and asked for the gate to be opened.

We went careening in and literally jumped out of the jeep and let it go on its own steam into a bunker. As we jumped out, about six artillery rounds landed. We were in the bursting radius. How it missed us I don't know.

We ran over to where the general was in the trenches directing the combat. The rest of the afternoon, this horrendous hand-to-hand combat took place. I was watching them, a hundred feet out, crawl through the grass, jump into a spider hole with the Khmer Rouge. They were stabbing people with knives and throwing hand grenades from one pit to another.

In the midst of all this, there were guys replenishing other guys with ammunition. And they were just walking through the field of fire with ammunition on their shoulders, standing full upright, almost as though they were expecting Buddha to protect them.

Guys on either side of me were getting shot, trying to go from one point to another around the perimeter. They had these rinky dink pits, trenches built for people shorter than I was. There was water in the lower half of the trenches. They were just slit trenches where you had to crawl on your belly. Because of the water, you kind of had to raise up a little bit. I was sure my butt was going to be shot off.

Finally this one captain, or was he a major then? His name was Chai. He led this patrol, of about a squad, around and came up behind some of the main Khmer Rouge fighters. He just went berserk, screaming and shouting. He made such a commotion I think it scared the hell out of the Khmer Rouge, who were already pretty well bloodied.

That broke the back of the assault and that was the day the siege of Kompong Thom was broken. When the battle was over and the Khmer Rouge had withdrawn—they didn't even have a chance to carry away their dead and wounded—I counted something like 320 Khmer Rouge dead just around our outpost.

We later found mass graves with hundreds of bodies in them. We estimated the Khmer Rouge may have lost as many as a thousand killed during that several week battle. We tried to get some journalists up from Phnom Penh to witness what had happened—not only the influx of refugees but the defense of the city. But no one was interested in this little outpost.

The day the siege of Kompong Thom was broken, with three hundred Khmer Rouge left dead on the battlefield, the headlines in the world press, one major newspaper—I can't remember which one—said: "Rebel Rockets Hit Phnom Penh; Three Killed."

These defenders had killed three hundred to one thousand enemy soldiers in bloody combat but there was never a story told about this.

For the rest of the dry season, things were pretty calm there. Khy Hak was promoted to general the final year, in 1975, in the final months in Phnom Penh.

He and I had worked out a plan where I would take his wife and children and set them up on an escape route I had put up in northern Cambodia for the civilians.

I didn't know when Operation Eagle Pull [the American evacuation] was going to go. When I found out, I was several hundred miles away from his family. I couldn't get to them directly. I had somebody else go over to the house to ask Mrs. Khy Hak to leave with them. She refused. She didn't know her husband wanted her to leave.

By the time he was able to get back to Phnom Penh, to the center of town as the perimeter was falling, there was no way to get her out. He put his wife and his five children—beautiful little children, from four years old to eight—in a jeep. The Khmer Rouge caught them approaching the airport and took them over to a pagoda.

One of my Cambodian soldiers who went back in and talked to witnesses said they killed the little kids. They executed the children, then they shot his wife. After making him witness that, they executed him. So they got their revenge on him.

We then started hearing of many atrocities being committed. [After Phnom Penh fell to the Khmer Rouge on 16 April 1975, as many as four million Cambodians were slain by the victors over the next two years.] The Khmer Rouge would get on the single sideband radios that had been part of the military network. After the Americans had made the evacuation in Eagle Pull, the Khmer Rouge would get on the radio and hold the key so you could hear the office people being tortured and murdered on the air.

Where were you when you heard these broadcasts?

By that time I was in Thailand. I had already left Cambodia, went to Saigon and was there when Saigon started falling. [The North Vietnamese took Saigon on 30 April 1975.] I left Saigon and went to Bangkok and then directed some of the early escapes from Cambodia of civilians and some military families.

Unlike Vietnam, the Cambodians could have held out. We, the advisers, were told we could supply the Cambodian army as long as they could fight. That's what we told them. After we evacuated the country, that order was rescinded.

The French died at Dien Bien Phu. They were soundly defeated but they fought and we just went out the back door.

We, the advisers who had lived with these people, sometimes for years, had to sit there and listen to them on the radio calling to us, saying, "Where are our supplies? We're still fighting. We're holding out."

Finally they ran out of ammunition. That's the only thing that made many of these people surrender and then they were executed by the Khmer Rouge.

One of the last transmissions—the last transmission I ever heard out of Cambodia—was a Cambodian colonel, just before they killed him. You could hear them breaking down the door. You could hear him say, "Vous les Américains sont pires que les Français"— you Americans are worse than the French.

SEALs Under the Seas

PART FIVE

Chapter 28
"Dead Before Sunrise"

In the mid-1970s, then-Lt. Comdr. Thomas Hawkins became one of the navy's most enthusiastic supporters of the use of small boats designed to carry SEALs to their targets underwater. These SDVs (swimmer, later SEAL, delivery vehicles) were sometimes called minisubmarines, but that was a misnomer since the occupants are not protected from the sea. Instead, the craft is free flooding and the crew must rely on bottled air or oxygen to breathe.

Hawkins, now retired from the navy, recalled a frightening incident when his career—and his life—almost came to an abrupt end:

In 1975 I was at the navy's operational test and evaluation force testing new hardware for the SEAL teams. We had these newly formed SDV teams.

The commanding officer of SDV Team TWO was Jack Schropp, a bright and funny guy, and I was the prospective CO to relieve Jack. He had taken the team to Puerto Rico for winter training and testing hardware. I was with the team and running test operations on a new SDV radio system.

One night we were going to do a night op in the SDV. The purpose of the op was to take the SDV out into Vieques Channel [east of the naval base at Roosevelt Roads] and raise the antenna. We had a standard PRC-104 UHF [ultra high frequency] radio in a waterproof can. We were going to try to talk to the Mark 3 patrol boats over in St. Thomas [Virgin Islands], a distance of about twenty-four miles.

The pilot was PO Rick Brown, who was an excellent SDV pilot. And the navigator was PO Frank Fetzko. These guys were the cream of the crop of SDV pilots in the navy. Back then, they didn't know me that well. But I have come to know and love these guys since then.

[The Mark 8 SDV is designed to carry six men, sitting two by two. In this case, the pilot and navigator sat in the two front seats and Hawkins sat just behind, leaning forward between them. The occupants are exposed to the sea and must wear protective suits and breathing gear.]

We were going to dive the Mark 15 UBA [underwater breathing apparatus], a closed-circuit mixed-gas system with a six-hour capability. That was part of the test.

It was a fairly routine operation. We were to launch, proceed a couple or three miles to the middle of the channel, surface the SDV, raise the antenna, and try to talk to the boat over in St. Thomas. We had these lists, a series of rhyming words: cow, now, how. They have to record what you say and it indicates the quality of your communication.

We went out in the channel as planned. When we came to the surface for the test, it was really rough. The SDV was being slogged around a good bit. The first thing that happened when the guys opened up the canopy, because you had to open the canopy to raise the antenna, I saw my swim fin float out into the middle of Vieques Channel. The seat belt had come loose.

We put up the antenna and tried to raise the boat. We couldn't do it. I was the test director and the sea conditions were very extreme so I declared it a no-test and told them, "Let's go back to the pier and regroup."

We closed the canopy. Rick Brown dove the boat and lined it up on course and headed back to the pier. The test was over.

We're down about twenty feet and going maybe four knots. It feels good to be down there after being banged around on the surface.

Frank and Rick are in the front seats and I'm right behind, leaning forward between them. We're all talking on the intercom in the SDV. [The SEALs' masks have a built-in microphone connected to the craft's intercom system.] Fetzko tells this joke. It had to do with the female anatomy. I'm not going to repeat it for you, but it's one of the funniest jokes I've ever heard and we're laughing like hell underwater. It can be very boring in an SDV during a long transit.

Frank is watching the OAS [obstacle avoidance sonar].

Right after he tells the joke, he says, "Rick, I've got this line going across the OAS. Have you seen that before?"

These guys are trained to alternate jobs.

Rick's going, "Oh, yeah, I see that every time I come in here. That's that sandbar that goes across right where the point is."

Frank goes, "Oh, okay."

And then ten seconds later, *ka-whoom!* We have hit something major.

As soon as we hit, Rick and Frank did everything correctly. They shut down the screw, checked everything.

It got real quiet. It's almost pitch-black except for a little bit of light from the instrument panel. And the water inside the SDV is getting real cloudy, with all this muddy debris flying around in the boat.

It is a surrealistic sight, made even more eerie by the view from the full-face mask, which created a tunnel-like view—like a small television screen—because the sides of the face mask's lens were intentionally scraped to a dull finish to allow the penetration of light but to prevent distorted peripheral vision.

We don't know what we've hit. Rick tries to maneuver in every direction but the boat doesn't move. We're stuck.

Rick says, "Whatever we've hit, we can't move forward or back out."

As a prospective CO, I watched two very cool guys do exactly what needed to be done.

Rick shut down the screw again. We don't want to use up our batteries.

There was no panic, but you could feel the adrenaline, the anxiety. We size up the situation: we are trapped under the water; no one knows where we are; we can't break loose from whatever we have hit.

It stays quiet for a very long moment. No one seems ready to speak, not really knowing what to say. It is clearly an unusual and unexpected event. We check to insure that none of us is injured. Then we discuss our situation, still disbelieving our predicament.

Again it gets very still. Each of us is uneasy but no one admits to it. We're all trying to think what we can do to get out of this mess. I look at my watch. It's a little after ten o'clock, with a long night ahead.

I calculate that, with the breathing gas left in our Mark 15s and the compressed air we have in the boat, we don't have enough life support to get us to daylight. My West Virginia math tells me that I'm dead before sunrise.

Rick says, "Let's get the canopy open and we can swim to the surface."

When we crashed, I saw the console [instrument panel] being pushed back. It was like a slow-motion movie and for some reason I was focused on the center of the console and the canopy handle. I didn't realize what that meant at the time. But now I look and I see what's happened. In those days, we had a single canopy with a U-shaped handle right up in front. When we crashed, the console came back with great force and locked into the canopy handle. We try, but the canopy won't open.

I say, "We're going to have to pry it open."

We take turns prying and banging at it, trying to make a hole big enough to squeeze through. We really tried everything we could do to get that canopy pried back and it wasn't working. We worked at it for some considerable period of time. For awhile, Rick and I tried to pry the canopy inward to make a hole large enough to get out.

We're working really hard. But then we have to force ourselves to stop and rest. When you breathe a closed-circuit rebreather, you cannot overwork the rig. You can't get yourself out of breath. You'll overbreathe and pass out from CO_2 poisoning and we've got plenty of problems without that. We're sitting there trying to breathe normally. We all have our own thoughts, but we keep them to ourselves.

What are we going to do?

Maybe we could communicate with the guys back at the base and tell them to come help us. But we're not sure where we are. First we have to try to figure out what we hit.

We decided we had probably gotten off course and hit the old sunken barge. Everybody knew it was there. When BUD/S training was still conducted on the East Coast, the trainees used to go dive on the barge, near a little island off the enlisted beach.

We tried communicating on the underwater telephone but the test was for the UHF radio. No one was monitoring us. After awhile, when we were overdue, we could hear them trying to call us on the underwater telephone and we were trying to call them, too. But they couldn't hear us.

By now, we had been there for more than an hour. We still have air for a while longer. But we've tried everything. We can't get the canopy open. We can't call for help. We figure that when we hit the barge, if that's what it is, these little bow planes on the SDV caught in the metal of the barge, holding us like a hook. The bow planes are designed to break away, but we figure they are still holding us.

Rick says, "The only thing I can think of now is to try to break those bow planes off."

He started doing what you would do in your car if you were stuck in the sand. He started rocking the boat: fast forward, fast reverse.

The power to turn the screw in the SDV comes from this big bank of batteries. We can only keep trying to break free as long as the batteries last. We decided we were just going to do that until the batteries went dead. We didn't have any choice. We had tried everything else. We were basically down there on our own.

He went forward-reverse, forward-reverse, forward-reverse, forward-reverse. The boat vibrates from the screw trying to move it, but it doesn't budge. I don't know how long this went on. It seemed like forever. Frank and I can't do anything to help. We just sit there.

And then, something gives. The boat moves. Just a little bit forward. A little back. We can feel it starting to move. Then it goes way back. It breaks free and pops up to the surface. Our ears feel the relief of pressure as we go up.

Now we are afloat on the surface. But with an SDV, this means only the very top is awash on the surface, while the remainder is under the water, and very difficult for anyone to see. Normally, this is a tactical advantage, but tonight no advantage at all.

But, at least we know we now have a chance to be found. We are adrift in the choppy, dark tropical ocean, being splashed around in a steady rock-and-roll motion. We cannot see because our compartment is enclosed by the black skin of the boat, lighted only from the soft green glow of our instrumentation panel. Our instruments are no help since we don't know where we are. If we got under way, we could steer away from rescue.

We're still in serious trouble. We're trapped inside this little black boat. We have no buoys, no lights. And we're being carried down Vieques Channel, wherever the currents carry us.

Actually, we are not much better off than when we were jammed in the barge, because we are still slave to our breathing apparatus. We are now only three inches from fresh air, but we are blocked from it by the jammed canopy.

Rick Brown and I continued trying to get the canopy off. Frank got on the radio to try to raise someone, anyone. It was our last remaining chance—unless we could pry the canopy open.

Theoretically, the canopy had to be open to raise the UHF radio antenna. It had not been tried before, but we hoped that it would work in the down position. It did. Suddenly, Frank made contact with the guys on the pier. We could hear the shouting and cheering in the background.

We were alive, but not yet found. We told them we were adrift on the surface, thought we had rammed and been captured inside the old Vieques water barge. That would give them a starting reference for search. Everyone knows our situation, knows we must be found before our breathing gas is exhausted.

They had already gone out searching for us but they didn't know where to look and we weren't sure where we were. We were like a small black log adrift in a large black ocean. We could do nothing but rest in place, and breathe very slowly to save our remaining gas. After some time, in the distance, we could hear the search party shouting out to us.

We could not shout back because of our full–face masks. Sometimes they would seem to be very near us, other times at a far-off distance. Immediately, we got on the UHF radio and told the people on the pier that we could hear the shouts from the search party, that they were close to us, to keep searching.

Finally, [PO1] Bobby Putnam, who was the diving supervisor for this operation, thought he saw us and shined a spotlight from the patrol boat in our direction. At last, we heard him yell, "I see the boat."

He quickly pulled his Boston Whaler beside us. We couldn't talk to him, but we could hear him giving directions to the crew of the boat to maneuver toward us.

As soon as they got close enough, he jumped into the water fully clothed. I remember him sticking his light through the section of the canopy that Rick and I had bent up like the half-opened top on a tin can.

The glare from that flashlight was one of the most welcome things I have ever seen in my life.

We still couldn't get out of the boat so they took it under tow, with us still inside. I remember how Bobby hung on to the boat as they towed us all the way back to the dry dock recovery area.

When Rick put his mask directly against the canopy, he was able to talk to Bobby along the way.

We had no idea where we were. As we proceeded under tow, the people on the pier began telling us over the UHF what would happen at the recovery point. Finally, they maneuvered us alongside a floating barge in the protected water of the old dry dock. We could hear a lot of activity and see the glare of floodlights penetrating the cracks of the canopy, and through the hole that we had pried.

Then, while safely captured alongside the floating barge (how ironic, a barge), they were able to pry the jammed canopy far enough open for us to escape through the area of our makeshift hole. To do this, we had to go one at a time: take a final lung full of breathing gas, ditch our MK 15 UBA and full–face mask inside the boat, and quickly squeeze through the small hole and to the surface.

Bobby Putman was still in the water outside the SDV, helping to pry open the hole for our escape. We rallied around Bobby and then swam together to the barge, guided by safety swimmers along the way.

We climbed up the ladder with assistance from the guys who had gathered there. A crowd of some size had come to assist in the search, and now to watch the recovery procedure. Once on the barge, we just stood there among our teammates, laughed, shook hands, and reveled in the familiar smell of the fresh, warm tropical air.

We learned from that. The SDV was redesigned to have a dual sliding canopy: a canopy over the pilot and one over the navigator to operate independently, and also a breakaway canopy. It was redesigned so if you stood up with some force you could pop the canopy off.

The next day was a Saturday and we had the day off, so we went out to do some lobster diving, and on the way back we dove down to the barge, which was pretty well rusted away.

We found one of the SDV's bow planes and the OAS window, so we knew for sure that's where we had been. I kept that bow plane and took it home with me, since it could not be repaired. Shortly after I took command of the team, I asked one of the team's corpsmen, HM1 Michael "Doc" Sabino, to draw me a cartoon on the bow plane as a memento, which he did.

Sabino was an artist of some fame around the team at the time, because he had designed the SDV team logo, which is still used by the command today. Doc was about to get out of the navy and return to his home in St. Thomas and I wanted to capture his talent before he left. He drew a picture of the SDV headed at full speed toward the underwater barge, depicting conversation between myself, Rick, and Frank. I keep it as a treasured memento to this day.

It certainly was a night to remember.

Chapter 29
One of Our Dolphins (SDVs) Is Missing

Even in the best-run navy, things sometimes go embarrassingly wrong. But, with luck, everything turns out all right in the end.

Captain William "Billy" Hamilton, now in charge of development of the navy's next-generation SDV, and Mike Bennett, recently retired, recall two such incidents. Hamilton well remembers the day Little Bit went AWOL:

I went to Naval Special Warfare Group One in Coronado in 1980 as officer in charge of the marine mammal program. The navy had three marine mammal programs, one with sea lions and two using Atlantic bottle-nosed dolphins.

Were you in charge of all three?

I was in charge of all three. I did that for two and a half years. We did a lot of harbor defense–type exercises, all up and down the West and East Coasts. I was a department head on the group staff, something called the undersea systems division. I had about fifty people. At that time the underwater demolition teams were 110 to 120 people. So my unit was half the size of a UDT. But my budget was twice as big as a UDT.

What did your marine mammals do?

At the time all that stuff was classified secret. But a lot of it has been in the open press since and confirmed by the navy public affairs people.

In a general sense, the unclassified program was the sea lions. It was called "quickfind." It has the same name today. We used them to find the electronics package from tests of missiles and other ordnance.

When they have quality assurance tests, they need to recover the electronics package. Before firing it, they attach a pinger to it.

Let's say it goes down in three hundred feet of water off San Clemente Island, which is where we do some of this stuff. If you use hard-hat divers, they need an overhead surface support platform—a ship.

We can take a rubber boat with these sea lions, which we work with all the time. We put them in the water near where it went in. They'll hear the pinger. They put a little attachment in their mouth, dive down, and attach it on the piece of ordnance. It has a line attached to it and you just pull it back up.

We also do that off Port Hueneme, the Pacific missile test range. They drop practice mines. You might drop twenty practice mines in one hundred feet of water. If you were to use divers, because of the depth and the time, you would burn up dive pairs pretty quickly. You can send these animals down, which don't breathe down there, obviously, and pick up all the practice mines in a couple of hours. It's a real cost saver.

The dolphin program had to do with some mine countermeasures. It was a defense mechanism against swimmer attacks against ships.

How did they do that?

I don't think I'll get into the specifics of that. They did have them over in Bahrain during the Gulf War. They did the harbor defense in Bahrain. That's been in the open press.

They used them to find mines?

Yeah, to find mines.

How do they find mines?

They echo locate. The dolphins put out a pinging noise. They can discriminate. You teach them what a minelike object sounds like. They're smart enough to discriminate.

What do they do when they find it?

They use their echo-locating skills to find things under the water and then there are ways we have to take care of the mine from there.

One report is that you would have a dolphin go out and run into a swimmer and blow them both up. Is that what happens?

No, that is not what happens. The animals, in the performance of their mission, are not harmed. It probably does not have to be said that if you're in a mined environment and a mine goes off, anything in that area is subject to shock waves or whatever. The animals do breathe air and they have voids in their bodies, such as chest cavities. The overpressure will certainly impact them. But the cartilage in the chest is a lot more flexible than that in a human so they can take a lot more shock.

With a diver, if you drop concussion grenades over the side, you bust a guy's ear drums and he gets disoriented. He doesn't know which direction is up. It is very difficult for a diver if you lose your orientation, to be able to successfully conduct a ship attack.

The same thing could harm an animal. But in the performance of their mission, they do not get harmed.

Have you had any unusual experiences working with these animals?

We took a group of the dolphins to Mayport, Florida, one year for a big annual exercise that CINCLANTFLT [Commander, Atlantic Fleet] conducts. They had blue-water warfare at sea and antisubmarine warfare and it culminated in a large amphibious landing.

Our portion of it was supporting a harbor breakout of ships from Mayport, where the aircraft carriers and some of the smaller ships are homeported.

What is harbor breakout?

You make sure that the enemy has not planted mines in the area— no mines in the lanes where our ships are going to go out.

These are Atlantic bottle-nosed dolphins. When we train with them, we're in San Diego or Hawaii. Now they're back in their home territory, the Atlantic. This was in the spring, March-April time frame. It is also the time when the animals come into heat. They call it rutting.

We had both male and female animals. Not surprisingly, they had their own personalities. The males are always very highstrung and the females are less aggressive, usually more dependable, more consistent.

We had this one female we were out working with. Her name was Little Bit. And this herd of wild bottle-nosed dolphins goes by. We've had experience with this before. Usually our animals will hear all this noise and stuff and they'll see them out there. Typically, they'll run out in that direction and then come right back. They were fairly dependable. But at that time of year it was tough to control some of them. You felt like you wanted to write them up under the UCMJ [Uniform Code of Military Justice] for being AWOL, but you couldn't do that.

This one particular day, I guess Little Bit, who was one of our better animals, decided she wasn't going to work with us. She was going to go stick with the herd. We looked and looked and looked and went all up and down the coast.

I finally had to call my boss, who was Bob Gormly, in Coronado. He was the chief staff officer and [Comdr. Cathal] Irish Flynn was the commodore. I had to tell my boss I had lost one of my animals. These are animals that had been in captivity for ten or twelve years. The navy had put a lot of time and effort into training them. If you added up all that time and effort, easily these were million dollar animals. We only had four of them and they were hard to replace.

A couple or three days later we're out in the same area working the other animals and our little animal shows up. She was bruised and cut and she had been bitten. She had been running with the wild herd. But because she was a stranger to the herd, she was not accepted.

I guess she got hungry or something and decided to come back. We saw her coming. We had these Boston Whalers with the side cut out with a kind of gym mat which they beached themselves on. All we had to do was slow the boat down and she jumped right on board without having to be cued to come in. She just wanted to come home. She was hungry and tired. She was happy to be back home.

You said it was rutting season. Did she come back pregnant?

No, she didn't. It didn't turn out that way. I'll tell you I worried about that one. Every time you put them out in the open ocean they can do whatever they want.

Bennett recalls a similar incident. This time, the loss involved an inanimate object, an SDV:

Let me tell you about the time we lost an SDV in Glorietta Bay. [Glorietta Bay is the body of water adjoining the amphibious base at Coronado.] At the time, the boats belonged to an SDV platoon of an underwater demolition team.

Tommy Bracken and James C. "Momma" Cousins had made a successful run and were coming back in. You bring the SDV out of the water up onto a trailer, just like any other boat.

When you're practicing with an SDV, you have an antenna with a little red flag on it. As they were getting ready to bring the SDV out of the water, Tommy unscrewed the whip antenna and Cousins went over to the trailer.

He got himself positioned and says, "Okay, bring her up."

Tom says, "I don't have the boat."

Cousins says, "You've got the antenna in your hand."

Tommy holds up the antenna. There is no boat attached. They both splash into the water looking for the boat. But the boat is headed out of the bay.

What happened was that the SDV has a little round rheostat as a forward and reverse switch. One of them, as he got out with his fins on, hit the switch and put it in full reverse.

The skipper was Captain LeMoyne. [Then-Lt. Comdr. Irve C. "Chuck" LeMoyne, who has since become an admiral.] He called the whole team in. All leave and liberty was canceled. This was around an Easter holiday.

The skipper called all of the team into the briefing room. We got the diving locker to pump up bottles. We were going to dive until we found that boat. Everybody was going to dive. The sick, lame, and lazy would fill bottles. Everyone else was in the water.

We did some frantic diving but we couldn't find the boat. In Glorietta Bay, you couldn't see much more than four feet.

Then we found tracks of the boat on the bottom, where it had gone scooting along the bottom in full reverse. It would hit a little bump and circle around and cross its path.

Robert Clendenning and I were tracking the boat. Everyplace the tracks crossed, we'd put a little flag in.

We dove all that day, all that night, and into the second day. We had flags all over the place. About ten or eleven o'clock in the morning on the second day, we had turned and were coming on a straight line.

We heard an M80 go off. That was the recall signal. An M80 is like a cherry bomb, an inch long, half an inch around. We stuck a stake in, put a life jacket on it.

Bill Wright had a handheld sonar. He was hollering, "Here it is."

We were only fifteen or twenty feet from it. It was full of mud. The little holes it has on the side to let water out were taking in mud big-time when it was going backward. It was heavy. We had to pump it up to bring it to the surface.

Chapter 30
Blocking Haiphong Harbor

For years, the navy's frogmen have had an often tempestuous love-hate relationship with the submarine force. They would seem to have been made for each other. Both operate under the sea. And both base their effectiveness, and their survival, on stealth.

But, for the SEALs, life aboard a submarine is often crowded, uncomfortable, and boring. Once they venture out into the ocean, their assignments are cold and often dangerous.

The submariners worry about the SEALs bringing aboard fuel for their boats and explosives, even when it is stored outside the hull. And working with the frogmen requires precise control of a barely moving submarine and involves the constant danger that their presence will be compromised.

With the end of the Cold War, the submariners have become much more amenable to working with the SEALs, seeing this as one way to make themselves useful and justify their existence. Frogmen from SEAL Team EIGHT, based in Little Creek, Virginia, recently conducted exercises with the USS *Flying Fish* off Puerto Rico, practicing the launch of two rubber boats perched on the horizontal sail attached to the submarine's conning tower.

This renewed interest in SEAL-submarine cooperation reminds some SEAL and UDT veterans of a kind of golden age in the 1960s and 1970s when a few submarines—among them the *Grayback,*

Tunny, and *Perch*—spent weeks at a time working with the frogmen in many exercises and a few daring real-life adventures.

One of the leading figures during that time was the late Capt. Fred T. Berry, a Naval Academy graduate and veteran submarine commander. Two men who worked closely with Berry in those days are Maynard Weyers, a retired captain, and James L. "Gator" Parks (see chapter 2). Weyers recalls a practice exercise off the California coast and preparations for a daring operation in Vietnam:

This was probably 1964 or 1965. Captain Berry had a submarine squadron on the West Coast and they were continually working toward something—some kind of real-world operation.

For one of these exercises, an individual from the CIA, a navy nurse, and I traveled out to San Clemente Island. For the exercise scenario, I was a sensitive foreign official defecting from an enemy island nation to the U.S. The nurse was to be my mistress and the CIA guy her brother. This exercise was observed by Captain Berry and was to test the entire system—submarine and SEALs.

We were on the island and the submarine was supposed to make contact and recover me. The SEALs locked out of the submarine and I signaled them in, using infrared signals. They came in in two boats. They were expecting to pick up just me and were rather surprised when they found this woman, her simulated "baby" and her "brother."

I said, "I'm not leaving unless my mistress and her brother can go along."

They'd go off and whisper and then we'd talk some more. They finally agreed to take the three of us and the baby. Then I told them I had my heirlooms. We had two big footlockers full of rocks to simulate the heirlooms. I told them I'm not going without my stuff.

Finally, they say, "Okay, we'll take you three in this boat and the footlockers in the other one."

It was dark out there. We got in the boat and left. But they tricked us and those heirlooms never made it off the beach.

They paddled us back out. The gradient there drops off sharply so the submarine could come in real close. But they couldn't lock my mistress and her brother and the baby into the sub underwater. So they came by, we threw a rope around the periscope and they dragged us out to sea so the radar wouldn't pick them up when they surfaced.

When they got out far enough, we pulled away, the submarine surfaced, and we got aboard. The CO and the crew didn't know what to do: a woman aboard a submarine! And my mistress is playing the role to the hilt. The baby has to have milk. So she has the corpsman heating milk.

They set us up with staterooms in officers' country.

Being a healthy American boy and to add to the confusion, I said, "I want my mistress in with me."

Captain Berry has been watching all this with some amusement. But he says, "Now wait a minute . . ."

While they're warming the milk and worrying about the staterooms, it turns out the brother is a bad guy. He had brought on a shaving kit and his shaving cream tube is full of C-4 [plastic explosive]. He says he's put the charge somewhere on the sub and that they must sail into the enemy harbor and surrender. However, the sub crew and the SEALs did a quick search and were able to locate and disarm the charge.

Those are the kinds of exercises we were doing. I think they were preparing for a real pickup of someone somewhere but they didn't tell us the details.

Captain Berry was the same person who was in charge of a plan to sink a submarine to block the channel into Haiphong Harbor. Since he had worked extensively with SEALs, he knew many of the people and their capabilities. He handpicked the people he wanted for this operation. They had a special boat made up for us. The plan was that they'd take the sub in with a small crew, sink it, and we'd pick them up and get them out of there.

I was in the best shape I've ever been in my life. I figured if anything went wrong, I'd have to work my way all the way down the coast to South Vietnam.

The whole operation was so secret that even those involved were told only what they needed to know. While Weyers prepared for his part of the plan, Parks was working on another phase of the same operation. His story starts many years earlier:

At the time the French got out after Dien Bien Phu, we took shiploads of Vietnamese out of Haiphong. We ran up that river. [In 1954 the French suffered a devastating defeat by the Viet Minh, as the Vietnamese force was known. The country was subsequently partitioned at the seventeenth parallel, setting off an exodus of Vietnamese allied with the French to the new South Vietnam.]

I almost got up that river again. During the war, we had a job that would have had us run SDVs up that river. It didn't come off but it was a very interesting scheme. It could have worked. We were going to take a submarine and sink it.

Captain Berry was in charge. We were great friends. He had been in the submarine business as long as we had been playing with SDVs. He had the foresight to see that was going to be a viable weapons system, eventually.

There were SDVs involved?

You bet there were. We were going to have two of them on the deck of that submarine. Also, we were going to do a reconnaissance before the sub went in.

You were going to sink that sub?

Yes sir, we were going to sink it right in the channel. We were going to take the people off in the SDVs. We were going to scuttle the ship, come topside, take the four men that were going to be running the submarine off, and go out and meet up with the SAR [search and rescue helicopter]. There were changes from putting SDVs on the deck to not putting them on deck. At the end, they were going to put them on the deck.

Sinking that sub would stop shipping for a year before they got that out of the channel. What happened, really, I think we would have done it, but the State Department got cold feet when Bucher got captured up in Korea—the *Pueblo.* Never been able to like him very much since then. [On 23 January 1968, the USS *Pueblo,* a disguised merchant ship under the command of Comdr. Lloyd M. Bucher, was captured, along with her crew, by the North Koreans while eavesdropping on North Korean radar and radio transmissions.]

Were you in SEAL Team ONE?

I had been in SEAL Team ONE and I had gone to the SpecWar [Naval Special Warfare Command] staff for this job.

Was Maynard Weyers involved?

Yeah, Maynard had the boat. He was going to run the surface boat. Him and Frank Flynn were going to be the boat drivers. They were the backup, actually, if something happened to the SDVs. They were going to get us anyway, when we came out beyond the antiaircraft range. Yeah, Maynard wasn't too swift about that.

We were actually on station to do the first reconnaissance, to get some photographs of the buoys and see how wide the channel was and how deep, of course. We were actually on station when Bucher got captured.

The old sub we were going to sink was waiting at Subic. We went up in the Tonkin Gulf in the *Tunny* [the USS *Tunny,* a submarine configured to carry two SDVs]. We were going to do a recon first [in the SDVs] to make sure if we sank this thing in the middle of the channel it was going to do some good.

That was a good plan and it was workable and it was going to work, probably without getting many, if anybody, killed, except maybe Maynard if he had come in in that boat.

That reconnaissance was the first phase of it and that was as far as it got. Then they wanted to take us up off Korea. So then our ten-knot submarine made a run for Korea. We went all the way from Vietnam.

I understand the North Koreans had a couple of submarines there the Russians had given them. They were to be the target. The plan was, we were going to fill one SDV up with explosives and leave it under the North Korean subs and take the other and rendezvous with the first one and take the people out. That was the plan. We were going to blow up two submarines.

But that too never got too far along. I don't think anybody was ever too serious about it.

Unfortunately, none of those things came to pass. I spent my whole life in those stupid little black boats and never did get to do anything real-world.

Underwater Demolition Team (UDT) members watch American planes strafe the beach as they prepare to go ashore in the Balikpanan operation in Borneo on 3 July 1945. *Photo by Lt. (jg) C. F. Waterman from the National Archives.*

UDT members plan an operation during the Korean War. *National Archives.*

UDT team comes ashore in Korea. Note the bulky dry suits in use at that time. *National Archives.*

Getting ready to destroy North Korean fishing net. *National Archives.*

A captured net is hung out to dry. *National Archives.*

Lt. Martin Every takes an awkward tumble during recovery of the *Gemini IV* spacecraft after the first American walk in space. *NASA photo.*

The *Gemini* capsule is stabilized with a flotation collar. *NASA photo.*

Every and Petty Officers Neil G. Dow and Everett W. Owl prepare the *Gemini* capsule for pickup by an aircraft carrier. *NASA photo.*

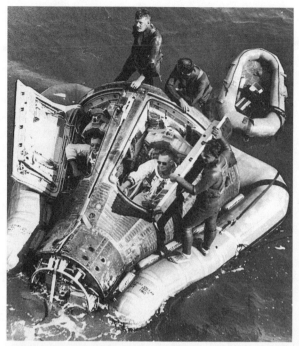

Navy frogmen assist *Gemini VIII* astronauts David Scott, *left,* and Neil Armstrong after their landing some five hundred miles east of Okinawa. Armstrong later became the first man to walk on the moon. *NASA photo.*

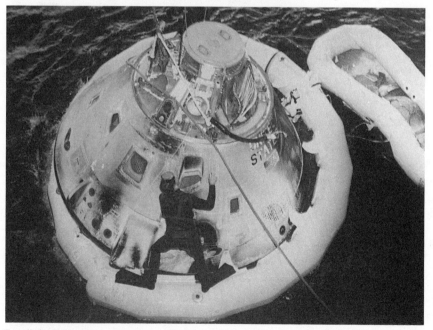

Lt. (jg) Chris Bent clings to the side of an unmanned *Apollo* spacecraft, preparing it to be hoisted aboard the USS *Boxer. Photo courtesy Chris Bent.*

Members of UDT Thirteen prepare to help the *Apollo 13* astronauts emerge from the spacecraft after their harrowing trip around the moon. *NASA photo.*

Members of UDT Thirteen take pictures and assist *Apollo 13* astronauts. John L. Swigert Jr. (back to camera) was the command module pilot. Fred W. Haise Jr., stepping into the life raft, was the lunar module pilot. James A. Lovell Jr., the spacecraft commander, is emerging from the capsule. *NASA photo.*

Command module pilot Swigert waves to a UDT Thirteen member photographing the recovery from the water. *NASA photo.*

Swigert, *left,* and Lovell, *center,* wait for a helicopter to carry them to the USS *Iwo Jima.* Haise has already been picked up. A member of the UDT recovery team is at right. *NASA photo.*

Norman Olson, an avid parachutist and founder of two SEAL parachute demonstration teams in a free fall over San Diego. *Photo courtesy Norman Olson.*

Members of an underwater demolition team prepare explosive hose for use during an operation in Vietnam. *US Navy photo.*

Putting explosive hose into place is heavy work for UDT frogmen. *US Navy photo.*

Two UDT frogmen stand guard as another team member prepares to blow up a bunker in Vietnam. *US Navy photo.*

A UDT member sets an explosive charge in preparation for the destruction of a Viet Cong bunker. *US Navy photo.*

SEALs climb aboard a landing craft after an operation in the Rung Sat Special Zone in Vietnam. *US Navy photo.*

SEALs fire on an ene-
my position in Vietnam.
US Navy photo.

His face showing the tension of the situation, a SEAL moves through a suspected
enemy structure. *US Navy photo.*

Two SEALs armed with M16 rifles prepare to move forward during an operation in Vietnam. *US Navy photo.*

Part of the U.S. riverine navy that worked closely with SEALs during operations in the delta formed by the Mekong and Bassac Rivers in South Vietnam. *US Navy photo.*

EM3 William Langley, a member of SEAL Team ONE, applies grease paint to his face before an operation along the Bassac River in Vietnam in the fall of 1967. *US Navy Photo.*

Two SEALs pause briefly before moving in on an enemy position during Operation Crimson Tide in South Vietnam's Vinh Binh province in December of 1967. *US Navy photo.*

SEAL Frank Scolise and friend in Vietnam. *US Navy photo.*

A navy Sea Wolf helicopter pilot and a SEAL plan an operation in Vietnam in the fall of 1969. *US Navy photo.*

Would-be SEALs in training crawl under a barbed wire entanglement as explosives are set off nearby. *US Navy photo.*

Men in training at the Basic Underwater Demolition/SEAL course in Coronado, California, paddle through the Pacific breakers. *US Navy photo.*

The USS *Grayback*, a missile-firing diesel submarine converted for use by SEALs. It carried SEALs and UDT members on Operation Thunderhead, a daring effort to rescue Americans from a North Vietnamese prison. *US Navy photo.*

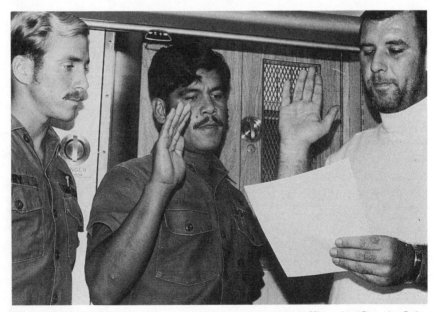

Philip "Moki" Martin is sworn in as a navy warrant officer by Comdr. John Chamberlain, skipper of the *Grayback*, in June 1962 as the submarine approached the North Vietnamese coast. Lieutenant Melvin Spence Dry, *left*, was killed a few days later. *Photo courtesy of Philip Martin.*

Chapter 31
Operation Thunderhead

In the spring of 1972, SEAL Team ONE sent a unit—the Naval Special Warfare Western Pacific Detachment—to Okinawa to act as the contingency platoon for the Seventh Fleet. This was a first step toward a peacetime routine after the SEALs' long involvement in the Vietnam War. But while the U.S. participation in the war was shrinking, one major concern remained: the fate of the Americans held captive by North Vietnam.

Philip Martin was the senior petty officer in the platoon and was soon to be promoted to the rank of warrant officer. A veteran of combat operations as both a member of the UDT and SEALs, Martin had a peculiarly appropriate nickname for a frogman, earned when he was a boy in the Hawaiian Islands. Because he was so at home in the water, the other boys called him Moki—Hawaiian for shark.

When the SEALs arrived in Okinawa, they immediately plunged into a strenuous training routine, involving everything from submarine operations to mountain climbing. But, as Martin and a few other members of the unit were soon to learn, their training was not just routine. Something was up. This is Martin's story of his part in Operation Thunderhead, one of the most daring—and, for many years, most secret—military exploits of the Vietnam War:

We went to Okinawa to be the contingency platoon for the fleet. We were to train there and be available for any ops that came up. So we trained on Okinawa for a few weeks and we went to Korea and did some cold water ops. Then we went to Subic [the major U.S. naval base in the Philippines].

We kept going back to Subic to work on the *Grayback* because the *Grayback* at that time had the two Regulus hangars, the wet side hangar and the dry side hangar. [A diesel-powered submarine, the USS *Grayback* had originally been designed to carry Regulus missiles in two large hangars on the deck. When the Regulus was superseded by the Polaris missile, the *Grayback* was converted for use by the frogmen.]

And they had the SDV, the latest model SDV. Mark 7, Mod 6. We called it the Six Boat. [The SDV was a four-man SEAL delivery vehicle.] We tried to stay away from the *Grayback*. We knew it was going to be wet and cold and you can't get away from the water. But we kept going back and doing SDV ops. Something was planned, something was coming up.

After a couple of months of that, we went to Korea to do some mountain climbing. We were halfway through the marine climbing school there when we got this message, this secret message, to get back to Okinawa. So we fly back to Okinawa and right there at the pier is the *Grayback* waiting for us.

We go aboard and there is a full SDV team aboard. [At that time, the SDVs were operated by the UDT and the SEALs rode along as passengers.] And when we get to sea, we get some briefings. We learned later it was to be an operation to possibly recover some POWs and it was going to be off the coast of Vietnam, near Haiphong.

The U.S. had received information that a small group of Americans hoped to escape from a North Vietnamese prison camp and make their way in a small boat down to the coast. Operation Thunderhead was the name given to the plan to have SEALs make contact with the escapees and help them to safety aboard an American ship standing by offshore.

We were briefed very little and not the whole platoon. It was just the two guys who were going to be involved in the first SDV, myself and Spence [Lt. Melvin Spence Dry]. And [Lt.] John Lutz and Edwards [Fireman Tom Edwards. Lutz and Edwards were the UDT operators of the SDV]. And the only people on the *Grayback* who were briefed were the CO, the operations officer, and the diving officer. It was so compartmentalized that everybody only knew what they were going to do themselves.

[Lt. Comdr.] Maynard Weyers was the officer in charge of the detachment, [to which a SEAL platoon and a UDT platoon were assigned] but he wasn't told what we were doing. Even when we came back and gave him the after-action report, he just kind of shook his head.

We didn't know exactly where we were going except perhaps the guys in the CIC [combat information center]. It's funny. I got a message just before I left that I had made warrant officer. It was going to be effective the first of June. On the first of June, in the midst of all these secret briefings, they baked a cake and cleared the wardroom out and all the officers stood around and welcomed me to the officer corps of the navy.

Now up on the surface were all of these ships, probably seventy or eighty ships. That's when they had a whole fleet of ships in the [Tonkin] gulf. We looked at them through the periscope. As far as you could see, there were ships. It looked like the World War II invasion of Normandy.

And no one knew the *Grayback* was there. This submarine snuck in under all these ships with her battery motors and nobody knew it was there. At that time the *Grayback* was one of about four boats still battery powered. Everything else was nuclear. The nuclear boats are noisy. I don't care how they try to quiet them down, they're very noisy.

So when we were sneaking through there the submarine crew just loved it. They're sneaking through this big fleet and nobody knows they are there.

Did you have to be quiet?

When we were close to a ship, we were real quiet. You can't use any of the machinery. You can't flush the toilet. The SEALs were bored. We were just passengers. We'd take all the movies up in the dry deck shelter and watch movies all day. Then they would come in and say, you guys turn the projector off because we have to go on silence. They snuck in and they did that extremely well. That submarine snuck under everybody's noses. You had all these ships up there and nobody expected a submarine.

How long did it take to get through the fleet?

They were doing it forever. When they ran the snorkel up at night, they would have to make sure they were not near a ship. It seemed like it took a couple of days. They let us look through the periscope. Not since D day in Normandy has anyone seen so many ships. It was scary. You go around with the periscope and they're all over the place.

Did the submarine crew know what was going on?

Everybody on the boat knew something was up, when you bring on a platoon of SEALs and a platoon of frogmen. [The term *frogmen* is sometimes used, as here, to refer specifically to UDT swimmers.] That's what the *Grayback* was designed to do, to sneak in there. They did it extremely well.

Basically, what we were going to do was, we—the SEALs—were going to check out a couple of islands. The *Grayback* was going to take us as far up as it could, as close into shore as it could. And then the SDV was going to take us the rest of the way.

Our instructions were to go on the beach and a friendly agent was going to approach us on the beach or there was going to be signaling by a red flag on a sampan coming down the river. Because of my previous experience in Vietnam, I was going to be the official greeter of the friendly agent, who would be leading one or two, three or four escaped POWs—we didn't know how many people there were going to be—and we were going to try to get them back to the submarine.

From my experience in Vietnam, I knew a lot of these guys fly a flag and a lot of them are red. So that was going to be a tough thing to call. They were going to be coming down the river and they were going to be on the coast, maybe on one of these islands. We were to go out and check the islands. I was going to approach them if we somehow came across them on the beach and somehow get them back to the *Grayback*.

Now, how were we going to get them back to the *Grayback?* It was going to be either a swim, after a five-minute lesson in how to use our equipment; it might have been a surface transit with the SDV; or it could have been an IBS—a rubber boat.

The idea was that the first SDV crew would go over and feel the area out, check the conditions. Look for anybody who might have a red light—it might have been at night—or a red flag. And then the two SEALs would stay ashore for a day or two and get relieved in a couple of days. And that was it.

Before we went, we tried to figure out the tides and the current from the river and everything. We laid it out with a compass. We said, we only have to go three thousand or four thousand yards. That's easy. Well, it's easy in San Diego or Subic Bay. But when you've got to work with that huge river current they have there and cope with the tides, even if you plan it with the tides, it could run against you. It ran against us. We launched about midnight. [3–4 June 1972.] But we underestimated the currents. The SDV kept going and going and going.

John [Lutz, the SDV pilot] says, "You know, we're not moving very far. We must have a hell of a current."

We made the decision to turn around and try to get back. The plan was, the submarine would send a signal out at specific times and we had a receiver so we could find them.

We ran and ran and ran all night. Finally, the SDV batteries gave out. We launched just before midnight and just before dawn the SDV batteries gave out. That means there's no way to get the SDV back to the submarine. Our contingency plan, in case we had to abandon the SDV, was we would stay in the water, swim as far out to sea as we could, stay together, and initiate our radio recall—we had these waterproof radios—and then they would pick us up by search and rescue helicopter.

So anyway, the SDV runs out of battery juice and we have to bail out. We actuate our call sign and the helicopters come by to pick us up. Even though we had turned around, we were still quite a ways off from the *Grayback*. It was farther out than I thought. It had to stay in eighty feet of water.

So we get picked up by a helicopter. The only thing we could salvage out of the SDV was the communications equipment and that was critical. We had to get those out. Some of those systems had regulators hooked up to them and that's how we talked to each other. It was hard to get a system and it was kind of expensive.

It was really the only thing we could salvage out of the boat. We couldn't get the motor, we couldn't get the batteries. We damn sure couldn't pick up the boat. It's seven or eight o'clock in the morning. Broad daylight.

John Lutz, the SDV officer, says we're going to have to sink the boat. The SDV kept floating, no matter what we tried to do in the water. Normally, you pump increments of water into the SDV to balance it and that sucker will sink. Well that boat just sat on the surface.

There was a minigun in the door of the helicopter.

So John says, "Can you shoot that thing full of holes?"

The air crewman naturally nods, yeah.

The guy shoots and he doesn't know where to shoot so John says, "I'll shoot it."

Poor John, there's almost a tear in his eye as he pulls the trigger. He just saturated it. He knew what tanks to hit. The boat sank finally.

So we go back to the [cruiser USS] *Long Beach* instead of going to the *Grayback,* for obvious reasons.

We tell the guy in charge there they have to let the guys on the submarine know they have to plan for the current.

John says, "Hey, whatever happens to the next operation, be sure they plan it with the current. Because that current—when the tide is ebbing, there is going to be a hell of a current coming out of the river. So you have to plan on that. You have to either move the *Grayback* or do this or that or do something to compensate so you can get to that island."

But the *Grayback* is on radio silence and they don't put their antenna up because the last time they did that someone shot at them. [The crew of a destroyer, the USS *Harold E. Holt,* spotted the submarine and fired at it but fortunately missed.] The *Grayback* only sticks their snorkel up at night to charge their batteries. The communication, when they did stick it up, was real sparse. Not very good. Somehow, they didn't get the word.

But on the *Long Beach,* we know that [Lts.] Bob Conger and Tom McGrath are going to launch the second SDV. Jesus Christ, that's going to be a problem if they do that. So we can't get the *Grayback* on the radio to warn them. Spence Dry and John Lutz and myself figured we've got to get back to stop them or brief them before they take off.

So the decision was made. They say, "Okay, we're going to send you back"—the SDV crew from the first op.

We got the sub to put up Nancy gear, the infrared gear, on the snorkel. They were going to put the snorkel up with an infrared light on it. The helicopter was going to home in and drop us before that other SDV was launched. We had to talk to the pilot and navigator of the SDV before they go out, before 2300.

We briefed the helicopter pilot. We told him the snorkel was going to be up, there's going to be infrared on the snorkel facing seaward. So the approach would have been from the seaward toward the shore.

The pilot flew around and he had trouble locating the *Grayback*. And when he finally found what he thought was the infrared signal, it was an actual red light. He flies toward it. And it's right on the beach!

Boy! The helicopter makes this 90-degree turn, a U-turn as quick as I've seen anybody do it. I'll tell you! So we flew around and as we came around, the pilot says, "All right, I see this light. I'm coming in on this light."

He was using infrared gear somehow. I look and I see, yeah, we're about two–three thousand yards offshore. It was real windy and it was real dark and the water was real choppy.

Prior to the helicopter taking off, we told the pilot we wanted to make sure that the height and the speed was clear, that it was no higher— absolutely no higher—and I'm looking at this guy. He had a red mustache, big lieutenant. I said, absolutely no higher than twenty feet, twenty knots.

And he said, "Well, I'll try to get you as close as I can to that."

I said, "If you've got to go lower, go lower, but absolutely no higher. I'd also like to have some control from the door. If I think you're a little too high, I'm going to ask you to come down a little bit."

I know how these pilots are. They don't like people telling them how to fly their airplanes. By the same token, I want to have my own life in my hands.

You took charge even though Spence Dry was senior in rank?

Yeah, I did that because of my experience. Out of all the SEALs there I was the guy who had the most experience with cast and recovery. But we did it as part of our training before going on the *Grayback*. So everybody knew how to do it.

Most people who have done a lot of cast and recovery, they can tell when a helicopter gets close to the water because the prop blast will blow water up. If it's right up to you, if that foam or spray is there, you're fine. That helicopter is probably five feet from the surface. He's real close, five or ten feet. We usually judge—we look out the back of the helicopter just past the tail. If you can see the spray there, you're ten, fifteen, maximum twenty feet. If you don't see any spray, that sucker is a little bit higher.

We told that to the helicopter crew.

We came around and the air crewman who was going to drop us on the command from the pilot, he says, "Are you ready to go?"

Then he says, "Go!"

I stick my head out and I say, "Hold it! Hold it! We're way too high! Ask the pilot to go around."

The helicopter makes a slow turn, comes around again, comes up on the pass again. Before, I had told the pilot, if at all possible, to try to drop us upwind. Chances for the helicopter slowing down would be a lot better. So he said, yeah, he was going to do that.

We came around the second time and I looked at it and I said, "Hey, bring this sucker down another five feet."

I feel it lowering. Another five feet. But I don't see any spray and I canceled the second pass. And then I canceled the third pass and I canceled the fourth pass.

Each time I cancel a pass, the helicopter is turning quicker and quicker. Finally Spence Dry comes up to me. I remember seeing his face in that red light.

He says, "Hey, Moki, we've got to get back there as quick as we can because these guys are taking off."

So I say all right. I tell the air crewman, "Tell that pilot to get down. Let's get some water spray on the tail of this sucker. We're way, way, way too high."

So he comes around and I look out and I think I can see some spray. Even though it's dark, that white spray will carry. Finally, I saw it. This is it. The pilot gives the word to the air crewman, go. And I look over and I say, "It looks good."

I step back. I was going to be the third guy out.

We waited a few seconds. That's critical, when we wait a few seconds because your altitude can change. So the guy says, "Go!"

Spence goes out. John Lutz goes out. I go out. Then Edwards went out. The plan was, the first two guys hook up and swim toward the second two guys. They hookup and swim toward the first two guys.

I go out the door and I turn in the direction of the helicopter. I hold my hand up so I can angle my body down.

I've got a wet-suit top on and I've got my camouflage uniform over that and then I had my web equipment and a Swedish K submachine gun. Our procedure is to unhook all your web gear so in case you get hurt you can dump real quick. Then we had swim fins under our arm.

So I turned and faced the direction the helicopter was going and I stuck my hand up and I counted: One thousand. Two thousand. Three thousand. And I didn't hit the water by three thousand.

I said, "Goddamn!"

And then I hit the water, wham! To me, in my mind, that's four seconds. Sixteen feet the first second, 32 feet the second second, 64 feet the third second. So I don't know how high we were. I do know we were way, way, way above twenty feet, twenty knots.

I also hit very hard. Boom! And I went sideways and I twisted my knee a little bit. And it was choppy.

The next thing I notice is that as I turned to find the guy who went out after me, I see the helicopter going this way and I turn and the wind is blowing the other way. The wind is blowing a good ten–fifteen knots.

So I say, "Goddamn, this sucker dropped us downwind."

I call for Edwards, the guy I'm supposed to hook up with. And I get no answer. Then I call on the other side, for the guy who went out before me, John Lutz.

John says, "I'm hurt, I can't hardly swim. My knee is hurt. My back is hurt."

I say, "Well listen, you try to find Spence and I'll find Edwards."

For about ten or fifteen minutes there are the two of us. I would zigzag toward the direction Edwards was in and zigzag back. We're supposed to be like twenty-five yards apart.

I swam up to John. I say, "I can't find him. You find Spence?"

He says, "No. I can't find him. He's not answering."

I say, "Oh, no, we lost two guys. Let me try to go find Edwards again."

So I swim down for the third or fourth time and on the way back, I get my head up and I'm listening. I remember bringing my head up and I hear a moan, and I'm not kidding you, probably less than five feet away from me is Edwards and he's kind of floating facedown and so I bring his head up. He was hurt so bad that he couldn't flip over on his back. And I just barely heard his groan and just barely saw him.

So I grab him, inflate his life jacket, and swim him back up to Lutz. And I say, "John, you hold him. I'm going to find Spence."

So I swim on the other side, downwind and zigzagging as much as five yards on either side of the track I thought he was on. And I had John call to me every few seconds so I wouldn't get lost. I couldn't find Spence. I did that three or four times.

I think, "Oh no, now what is going on? This is something that has turned into shit."

I get back and John and I are sitting there and we are calling and calling. About an hour goes by after the drop. We're still calling and we hear, "We're over here!" [Martin learned later that the second SDV had launched about the time he and his colleagues were preparing to jump into the water in an effort to warn the other crew about the dangers they faced.]

So we swam maybe fifty or seventy-five yards—not far away. We find the second SDV crew. We find Tom McGrath, Bob Conger, and Steve McConnell, who was the navigator.

I go, "What the hell are you guys doing here? You guys were not supposed to launch. Didn't you get the word?"

Well, they say, we wanted to go on the op and this and that and find these guys and we got carried away. They didn't say that but that's what happened. Everybody got carried away with the whole prospect of liberating some American people.

I say, "Where is Sam Birkey?" He's the other SEAL.

They say, "Well, we lost the SDV."

I say, "What do you mean you lost the SDV? I can tell you how we lost ours. How'd you lose yours?"

"Well, we launched off the *Grayback* and the thing sank like a rock so we abandoned it."

So I go, "Jesus Christ, has this thing turned into shit or what?"

They had left Birkey in the SDV. They didn't want to admit they had left him in the SDV.

I'm thinking, "Here I am, I've been in Vietnam for a little over two years, been shit at and shot at and you name it and I've done it and I'm going to die with a bunch of these dummies."

I didn't mean that literally. But I have no control. When I put my life in somebody else's control, I've lost my destiny. That's exactly what was happening on that operation.

I'm in the water. I'm less than two thousand yards from shore and all night long we hear these patrol boats start up because we're near this one island that has these patrol boats. I could see myself behind bamboo bars.

So I said, "All right, everybody, let's swim to sea."

So we're swimming to sea. The obvious thing is to swim to sea. So somebody pulls their radio out and starts calling the helicopter. This is one o'clock in the morning.

I say, "That sucker is not going to come out until seven."

"Well, let's try."

So they turn on the radio, which has two modes. One is voice mode in which you can actually talk to them. And there's three or four different channels for it. And then there's the other one that sends out a continuous signal. So they're doing all of this. And I say, the only thing you're doing is telling those guys over there.

You could see the lights on shore.

The wind died down about an hour later and it was relatively calm. There's all this pissing and moaning. And I hear this, "Get your foot out of my face!" And I think, now what the hell is this?

I looked across this tight group of guys. I've got Edwards on one arm and we're swimming. These other three guys are, I guess they are following.

I hear this, "Get your foot out of my face!"

I reached over and there's this foot and the toes are pointing down. Someone is floating in the water with their toes down, which means he's on his stomach. I reach over and grab him and pull him real quickly and flip him over and it's Spence Dry. He was floating all that time, at least an hour, maybe an hour and a half, floating on his face. I figured, if anything, he might have drowned. I thought I could see blood in the moonlight. There was something dark coming out of his nose. [A subsequent navy investigation determined that Dry died from a broken neck suffered in his drop from the helicopter.]

We kept swimming. I knew the current would, if anything, be pushing us between the mainland and the island. So we kept swimming, kept swimming, kept hearing all these boats starting up.

I figure, it's dark and I can swim. I'm going to shoot what I can and then haul ass.

I hear these people, these people in this little swimmer pool. Someone says, "It looks like they're going to capture us. Let's get rid of our weapons now."

I say, "No, don't get rid of your weapons now. Hold onto them."

They say, "Oh no, if we get captured . . ."

They're talking capture, you know? It really kind of pissed me off.

We just kept swimming and kept swimming. And finally at seven o'clock in the morning come these helicopters, just as planned. These guys ain't going to change for our benefit and rightly so. The plan was, swim to sea. If you can swim, swim to sea.

We get on the radio. They say, "We've got you now."

So the two helicopters come toward us and I see the helicopters about five hundred–six hundred yards away make a turn away from us, a 90-degree turn, and stop and hover. What the hell are they doing that for? They started picking up a guy in the water.

Well, here's Sam Birkey. They picked up Sam. Then they come over to us. Birkey, he sticks his head out the door and smiles at us. So we get picked up. They pick up Dry first and they pick up Edwards. Then they pick us up.

Did you find out what happened to the second SDV and Sam Birkey?

Yeah, I talked to McConnell and McGrath. Apparently there was a problem with communication signals on the *Grayback*.

The SDV is relatively light when it comes out of the wet deck so the swimmers can pick it up and bring it out. The *Grayback* crew actually does that for you. Some of the UDT guys also helped because it was a real big important op.

Then they put water in tanks on the SDV as ballast. That balances the SDV so you can maneuver it. We had signals. You point your finger down, you need more water, more ballast. Or, you point it up, it means take some ballast out. Hold your finger across and that's it: we've got enough ballast to take off. They do it by increments of water, trying to get this thing neutrally buoyant or slightly heavy.

I feel, and this is my own personal opinion, that there was too much miscommunication on the deck when they were getting ready to send that second SDV off. They were too heavy. So they're telling them to take increments out.

Well, the pilot is the very first guy and then the SEAL passenger and then there's the next compartment with the other SEAL and the navigator. The two guys in back—including the navigator—face the rear and there's a big tank in between.

The only way you talk is the hydrophones we had or you get out and punch the guy in the mouth to get his attention. The communication between the *Grayback* crew and that pilot and navigator was not clear. Instead of taking water out, they were adding more and more water.

Finally, the decision was made, get this boat off the deck. Somebody made that decision.

I talked to the divers later and they said, "Goddamn, Moki, that sucker was heavy."

They picked it up and they shoved it off the side and it went straight down to the bottom. The crew tried to power the boat up but it was too heavy. It just went nose down and set there. Then they tried to get water out and they couldn't get the thing deballasted. They couldn't bring it up. They tried for fifteen or twenty minutes.

McConnell, the navigator, gets out and he goes up front and tries to help. They couldn't get it up.

They make the decision to abandon the SDV and go back to the *Grayback*. Well, they'd drifted some. They couldn't find the *Grayback* even though they must have been close. They even thought the *Grayback* might have bumped the SDV at one time but they weren't sure.

I'm finding this all out later.

They decided to go to the surface and the communication McConnell made to Birkey when he got out and went up front was not clear. Birkey heard, "I'm going to check on what's going on. I'll be right back." Well, he didn't come back.

Birkey is in the back compartment. He's on boat air and boat air is eight hours. So Birkey says he waited fifteen or twenty minutes and nothing happened. So he gets out. You have a bailout tank, a little single-cylinder tank that you take with you and he bails out. And he goes up to the front and there's nobody there. So now what the hell's going on? So he said he waited there five or ten minutes, being faithful. Nothing happens.

Finally, he goes to the surface. All this time the eddies from the river and the ocean currents send people in different directions, but keep them in the same general area. That's why the helicopter went to pick him up first and then they picked us up.

Was the SDV in danger of having the* Grayback *roll and smash it?
I believe that could have happened. Because the *Grayback* would
every now and then rise real slowly because it was sitting on the bottom.
And, as I learned later, they didn't want to just sit on the bottom because
that might cause structural damage. So they were basically just slightly
negative and they would rise up and move, not a lot, not so you would
notice it much. We spent nearly two months on the *Grayback*. You could
feel it move. If the SDV went right off the side and lay there, the
Grayback could conceivably come up and land on it.

Anyway, they pick us all up and we all go back to the *Long Beach*.
We had a debriefing there and I tell them we were too high and too
fast. I estimate our height to be in excess of forty feet—and that four
seconds I counted meant we could have fallen something like a hundred
feet. I could have counted fast, but I didn't. I've got 850 sky dives.
I know when you're falling how fast you go the first few seconds.

I don't blame the pilot or the helicopter crew at all. He told me later
on that he was using instruments to try to get his height off the water. You know, it's hard to read off choppy water. That's why you have
to depend on somebody at the door. You have to know, if you're too
high, there's no sense putting them out because you're only going to
get someone hurt.

But there was the whole romanticism of that whole operation.
Everybody wanted to get it going. Everybody wanted to get something
done. It's June of 1972 and everybody's thinking POW liberation.

It would have been a classic SEAL operation: to go into the enemy's
front yard, not his backyard, and try to recover some American prisoners of war.

The op sounded good. We all got caught up with it. But I still believe
there's no reason for anybody to get hurt or get killed.

Later, the pilot says, "I had you down to twenty feet; I had you lower
than that."

I said, "No you didn't. Let me tell you how hard Edwards hit the
water. He hit kind of chest first. He hit so hard he blew holes out
the back of his wet suit. The air that was trappped there just blew
out the back of his wet suit. I had part of my web gear just ripped off
the side of my body because I hit so hard. I still managed to hold onto
my gun and my fins. Everybody hit way too hard."

What happened after you got back to the **Long Beach?**

We spent three or four days on the *Long Beach.* We were walking around with new dungarees. They knew who we were.

Then the *Grayback* sent a rubber boat for us. That was another screwed-up operation. They pick us up about one o'clock in the morning. It was one of those big boats, like a Zodiac. The motor broke down so all of us end up having to paddle the thing back to the *Grayback.*

We paddled forever. We finally got on board and sort of licked our wounds and packed our gear.

We had a memorial service for Spence Dry at Subic. Almost the entire *Grayback* crew was there. To have a submarine crew not to go in town on liberty and come to a memorial service, that was asking a lot.

Later the thing that bothered me was that Spence Dry's father kept writing to me. And I couldn't answer him because it was still secret. He wrote me off and on. He even had Spence's old girlfriend come and see me one time and she gave me his address. He was a retired navy captain, a boat commander, submarine squadron commander, well respected in the submarine force. I was still afraid to tell him. I wrote him one letter and told him we were doing what we were trained to do and had it come off . . .

He wanted to know how he died. He wanted to know how high the helicopter was. He wanted to know the *Grayback*'s role. Could he have hit the snorkel? Later, I got another letter from him, that he had moved to Florida. I kept it for a long time and I finally decided to write him a letter and tell him as much as I can. And this letter came back. From the letters, he sounded very brokenhearted and I would be too.

Chapter 32
"An Electrical Shock . . ."

After his participation in Operation Thunderhead, Moki Martin spent three years on destroyers in the fleet before returning to the SEALs as an instructor at Coronado. He advanced from warrant officer to lieutenant junior grade and served in SDV units in Coronado and the Philippine Islands.

In 1982, he was SDV, maintenance and diving officer for Naval Special Warfare Group One in Coronado and an avid competitor in the triathlon—the grueling test of endurance that involves running, bicycling, and swimming long distances.

He had survived combat in Vietnam, jumping into the Tonkin Gulf off the port of Haiphong, and the constant dangers of life as a SEAL. And then, one peaceful morning, his life changed dramatically. Moki Martin continues his story:

In October 1982, I was in training for the triathlon. I rode my bike every day, early in the morning, from Coronado to Imperial Beach and back.

I was on my way down to Imperial Beach about 6:25 in the morning. I saw this bike rider coming right at me. I was going with the traffic. He was going against traffic. I was probably going maybe twenty-five miles an hour, which was reasonably fast. There aren't many curves on that road but there was one curve there and I happened to be on one side and the guy was on the other side so I didn't see him until the last minute.

From what I saw of him, he was up on his pedals, standing up, looking at the ocean. He was a seventeen-year-old kid looking for surf. He didn't see me. I yelled at him. He didn't see me.

I tried to avoid him, to go around in the street. As I turned to go out in the street, he turned into me and we had a head-on collision.

An electrical shock went through my whole body and I knew something was wrong.

I had damaged my spinal cord at the C-5 level and become a quadriplegic.

As I learned, the first twenty-four-hour period is critical—if you can get the nerves to stop killing themselves.

Fortunately, I was the diving officer for the group. Within four hours, the diving doctor came to me and said, "I read this thing about hyperbaric treatment, where you put someone in an oxygen-rich environment under pressure. It superoxygenates the blood and the oxygen in the blood minimizes the damage."

This basically heals things from the inside out. The Russians had been doing that since the late '40s. Even though it hadn't been accepted by the navy, he said, "Let's put him in the treatment." [In the chamber used for decompression of divers.]

Well, I went there. I did hour-and-a-half treatments twice a day for ten days. And then after that ten-day treatment, they sent me to the Veterans Administration and they said, "We don't use that method. We have the hyperbaric chamber, the only one in the system, but we use it for burn treatment."

Our doctor goes up there and he convinces them to give me two more ten-day treatments.

Basically, I think it stopped the damage from the inside out. The outside of your spinal cord is the upper part of your body. And as you get to the inside, it's your tailbone, legs, internal organs. It healed it from the inside out.

I'm now known as an incomplete quad. I'm like an upside-down paraplegic. I can actually walk but I can't use my arms or hands. I can move my legs. I can actually ride a bike, a three-wheeler, anyway, and I attribute that—not to the common belief that my injury would have killed the average man—but to the fact that I began that treatment within four hours of my injury.

I'm a firm believer in hyperbaric treatment. Between that and steroids, that's the future for treatment of spinal cord injury. It has to be done in hours. None of this, let him lay here and put him in one of those striker bed frames.

My internal systems work a lot better—not 100 percent, but a lot better because of that treatment—thanks to Naval Special Warfare and the diving doctor—and there's nobody in this world who can convince me differently. I know a lot of quadriplegics and they are just amazed that I have this.

After a year in rehabilitation, Martin went back to college and earned a degree in fine arts. He has gained enough dexterity with his hands that he is able to draw and paint and embark on a new career as an artist. He also organized and manages the annual Superfrog Triathlon competition held annually at the North Island Naval Air Station in Coronado.

Chapter 33
Target: Libya

In the fall of 1987, press reports told how SEALs, operating from submarines, had staged a series of raids on the coast of Libya, blowing up electrical power and telephone poles. And, to confuse the Libyans, the reports said, the SEALs had used explosives of Soviet and Israeli manufacture and had left behind a collection of disinformation clues—such items as Israeli and Syrian cigarette butts and American facial tissue.

SEALs at Little Creek, who almost certainly would have been involved in such secret operations, laughed. They had not set foot on Libyan soil. But they also recalled plans for even more daring forays against Libyan targets.

In the early 1980s, U.S. intelligence received reports that Col. Mu'ammar Qaddafi, the Libyan ruler, had dispatched a team of hit men to the United States with orders to assassinate President Reagan and other American leaders.

The information was later learned to be false. But, at the time, it was taken very seriously, with heightened security at the White House and stepped-up protection for the president and other officials.

A small group of SEALs was hurriedly called to a secure intelligence building at the Norfolk Navy Base. They were ordered to draw up plans to destroy two diesel-powered submarines that had been supplied to Libya by the Soviet Union. The U.S. wanted to send a message to Qaddafi, but they wanted it to be nonattributable.

The SEALs were given free access to aerial and satellite photos of the harbor where the submarines were anchored. They spent hours leaning over the photos with magnifying glasses and special loupes of the kind used by jewelers. They saw the two submarines and, nearby, a white boat. They asked what it was. They were told it was Qaddafi's personal yacht.

It was a frustrating night. Photos taken from a high-flying plane or a satellite, while technically impressive, weren't detailed enough to plan a SEAL operation where the frogmen would actually have to come in contact with the target.

"Planes and satellites can't tell you shit about what's on the ground. We weren't getting anything to plan a SEAL mission," says one of those involved.

They worked through the night and came up with six options—none of them very good. The options included two operations using SDVs and four non-SDV operations.

There were a number of difficulties. The only submarine capable of delivering an SDV was the *Grayback,* but it was in the Pacific and its top speed was only five knots. It would take too long to bring it to the Mediterranean.

Another problem was that the navy had no limpet mine that had been tested to be sure it would take down a submarine on the surface. The antisub mines they had were designed to sink a submerged sub. They had the LAM—the Mark 5 limpet assembly modular—designed to sink a surface ship. But it was big and heavy, a tough job for the strongest swimmer to push or pull to the target.

If the SEALs went in by rubber boat from a sub, they would have to go over or around a long jetty and pull or push their limpets to the subs. Then they would have the problem of getting away again.

Still another complication was that the weapons they had were not nonattributable. If the SEALs sank the subs, the Libyans might dive down to inspect the wreckage and find parts of the explosive devices that would identify them as American.

The team worked through the night. About 8:00 A.M., they presented their proposals to the commander of the surface fleet, Atlantic.

Despite the lack of a submarine, the SEALs' recommended plan was to use an SDV rather than attempt a swimmer attack. They proposed that the U.S. acquire a foreign flag merchant ship and put the SDV aboard. Then the ship would feign engine trouble, ask permission to enter the Libyan harbor, and limp toward the harbor.

This would be done at night. If the Libyans sent out helicopters to inspect the ship, they could not see much. As the ship came within range, the SDV would be lowered into the water. The SEALs would enter the harbor, place their limpets on the two subs, set the timer, and then go back out to sea. There, they would be met by a submerged fast attack submarine. They would climb out of the SDV, sink it, and lock into the submarine.

The plans included sinking Qaddafi's yacht, as well as the submarines. This caused serious objections: What if he was on it? What if he was killed? What if he was injured? What if there were other people on the yacht? The SEALs thought those were all pluses, but higher authorities disagreed.

Qaddafi, it was assumed, would blame the Americans and they would deny it. He would know the U.S. had done it but be unable to prove it. The U.S. would know he knew who did it and would get the message.

The proposal was reported to the office of the Chief of Naval Operations in Washington by secure phone. The go-ahead never came. The SEALs thought that was just as well.

A few years later, in 1986, an even more ambitious plan was developed for an attack on Libyan terrorist training facilities.

The assignment was given to SDV Team TWO in Little Creek.

The USS *Cavala,* an attack submarine converted for use by the SEALs, was operating in the Pacific. She was brought around to Puerto Rico and the SEALs began their training there. The *Cavala* was equipped to carry only one SDV, and that meant only half a dozen SEALs could be put ashore. The newly reconditioned USS *John Marshall,* a large converted ballistic-missile submarine capable of carrying two SDVs, was alongside but not ready to be used.

In the midst of the training, it suddenly dawned on those in charge that the time for a scheduled change in command of the SDV team was fast approaching. They faced two alternatives: delay the changeover or put up with the inevitable disruption caused by bringing in a new commanding officer to complete the training and supervise the operation. The decision was made that delaying the changeover would cause more operational security problems than it was worth. The change of command went ahead on schedule.

The SEALs involved considered the operation doable. But there was one major worry. This would require not only entering Libyan waters but landing and operating there. If a SEAL were caught, would he be treated as a prisoner of war? Or would he be treated as a spy and executed?

Officials of the Reagan administration, acutely aware that the long hostage crisis in Iran might have cost President Carter the White House, were determined to avoid any situation in which Americans might be held by a hostile power. They decided not to use the SEALs. Instead, air force F-111 bombers flying from England and navy bombers flying from the USS *America* and USS *Coral Sea* hit targets in Benghazi and Tripoli on 14 April 1986.

Chapter 34
Shadowing the *Achille Lauro*

Lieutenant Brian Lippe is a veteran SEAL, with experience on both coasts and in almost every kind of SEAL assignment. In an interview in Coronado, he reflected on his experiences as an SDV operator and recalled what happened when a cruise ship, the *Achille Lauro,* was seized by terrorists on 7 October 1985.

Have you spent a lot of time in SDVs?
I've been in both the Mark 8 and the Mark 9. Mostly as navigator.
Did you like operating in SDVs?
Some things I liked. But I thought it was pretty dangerous and was happy to have survived it. It's a lot harder than other things we do, to me the hardest thing we do. You can't do a mission that doesn't take about thirty-six hours from start to finish. There is a lot of prep time and cleanup time. It wears you out.
What did you like about SDVs?
I liked the notion I could sink an aircraft carrier. Just myself and one other guy could really do some pretty serious damage to a fairly large asset. I really enjoyed the missions like that.

You can put enough explosives together to sink an aircraft carrier. We have done exercises where we have "sunk" ships in training. It's just a matter of putting a mine and a timer on a ship.

Our charges are set up to do a couple of things. One of them is it just blows all the water out from under the ship. And the ship basically breaks its own keel by its own weight. That's how you can get away with that big amount of damage. You'd need a lot of demolitions, more than you could carry, to blow up a big ship itself.

Have you done any actual real-life missions in the SDV?

Almost. At the time of the *Achille Lauro* incident in 1985, I was assistant commander of the 7th Platoon of SDV Team TWO. We were in the Mediterranean and we pulled into the port in Genoa to switch ships from the USS *Pensacola* onto the USS *Hoist* so we could run our SDV training missions. The *Hoist* is a diving salvage ship.

We didn't pay any attention at the time, but the *Achille Lauro* was at the next dock, right next to us. That's where the hijackers got on board.

We went off to do some SDV diving ops and some demolition work, just to keep our skills up.

After that we were supposed to rendezvous several weeks later in Venice with the *Pensacola*. A week or so after the *Achille Lauro* was next to us, the terrorist incident occurred. We were within four or five hours of the ship.

There was a period where they went dead in the water, just turned off the engines. We thought we had an opportunity to go in with the SDV and either do some ship boarding or disable that ship, make it so they couldn't get it under way.

We were really excited about getting to go in there with the SDV. It was a perfect mission for the SDV. We could have had some SEALs—four SEALs—come right out of the SDV and they wouldn't know it at night.

We'd have these telescoping poles of some type and climb aboard that way. Unless a guy happened to be right there, we'd probably be able to do that mission. Or we could just wrap some cables around the propeller so they couldn't get under way and let one of the other SEAL teams come in from the air, board the ship, and take it over.

We did our own planning and were steaming toward the ship. All I can tell you is that we were considered but our plan was not chosen.

I've had both coasts, boat, SDV, and SEAL experience but nothing seems to happen when it's my time to go do something. Which is probably okay.

After the hijackers killed Leon Klinghoffer, an American passenger, they forced the ship to sail to Egypt. They were placed aboard a plane by the Egyptians but the plane was intercepted over the Mediterranean by U.S. warplanes and forced to land in Italy. Members of SEAL Team SIX, the hostage-rescue experts, were at the airport, where they had been standing by for a possible effort to board the ship at sea and rescue the passengers. When Italian authorities took custody of the hijackers instead of turning them over to the Americans, the SEALs became involved in a standoff with the Italian military that almost led to bloodshed. The Americans finally backed off. The Italians took the hijackers into custody, but they were soon released and permitted to leave the country.

Chapter 35
A World-Class Swim

When then-Comdr. Rick Woolard became commander of SEAL Team TWO in 1982, one of his top priorities was to upgrade the team's ability to carry out complex combat swimmer attacks. Woolard tells what happened:

When I came on SEAL Team TWO, they were unable to conduct a good ship attack that involved anything more than a straight line compass swim against a stationary ship target. We—SEAL Team TWO—had embarrassed ourselves in a Flintlock exercise in 1981 with both the Germans and the Dutch.

The caliber of our combat swimming was so low we were unable during this Flintlock exercise to complete our combat swimmer operations. I was there monitoring it and I was really embarrassed. Right around the same time I checked into SEAL Team TWO as commander, a really lucky thing happened. For the first time in about ten years we had an exchange with the French. We had been sending SEALs to Toulon who had gone through their course in *Commando Hiver*. They had never sent a one of their officers here.

They sent a wonderful man, François d'Avout—an aristocratic Frenchman, a great teacher. He was very patient but with high standards. This is what I needed to get my guys to learn how to conduct proper swim attacks. I kept him running combat swimming courses from the time he arrived till the time he left with a few short but enjoyable forays into free fall parachuting and winter warfare.

We ran a very tough course. I didn't pick the old and bold. I picked the young, hard-charging guys who were E-4s and E-5s that had the force of personality and the leadership characteristics, the enthusiasm and capability—the guys who had the best reputation among the younger men in the team—to go through this course.

I sent these smart enlisted men through the course. Then they taught the rest of SEAL Team TWO how to do it. The entire standard of combat swimming changed to the point where we were able to do with absolute certainty a mission such as we did down in Panama. [During the U.S. invasion of Panama in December 1989, four swimmers from SEAL Team TWO attached explosives to a Panamanian patrol boat and blew it out of the water.]

In a 1983 Flintlock exercise I sent a platoon over under a lieutenant named Joe Maguire who is currently the CO of SEAL Team TWO and his platoon conducted, in Flintlock 83, an operation with the same [German] Kampf swimmers with which SEAL Team TWO had embarrassed itself two years before.

The operation went like this: four SEALs, four Kampf swimmers were dropped into the ocean, the Baltic. They conducted a rendezvous with a German coastal submarine. It locked them in through the torpedo tubes. On the second night, the SEALs and the Kampf swimmers, all eight of them, locked out of the submarine, again through the torpedo tubes, about two miles off a German naval base called Olpenitz.

The swimmers' mission was to penetrate the harbor, which itself was about a mile deep in an eastwest orientation. These guys were coming in from the east. There was a net or boom across the narrow part of the harbor entrance. The SEALs were tasked to penetrate the harbor, work their way in, blow up a couple of patrol boats, and then get back out and rendezvous with a German fishing boat.

There were six or eight different compass legs they had to effect, compass course changes they effected underwater.

That was a world-class combat swimmer op. If we had been able to do something like that in wartime, that would be a major, major commando operation.

The German base at Olpenitz is situated on a flat headland jutting into the Baltic, or as the Germans call it, the East Sea, near Kopeln, a picturesque fishing town that rises from the harbor to a small hill dominated by a brick church of the type common to northern Germany. The naval base lies where the German coast extends almost due north toward the Danish border, in a strategic position astride the passages from the Baltic into the North Sea. The base surrounds its own separate small harbor, whose entrance is protected at the seaward side by two stone and concrete breakwaters. The land borders are defended by high, wire fences.

Master Chief Charles "Chuck" Williams was one of the young hardchargers who went through d'Avout's course and later participated in the simulated attack on Olpenitz. He recalls d'Avout as a tough task master in this account of their training:

I can remember in Puerto Rico doing dive training. There was a severe thunderstorm came in, a squall front. Everybody was happy. We don't have to dive tonight.

Mr. d'Avout comes in. "What is going on? Why aren't you guys ready to go diving?"

We said, "There's a big storm."

And he goes, "If you have been struck by lightning, zen you have made zee bad peek." [When a swimmer surfaces for a moment to get his bearings or check his target, that is called a peek.]

He didn't cancel dives for anything!

Williams was slated to swim for the U.S. in the 1980 Olympics in Moscow until the U.S. and sixty-five other nations withdrew to protest the Soviet invasion of Afghanistan. In the 1983 exercise, he teamed up with his platoon leader, Lt. Joseph Maguire. Maguire, now commander of SEAL Team TWO, and Williams, a master chief in charge of swimming training for the team, tell about that "world-class swim."

Williams: To get to the submarine, we linked up with a Combat Talon MC-130 and did an equipment airdrop in a deserted portion of the Baltic Sea.

Maguire: There were four American swimmers and four German swimmers. It was a joint—a combined—op.

Williams: We did a low-level airdrop into the Baltic. At night.

Maguire: We flew in at water level and as soon as it came within the window, the plane just jumped on up, the green light went, and we went on the green light. As soon as all eight guys were out of the aircraft, he dove back down to the surface. He popped up for a minute or so.

Williams: It was between eight hundred and one thousand feet that we went out. We jumped with a static line and our Draegers [underwater breathing rigs]. We jumped with equipment on our legs. You put your reserve parachute up front and equipment on your thighs. After that, we linked up all eight swimmers in a swimmer pool. We had a long wait, about a four-hour wait. The German U-boat was late getting to us. It was four to five hours waiting on the sub. The fog rolled in. You couldn't see more than about fifty yards. There's nobody out here but us and if the sub doesn't show up, we're going to have a long wait.

Maguire: What we did was, we banged our weights against the bottles [on the breathing apparatus]. That is a good frequency for the sonar on the submarine. So he was able to come in on that and found us pretty well. The first thing I noticed was, about twenty yards off from us, the periscope came up. And then came down. Just to let us know he was there. So we swam on over and the submarine was submerged. And then we—what was his name, Uve—went down. He gave tap signals to the submarine. It was bona fides so they would know it was the right guys coming in. You don't leave anything to chance.

Williams: It was a German U-boat and a German did the signaling to let them know we were the right guys and we want to come in. Now.

Maguire: They opened the torpedo tubes. There's eight torpedo tubes. And they emptied two of them, to put four swimmers in each torpedo tube. We put two Americans and two Germans in one tube, two Americans and two Germans in the other. The first guy backs in, then the second guy comes in so the two are head to head. So that if you break your rig during the lock in, you can buddy breathe off the Draeger. And then the other guy backs in and he lays his legs over yours and then he's head to head with his buddy. And he comes all the way in. Because with the shutters for the torpedo tube, we don't want the last guy to be exposed. So the fourth guy in is going to come in and then he is going to curl up in the fetal position until they have shut the doors. Just to make sure he doesn't get caught there and lose his foot. The two swimmers who are head to head can communicate with each other. The German can communicate with you by tap signals on your legs.

Williams: The tube is twenty-one inches in diameter and seven meters long, a little over twenty-one feet. The last guy in our tube was the German officer, Uve. But first, he made sure all the guys were in the other tube, all four. He came over to our tube. The two Americans were in. The other German was already there waiting. And then he gives the tap signal. "Everybody is clear. Close the shutter doors."

Maguire: We're locking in at eleven meters [about thirty-five feet], which is pretty deep for oxygen. When they close the torpedo shutter, you're at eleven meters depth. Which already puts you on the extreme O_2 table. [In the Draeger breathing apparatus, the swimmers breathe pure oxygen. The carbon dioxide they exhale passes through a lime canister that cleanses it and returns pure oxygen. But breathing pure oxygen below a certain depth can cause convulsions and even death.]

Williams: Once he's given the signal that everyone is in, they shut the shutter doors. There's about a thirty-minute wait. It took about thirty minutes for them to drain the tube, bring the pressure from eleven meters up to zero. [This equalizes the pressure in the tube with that in the submarine.]

Maguire: That [change in pressure] was instantaneous. That's what the slam was.

Williams: The pressure change was instantaneous but the duration of the whole evolution took thirty minutes so you were lying there in the tube for thirty minutes waiting to be taken out. It seemed like things took forever when you were inside there. They were supposed to give tap signals when they were doing things. But for some reason, the Germans in the U-boat didn't understand the tap signals or when they were supposed to give them. So you were laying there waiting for something to happen but the signals didn't come.

Maguire: This is not for everybody.

Williams: You go from eleven meters to the surface pressure. It happens so fast. In a second. So you can imagine if you're breathing compressed gas at eleven meters and you go to zero or even past zero in a split second, everything is expanding.

Maguire: It was like a quarter-pound or half-pound block [of explosive] going off in the chamber. It literally picked you up and rattled you.

What was happening in those thirty minutes?

Maguire: They've got to drain it. The torpedo tube is designed for a machine—for a torpedo. The human factor is not a consideration. Stealth and quieting is also a part of their thing. The draining process is quiet.

Williams: Water was still in there when we came to the surface and then they drained it. I remember, in rehearsal, I wasn't expecting that. I took the head strap off of my mouthpiece so we could buddy breathe if we had to in an emergency. And I was just laying there waiting for the signal to take the pressure from eleven meters to zero. And when it happened, everything expanded so fast, my mouthpiece flew out of my mouth. And the first thing I thought of was, I have to put my rig on because there is still water in here. I'm laying there going, "That was interesting!"

Maguire: The way it is supposed to work is: The tap signals were, "We're about to depressurize. Are you guys ready?" He'll squeeze me. I'll kick the guy behind me. The guy at the end of the torpedo tube will signal, "We're ready to go." You took your straps off and the two of you were ready to buddy breathe but what you did is you breathed your breathing bag down to a pancake, purged all of the O_2 out of your lungs and signaled, "We're ready to go." You take the faintest breaths and your breathing bag just about has nothing in it. When you go from eleven meters to the surface instantaneously, your breathing bag goes whoosh and your lungs go whoosh. The expansion shot his mouthpiece on out. The reason he didn't flood his rig is the bag expansion had so much O_2 still coming out he could put his mouthpiece back in and the rig was not taking on water yet. It's something you have to know what you're doing and you have to be very comfortable in the water.

Then I ask, "Are you okay?" with a squeeze. He says, "I'm okay," [weary sound]. Then they open up the torpedo hatch and they have to carry you out. You're up about five feet. So they take you out and they stand you up. You were first, right? They took Chuck out and I kind of shimmy to the front. I remember being carried out at the same time the other American swimmer, this guy Ron Pierce, was being carried out from the other tube. And I remember the look in his eyes like, "Wow! This is a fun ride!" I had to have a little talk with the boys [the sub crew] and say, if at all possible, just give us a little stop along the way. Give us even a half a second. It is important to us.

Williams: We had no idea it was going to be quite that fast a ride.

Maguire: The German swimmers had not done this either. They were able to use the fact that we were there to train with them to get the submarine. Nobody was really up on that. We were the most experienced. So we kind of talked to the guys on the submarine and got a pretty good routine. We got it down pretty good.

Williams: We did two or three rehearsals. I got so, once we got in there and knew the torpedo door was shut, I just had my breathing bag down to nothing. In case they did it before they gave the signal, I was ready for them.

Maguire: He held one hand on his mouthpiece and the other hand on my arm. I did the same thing. Just in case it blew out, we had a signal, "I've just blown out my bag. I need to buddy breathe." Once you had one good rig, you were okay. If you blew out both bags, you were dead. It was as simple as that. But we felt comfortable with it. It was a risk, but, too, we're in the risk business.

You have to consider the times. We still considered war with the Soviet Union, if not likely, at least a possibility. Training was very arduous and very serious. We took risks.

Williams: Just like coming in, going out was also a good ride. You get loaded from the inside for the actual op. You go back in the tube the same way you came out. You're laying there, they close the torpedo door on the inside. They give a signal and they flood it. You're sitting there in water now. They give the signal they're going to pressurize. The pressurization was just as fast as the decompression. You go from the surface, zero feet, to eleven meters at the snap of a finger. You have to be clearing your ears, waiting for it to happen, or you can rupture an eardrum. The ride down to depth was just as good as the ride coming up. Once they had it pressurized, they would open the doors and everyone starts floating out.

Was the inside of the tube greasy?

Maguire: Yeah, and pitch-black. Absolutely no light whatsoever. We had lights in there for the rehearsal and our lights would not shine on anything. Even a flashlight would just be absorbed.

Once we got in the submarine, we had a two-day transit to the target. I forget where it was that we linked up. It was pretty much in the western part of the Baltic. Probably around Denmark. We transited to Olpenitz.

The transit was interesting. The submarine had a very small crew, about twenty-one people. The racks were in the mess deck and the mess deck was in the torpedo room. I mean, this submarine is tiny, tiny, tiny. The sausages hung everywhere.

Williams: It reminded me of the movie *Das Boot.*

Maguire: Absolutely professional. You really felt like you were part of an outstanding—I mean, these guys were good. The commanding officer of the submarine was very impressive.

Williams: He was young.

Maguire: I think he couldn't be over thirty-five. The white cap with the scrambled eggs, beard, turtle neck, and the jack boots. Absolutely professional. Those guys were right on the money.

Williams: Just like being in the movies.

I think one of the most interesting things, showing they were squared away and really professional, was when we were in the target area where we were going to get inserted—they had the subchasers, the old diesel-powered subchasers.

Maguire: They knew we were coming. They had been alerted.

Williams: I remember we were in the process of putting our rubber wet suits back on to insert. All of a sudden, everyone said, "Stop what you're doing. Freeze. Freeze. Don't move." I can remember sitting there with my rubber half on and the U-boat bottoming out on the bottom of the Baltic. And all you can hear is those engines. Like in the old U-boat movies. You could hear those engines get louder, right overhead. I was thinking, okay, a depth charge should be next.

Maguire: They ate four meals a day. Breakfast, lunch, and dinner and midrats. They only had about six racks. The mess area was also the berthing area which was also the torpedo area. So they were either setting up for a meal, serving the meal, or breaking down from the meal. So the racks were only up for no more than one hour at a time. We put up with that for two days before we had to do the mission. It was a lot of fun. We just sort of sat up, drank coffee, ate sausage, and ate cake.

Williams: I remember wandering around in there, I found an empty rack someplace else. I crawled in that empty rack. I was like, I've got to get some sleep. And every time I'd fallen asleep, they were going *raus, raus.* It was always, what? Time to eat, you know. So I get in this rack and it had a dry blanket and I'd been wet for a day and a half. In the torpedo room it was basically raining all the time. And I was laying in this rack and I was sleeping good and all of a sudden

I heard *raus, raus.* And I was like, what, time to eat? And he says, "No, you're in my rack." And I had to get up.

Maguire: When it came time to do the mission, we fine-tuned it with the officer of the submarine who was in tactical command. We had the limpet mines pre-staged on the outside of the submarine. They put blankets all over the deck. As we got dressed, we had men holding us. The submarine was tactical. We were going into the high-threat area. With the ASW [antisubmarine warfare] vessels and ASW aircraft against us. As we went in, the guy in control, when we were in a high-threat situation, he would just bottom out the submarine. You could feel the destroyers and the ASW aircraft coming closer. You could hear the ping. There was absolute quiet.

Then once they went by you, the commanding officer would give the signal to continue getting us dressed. We put the weight belts on ever so quietly. They opened up the torpedo tube. They start loading you. They pick you on up and silently start loading you in. There's no talking. We know the courses, we know the speed. Finally, I'm in there and the commanding officer comes to me and says: "Right now, our present location is such and such, your target bears so and so, here at this distance. Good luck and good hunting."

It was good. And they put us right on the money. We flooded, instant pressurization, just like ka-boom. And then it was time to go to work.

One German swim pair tore a life jacket on the way out so they had to abort the mission. They tried it for awhile. The submarine had left. Once they tried to do a turtle back, they found they had a catastrophic failure. Turtle back is where you inflate the life jacket and just lay on your back and you're still maintaining your course. The driver is still driving. But you're conserving your O_2. You're swimming tactically.

Williams, the stronger swimmer, was the "driver," holding a board with a compass. He had the entire course—all of the compass headings he would use over the next six hours—memorized. Maguire followed close behind, linked to Williams by a cord.

Williams: We were two miles out from the harbor at that point, in total darkness. The water was pretty flat, a one- to three-foot chop. It got calmer as the night went on. There had been storms during the day. But as we came out, it was pretty calm.

You're ready at any time. If a patrol boat comes, you deflate your life jacket and sink out of sight.

Maguire: We've got our canteens and our food. We're taking our time, taking a look at the harbor. We're drinking water, eating food. We try to finish one canteen before the swim and then we flood the canteen with saltwater because you use that canteen as ballast. That's part of your trim.

Williams: We sat there about five hundred yards outside the harbor. You could see the opening into the harbor, just barely, in the darkness. We had a power bar and then a canteen of water between the two of us.

Maguire: And then all of a sudden a patrol boat came up on us. Obviously he didn't see us, but we decided, hey, it's time to go to work. We made an emergency descent, put our rigs on, purged, and started the swim from there.

Was the harbor blacked out?

Williams: It was blacked out for a ten-mile radius.

Maguire: You know, these people went to war twice in this century so they play these exercises for real.

Williams: All your channel lights, all the navigational aids were blocked out. All lights.

Maguire: Street signs had been removed on the base.

Williams: They had even turned off a lighthouse on a point.

Maguire: They issue a notice to mariners: In this place for such and such a time, we'll be conducting an exercise. Or they might go as far as to move the navigational aids. They take this very seriously. They had two world wars and they're not far from East Germany.

Williams: After we had locked out of the German U-boat, I remember checking the bearing they had given us to the harbor. And I remember looking at that bearing and thinking, I don't see anything we're supposed to see. And then we looked around and it was all dark over there. The harbor was like a dark hole in a dark hole. That had to be it.

Maguire: We just went for the nothing. We started swimming for the black hole.

Williams: The success or failure of the mission is based on that bearing we got off the German U-boat commander. If he's right or wrong, that's going to be the success of the mission.

Maguire: We had a good first leg, from two miles out. One of the

German swim pairs went on dive status before we did. They just never found the harbor. They spent a significant amount of time in the water and finally suffered hypothermia and had to get out. They had to get on out and one of them was hospitalized for hypothermia. The water temperature was forty degrees. But it didn't seem that bad.

Williams: I think it was because of the adrenaline rush.

Maguire: It was as black as could be. No bioluminescence, no ambient light. Even after your eyes really got adjusted, even after an hour into the swim, I still couldn't see anything. All I could see was a faint glow off his compass.

Williams: It was so dark, I had that compass against my face mask and that was all I could see.

Maguire: When we got into the threat area you could see the flares going up in the air. They didn't do that initially. And we were concerned. For the two-mile swim in, we didn't see anything. All of a sudden flares started going off. And then our concern was that one of the swim pairs was compromised. Should we continue with it or get the hell out? No one was compromised yet, I believe. It was just that they knew we were coming and damnit, they were going to catch us. There's a great incentive for them, the people guarding the port, to catch Kampf swimmers and to catch SEALs. It would be a great loss of face when this is your job, this is what you do for a living, and guys can get into your harbor when you know they are coming. So there was a real incentive for them to catch us.

Were you in contact with the other swim pairs?

Maguire: No, never. Once you're gone, you're on your own. And that's why you have to make sure the guys you're going with are reliable. Because if one swim pair is compromised in the swim, there's a chance they're going to set up the harbor defense and kill everybody.

Williams: In this exercise, the senior swimmers [in rank] are not necessarily your better guys. Ron Pierce was an E-6. The thing is, they are better divers so they are more reliable. You like to have someone in there who is a chief or above, even an officer, just for the planning phase, for liaison with the submarine. And then you're on your own. But there have been times when it was a chief or even an E-6 who was the senior guy out there. That's a lot of work for an enlisted guy to be doing all the liaison work. We were lucky Mr. Maguire was out there, one of the top-notch divers in our platoon.

What time was this swim?

Williams: I want to say we hit the dive status between ten and eleven at night. When we launched from the sub it was about seven-thirty or eight o'clock. At seven-thirty we loaded tubes. We were out of the tubes by about eight and started to turtle back by about eight-fifteen. It was about an hour and a half turtle back so it was right around ten when we started dive status. At the five-hundred-yard mark it was a good ten or ten-thirty. Then we dove for almost a good four hours. Then we swam for another two and a half hours, basically, to get to the extract point.

We were hitting targets of opportunity. Basically, our plan was to come to a place where we could have a shallow water peek underneath the quay wall. We took a look to see what we could see that would be a good target. Lo and behold, it was kind of a good thing that we had the target of opportunity because they had taken all the ships out of the harbor as a ship defense. There were no targets.

Maguire: Everybody plays over there. So we came in from sea, from the German U-boat, and we were able to find the target because the whole city was blacked out. We just went for the darkest center of the beach. And all the local police were notified. All the harbor was notified. And there were also ASW aircraft chasing the submarine on the way in. Subchasers were out after us. So from start to finish it was pretty sporty.

Williams: We hit the only target that was in the harbor, which was a salvage tug. That was the target that we took. It was about the three-hour-and-fifty-five-minute mark, I think, that our scrubbers [the lime canisters that purify the oxygen] started failing. At that point we were about halfway out of the outer harbor. I just immediately did a ninety-degree turn and took us to the quay wall. That was part of our plan. If we had a problem it would be in that area. So the plan was to get over to the quay wall, come up, see if it was safe, see if there were any patrols on the quay wall area. Basically, it was fairly large boulders at the water level and then it went to a wall that went up about seven or seven and a half feet and on top of that was a road. That was the outer harbor quay wall area. What we did was a ninety-degree turn, went over and hit that, came up, assessed that it was safe, that there were no guards right there in that area.

You have an opening to the harbor which is maybe 100 to 150 yards wide. And in that opening, you have these two quay walls which come around. And there are boulders at the bottom of the quay, which are humongous. Then basically a concrete wall that comes up about seven feet. It is wide enough that vehicles could drive down to the sentry post.

I pulled my buddy up, Mr. Maguire, and told him my scrubber has quit working. I have a serious . . . like, you know, somebody has hit me in the head with a sledgehammer. He said the same thing. He said, "Yeah, I think I've got one too. My scrubber's quit." By that time, in that water, it should have quit.

Maguire: It was about forty degrees.

Williams: It should have quit long before that. What happened was that the canister had basically stopped scrubbing out the CO_2. We were getting a CO_2 buildup in our bodies. There are symptoms you are trained to notice. It was a pretty definite symptom. Instead of pushing and possibly going unconscious, we went over and got on fresh air. About the only thing you can do at that point. We could have kept going. We still had oxygen but we would have been making a mass of bubbles then. [If they breathed the oxygen and then expelled the carbon dioxide into the water.]

Maguire: There were guards all over the harbor, picket boats. They were shooting off flares all night. At the mouth of the harbor there were security guards. We never would have been able to make it through.

Williams: What we did was take off our Draegers and our life jackets and fins and put them all on the buddy line, which is what keeps us connected underwater. In case one of us should go unconscious, you're attached by a buddy line. For about ten or fifteen minutes we sat there and assessed to make sure there weren't any patrols around.

Maguire: There were guards everywhere. So we just sat back among the boulders and sat there listening and seeing what was what. We still had some time left on our window for the rendezvous with the fishing boat. We took our rigs off. Then we went on over, dragged the rigs, and got on the other side.

Williams: I pushed him up on the high wall. He crawled up.

Maguire: Then I pulled him up and we crawled across.

Williams: Then we just dropped down on the other side. Which basically was open water at that point. So all we had to do was put our gear back on and swim back out.

Maguire: It was at this point in time things got tough. I had broken my back and my pelvis about six months earlier.

How did you do that?

Maguire: Fast-roping. The line broke. We do it regularly now. But we had just got it in the team and the line was defective and it parted and a bunch of us got banged up. So it was okay. They gave me thirty days off and I was able to watch *Oprah Winfrey* and *Geraldo*. And then come on back.

I was fine until we made it to the primary extraction point and the extraction vessel was in the wrong place. We didn't know what the heck to do. There was one boat out there. He wasn't where he was supposed to be. It was about another mile to a mile-and-a-half swim. We just figured, hey, we have to go for it. We had to do some real good swimming at this point. Willie's an Olympic swimmer. I was a college swimmer, but not an Olympian. To tell you the truth, I was just about being towed at this point.

Williams: You said, "I don't think I can make it that far because my hip is killing me."

Maguire: My hip had finally given on out. My accident was on Halloween and this is the first of April.

Williams: I was like, you aren't going to quit on me now, damn you. I didn't want to be a failure. I wanted to do the whole thing and make the extract. We swam away from where that boat was supposed to be to make it to the extract point.

Maguire: That's the way it is. We've got a civilian picking us up. Who knows what the problem is? He's got to be in the fishing area. Or maybe security moved him to there.

Williams: I remember that. I was a lot discouraged. But I was real determined because I'm competitive. I don't like to lose or get beat on anything. He was going, "Hey, my hip is hurting me. I don't know if I have enough left in me to go that far."

Maguire: We had another mile and a half and we only had twenty-five minutes to make it in. You still need 100 percent and my battery was starting to run low. Chuck was swimming and I was sort of drafting on him. He was breaking the tension in the water and I was kind of tucked into him. It was not like we were just kick-stroking and gliding. We had to stroke on out. So after six hours in the water now, we have to swim all out at our best to make the window.

At six o'clock the window closes out and off he goes. We have to go into the E&E net. That was not kidding. We had to go ashore to an emergency shore rendezvous, contact agents. And then go into a net. Which would have been played out in the exercise. It would probably have put us in the net for two or three days, as opposed to linking up with the fishing boat and just go below decks. So there was a real incentive to make it to that damn boat.

We got to the boat. I think we just about caught it, just at the end of the window. It was a fishing boat with a [German] swimmer for the bona fides. And we had a chem light underneath the fishing boat. We had to go back on bag [oxygen] and swim underneath the boat and make sure it was our boat. And then we came up to the side of the boat and gave the bona fides, challenge and reply, and then they took us down below decks. We had to make sure it was the right boat because it was in the wrong place.

Williams: You get the wrong fishing boat and this guy is sitting there saying, "Who are you?"

Maguire: With marine radio. You have just put some charges on somebody's ship. So you want to make sure you've got the right guy.

As soon as we gave the bona fides, it was immediately, "Come on in." They took us below deck, in a void below deck, and covered us on up and hid us down there, in case the boat was searched. So we came on board and our other American swim pair was there and the one German swim pair that aborted the op [because of a torn life jacket]. They just hovered in the area for about three or four hours until the extraction vessel came. It was just prudent. Your life jacket is your safety equipment. You didn't want to go messing around getting into extremis without your safety equipment. That was the right move for those guys. And the other [German] guys ended up with hypothermia. One of them wound up in the hospital.

Williams: That one pair, I think it was Uve who ran down and got help at the harbor. By the time that happened, we were clear of the harbor.

Maguire: Again, too, if you have a bad initial leg . . . They just had trouble finding the mouth of the harbor. It was pitch-black. We just had good luck, I guess.

What happened to the other American swimmers?

Maguire: That was Ron Pierce and Caleb Esmoil. Caleb was a seaman and Ron was an E-6.

Williams: They had gotten in the harbor and then Ron had a problem with his rebreather and got sick. All of us knew the only place in the harbor you could come up. The place where they came up was the place where we came up to take our peek for the target of opportunity. It was a pier facility with about a foot of headroom from the water to underneath. They went way back under, twenty or thirty feet. From all the photos and the Germans who knew the harbor, that was the only place you could come up. Everybody knew if you had a problem that's where you were going to go to. So when they had the problem, that's where they went. They got under there about the same time we were. We never ran into them.

To avoid making a noise that might alert the guards, when Pierce became nauseous, he ducked his head under the water, threw up, and then came up for air.

That's when they looked out in the harbor and saw all the ships were gone. There was a captain's gig on the first pier and a fleet salvage tug. We took the tug because that was the most feasible target. And since they were sick, they saw the captain's gig, only maybe sixty yards away. And they swam over and hit that. And then they went back and Ron got sick some more.

And they had to make a decision whether they could swim and dive out of the harbor. They couldn't dive out. There was a ladder and they went over to the ladder, took their Draegers off, and ditched them on that ladder.

And they actually exited the water in the harbor right there stealthily and E&E-ed across the base over the fence out to the beach and open water.

Maguire: It was blacked out, so with a wet suit and a camouflaged face, it went in their favor. They were just about invisible.

Williams: The Germans' harbor defense was one, to get the ships out to sea and, two, to black it out. They figured if you couldn't see it, you couldn't hit it. But if you do find it, it becomes our favor because it's so dark there's lots of darkness to hide in. So Ron and Caleb were able to get out of there without being detected.

Maguire: They went through that whole base.

Williams: Lying in flower beds, letting guards walk by. They were belly crawling and sneaking all over this base to get back to the beach area to get out to open water to make it back to the boat. They probably covered about a mile on base.

Maguire: On a military installation. It was pretty sporty.

Williams: Especially a military installation that had brought an extra hundred men on base.

Maguire: When we all got to the fishing boat, the Kampf swimmers were trying to take good care of us. We were tired and dehydrated. They had these liter bottles of beer for us and chocolate. Which were the two last things I wanted. No clothes for us. Right now, we're getting cold. The fishing boat is not heated. We've been in the water now for over six hours. It was beautiful German beer, dark German beer, but it was not too appetizing. We tried to stay tactical, stay below decks, and stay covered up. They finally brought us back into Eckernförde, the city where the Kampf swimmers are located. It is a large German naval base, about a thirty-minute drive from Kiel on the Baltic.

Williams: The thing I remember in the debrief was those guys sneaking across that base. These Germans couldn't believe that these guys . . . Like the CO of the harbor defense, he called them liars in the debrief.

He said, "There's no way you got out in that harbor and made it across my base and got out that way."

And they said to him, "Well, you can go back in your harbor and you can retrieve our Draegers for us because they're on that ladder."

And they went back and picked the Draegers up and said, "Well, they didn't dive out of here." That was what convinced everybody. They were right where they said they were.

The French diver, Mr. d'Avout, who was helping us in training, was one of the mission coordinators. In the debrief, he was in the back, beaming.

Maguire: Just like a proud parent. No doubt about it, we were fish. But we owed the whole thing to d'Avout.

What was the reaction of the German swimmers when you made it and they didn't?

Maguire: They were happy for us, I think. We were a team—an eight-man team.

Was this your most memorable swim?

Williams: Not mine.

Maguire: Oh, I don't know. Probably the only one we can tell you about.

You've been places you can't tell me about?

Maguire: That's what we do for a living. The country pays us well, gives us good stuff. And our country uses us. Our commander in chief and our admiral put a lot of faith in us. They believe we can do it and we never let them down.

SEALs from the Skies

PART SIX

Chapter 36
A Shocking Takeoff

During World War II, the underwater demolition teams and the naval combat demolition units worked in or close to the water. After the war, they began experimenting with helicopters and a few of them made parachute jumps. By the mid-1950s, as they expanded their capability to function as commandos, more and more of them took jump training. By the time the SEALs were formed in 1962, parachuting was one of their standard skills.

Often, the frogmen have been the pioneers in developing new techniques. In the following interviews, five frogmen—and one wife of a veteran SEAL—tell of their experiences in jumping out of airplanes and, in several instances, being plucked from the ground and hoisted into an airplane.

Norman Olson was a pioneer in the use of parachutes by navy frogmen in the 1950s, before the creation of the SEALs. He later founded the SEAL demonstration parachuting teams, the Chuting Stars on the East Coast and the Leap Frogs on the West Coast. This is his account of his involvement in parachute work:

I took the first detachment that went to jump school from Little Creek. They had sent one guy, to go through jump training and evaluate it. This was in 1956.

I was selected to be the officer in charge. There was one other officer and twelve men. We went all through jump master training.

251

I brought a dry suit and German Draeger. We made test jumps from the thirty-four-foot tower to see the impact on the scuba gear. The test was to see how the closed-circuit scuba, which has a bag, could withstand pressure.

We came back to Little Creek and did a lot of testing in the pool.

Then in 1958, a bunch of us made a deal with the [army] Special Forces to train some of their guys in scuba if they would teach us advanced chuting.

Eventually, almost everybody on the East Coast was qualified, so when the SEALs came in [in 1962], most people were well qualified in jumping.

I went to advanced HALO school. When I came back, I got very active in sport parachuting, really enjoying it. I've got about twenty-three hundred parachute jumps. A master chief and I, we'd go out every weekend and we thought we could put a demo team together.

We were out at Coronado then and we'd go off on weekends all through southern California and Arizona, putting on demonstrations. Everything we had, we stole. We had no support. We called it the UDT/SEAL parachute team and that became the Leap Frogs on the West Coast.

When I moved back to the East Coast, I started another team and it eventually became the Chuting Stars.

Those teams developed the most qualified chutists we had.

Did you ever have any problems parachuting?

I had several malfunctions—three of them. When you go for eight hundred jumps or so, you start knowing you're going to get one some time. I finally got it and got it over with. It was sort of a relief, in a sense.

You have a problem with the main parachute, you get rid of it, and use your reserve. It's not that big a thing. You're trained well and you react very fast.

At the time it's happening, you see the whole world flashing before you and it seems like forever, but people on the ground say, wow, I never saw anybody activate a reserve chute so damn fast.

I did a lot of sports parachuting and went to the national competitions, representing the navy, two years in a row. I was in on all the all-navy and all-military records for formations—the number of people they put together.

I had a malfunction during a demonstration at one of the SEAL reunions and everybody still remembers it. My wife was there. I was going out with five guys and I was the center of this formation and they were going to build this thing around me. At a certain altitude, they would break away and I would continue to take it down from the center so their parachutes would be open and I would be going down, for added effect.

It was a very windy day so we were way out [from the grandstand] to compensate for the wind. When you look at them out there, at a distance, as compared with up close, they look much closer to the ground. There was a tree line. I was coming down and I activated my parachute and I had a malfunction. Of all times.

The crowd is going "Pull!" And all this stuff. And my wife is watching.

I was lower than I should have been, probably a thousand feet from the ground. So I dumped the main parachute and went to the reserve. I ended up in a tree. They dug me out of the tree and I was so pissed off.

We got back to the drop zone and I said, "Let's get another parachute and go right now. Because if I don't go now, it's never going to happen."

You also did the Fulton sky hook recovery, didn't you?

[The sky hook, invented by Robert E. Fulton Jr., is a system for picking up men from the ground or water. A plane drops a nylon line and a balloon. One or two men fasten themselves to the line, inflate the balloon, and release it. The pilot hooks the line with a special attachment on the front of the plane and the men are reeled in through a hatch in the plane.]

Yeah, we did it off Coronado. A night pickup. Peter Slimpa and I. We're in the water and the plane came over and dropped the bundles. They dropped them way the hell off and we had to swim to them. We got there, got the stuff open, put on the harness.

There are these three humongous bottles. One guy had to hold the dirigible while the other puts the gas in. I'm holding it. We got about one and a half bottles in and it wants to go up.

I say, "Pete, I'm losing it!"

He jumps over and punches his thumb in it and it sort of falls over us.

The boat comes over with Fulton. He says, "What happened?"

We say, "Something's wrong here." We wouldn't admit we punched a hole in it.

He says, "I've never seen anything like this happen before." They
lug it onto the boat and they patch it up. Meanwhile, they pick up the
other guys.

We let this balloon up finally. I was sitting in the front. Pete is tied
to an umbilical cord to me and I'm tied to the dirigible. They have
strobe lights. The balloon goes up about five hundred feet and about
a hundred feet below this are the strobe lights the plane focuses in
on. You have a power pack for the lights.

As I see the plane coming in, my feet are dangling over the side.
I turn the switch on and I get this shock. I was leaping all around. We
turn the thing off, the plane aborts, Fulton comes over. He says, "What's
the matter?"

"Something's wrong with the power."

He says, "We've got to get the dirigible down."

This goddamn thing is five hundred feet in the air. We're pulling
this mother down. Each of us lost about twenty pounds. We pull it down,
he does some adjusting. We let it up again.

I say to Peter, "If this happens again, screw it, we're going! Because as soon as that plane hits the cable all the juice will be gone.
I'll take whatever is necessary."

It happened again. I said, "Screw it, Pete, we're going this time."

What does it feel like to be picked up?

It happens so fast! It's like somebody grabbed you by the top of
the head, and whup, you're up there.

But you're being pulled in slowly. It took about nineteen minutes.
While they were pulling us up, I had some thoughts about when Fox
was killed.

The pickup occurred a short time after Photographer's Mate Third
Class James Earl Fox was killed on 24 June 1964 when the nylon
line snapped as he was about to be pulled into a plane after being
lifted from a boat near the SEAL base at Little Creek, Virginia.

You get up under the fuselage and they have to shift that gear so
you can get inside. And you put your hands in that manhole and you
think, "If it goes, I can hold." But no way, you're not going to hold.
And finally they get you in there.

Chapter 37
"I Started to Black Out"

Although his primary assignment was as a medical corpsman, Robert P. "Doc" Clark also specialized in parachuting and teaching other SEALs to jump. He told about that part of his career in an interview:

You know who Dick Marcinko is? Well Rick and I were both second class together. We were in UDT Twenty-two in the Buzzard Platoon. Eventually he ended up as my commanding officer in SEAL Team TWO. I was in charge of the medical department from 1974 to 1976.

I walked into his office—we were friends and we still are friends. I said, "Skipper, I need another job. I'm just bored of doing this medical stuff."

He said, "Well, Doc, what do you want to do?"

I said, "Just put me in another department. I can run it."

He said, "Well, you're a big sky diver. You go down and run my air ops."

So for two years I was the air ops officer at SEAL Team TWO. That was great. I got to teach a lot of guys skydiving. And I had a great time.

We used to teach guys about cutting away if they had a malfunction in a free fall. I taught this for years and years. I had one malfunction in twenty-some years of free fall. My reaction was automatic, the minute I looked up. I had what they call a cigarette roll. My lines were all wrapped up.

I was jumping a Paracommander at the time. I tried to work my risers and get an air channel up into the parachute. I had a wrist altimeter on. I was kind of looking at that, too, to see where I was falling. It just came into my head in a matter of a second, at most. I had reached down. I had pulled down on my capewells, got rid of my main chute, came in, and pulled my reserve. [A capewell is a fastener that permits a chutist to release his parachute quickly, either after a malfunction in the air or immediately after landing.]

It was nothing I had to think about. It was just automatic. I had taught it for so many years. The same is true of the medical training. We just automatically react. And that's because of repetition in our training. I believe in repetition. That's how you get good at what you are.

You're a hospital corpsman. How did you learn to run air ops?

When I was in UDT, I convinced the CO and the XO to send me to HALO school at Fort Bragg. That was in '66 or '67. I had made thirty-seven static line jumps—what we call rope jumps. But I had seen a lot of jumps where the guys were free-falling. And I thought, boy that is exciting!

I didn't have the money to become a free faller at the sports parachute club. I convinced them the reason to send me to HALO school is, if you have a mission where you have to free fall, you don't have any medics who are free fall qualified.

They said, "Guess you're right."

I had four parachutes of my own. We were jumping what we called "rags" back in those days. We were sewing them up on a sewing machine, putting different modifications in them. We made modifications, put them in the bag, took them up, and jumped them. The whole rig probably wasn't worth twenty-five dollars.

We used to go out here to Oceana and get the reserves to fly for us and we used to jump. I'd take my wife and two little kids and they'd watch me jump. I liked to jump, so I jumped every time there was a chance. I got jump master qualified. And HALO qualified. Also HALO instructor.

What is it you like about jumping?

Well, I like individual sports. I guess that's why I became a marathon runner. Skydiving is just neat. Falling through the air at 125 miles an hour. It's a thrill. Opening up the chute, trying to hit a target on the ground.

I quit logging jumps after—I quit logging after two hundred. I've got maybe four hundred. The highest I ever jumped was 21,000 or 23,000 feet at Fort Bragg on oxygen.

It was over 20,000 and that's a ninety- to ninety-five-second delay. You just fall and fall and think you're going to fall forever.

You mentioned the time you had the cigarette roll. Have you had any other close calls?

I was jumping at Suffolk one day. We had kicked out the static liners. Myself [and Petty Officers] Stan Janecka and Joe Hulse were in the airplane. I had never done any relative work, where they come in and do a hookup, touch hands.

I was going to try it this day. I was going to go out, lay out in a stable position, and Stan was going to come down and hook up to me.

I was out of the plane. Stan came down to me. And Joe dove out of the plane after us. We were jumping from about 12,500 feet, which is normally about a sixty-second delay. Joe decided to make it a threesome. He tracked in just before I was hooking up with Janecka and he came in too hard. He spun off as he saw he was going to crash into me but his boot hit me.

It hit me so hard that it spun me around. You have a radial artery and the nerve runs down your arm. You know how your arm goes to sleep and you can't do anything with it? That's what happened. And all of a sudden this arm is just flopping.

I'm trying to stay stable but I spin around. I went into a real uncontrollable spin. And I started to black out.

It was my right arm and I had a right outside pull. This arm was flopping. The last thing I remember before I started to black out, I reached over with my left hand and pulled my rip cord. Of course my chute must have opened because I'm here to tell you about it.

The next thing I remember I'm sitting in the saddle. I looked at my altimeter and I was about five thousand feet. I looked at that beautiful Paracommander over me and you know how your brain thinks, you've got to get your arms up and steer the thing. But this arm [the left] is the only one that goes up. This one [the right] has no feeling. I couldn't feel anything. I thought maybe it was broken.

I'm trying to steer with one toggle. Then I started getting some sensation in my fingers. I lifted my right arm with my left hand and I grabbed the toggle and the weight of my arm brought it down to half brake position. So I could turn and make a landing. Of course when I got on the ground, Stan and Joe Hulse came over. Joe was all apologetic.

I said, "Don't you get near me!"

Chapter 38
"Your Adrenaline Pumps"

Rudy Boesch was for many years the SEALs' Bullfrog—the longest-serving member of the teams. He retired in 1990 after serving as command master chief for the U.S. Special Operations Command. He tells about his experience in parachuting:

Have you done a lot of parachuting?
Quite a bit. But I wasn't a fanatic like a lot of people were. Some of these guys, once they started, they'd go out on weekends. I did it when it was necessary or on a nice, sunny day, maybe, when there was nothing else to do. I didn't really go out of my way to make parachute jumps.

How many jumps have you made?
I don't even know. I told myself a long time ago, when I get out of the military I won't be jumping again so I don't care how many I've had. I wish I did keep it, now.

Do you still get nervous after all the jumps you've made?
Your adrenaline pumps. I always looked forward to the jump master inspecting me to make sure I was dressed right. You can always make a mistake. You probably don't really feel at ease until you get out of the airplane and you get stable. You're standing on the edge of the door, looking down ten thousand feet, and you dive out.

Did you ever get in trouble on a jump?

Three different times I had to pull my reserve. One time, the main chute didn't come off my back. The flap opened but the chute stayed in there. They call it a burble. The suction keeps it in. You do a couple of flips, twist around, and try to shake it loose. And if you can't shake it loose, right about then you pull your reserve. I pulled the reserve and the shock when that opened knocked the main chute out. The main fell down, the reserve is up there. But the main is bigger than the reserve and that started coming up and filling with air and then the reserve fell down.

Aren't you supposed to get rid of the main chute when you pull your reserve?

This was the MC-1, before they came out with the squares. When you pull your reserve now, it cuts away your main. It's automatic. The square is like a Cadillac compared with those round parachutes. It's almost like flying an airplane. You can land on a tabletop.

You said you had several problems?

I had some panels blow out. There are thirty-two-some panels. Some panels blew out. The chute started twisting, getting smaller and smaller. So I pulled my reserve. The other time I had a line over the top—what they call a Mae West. All the malfunctions were with round chutes. I never had any with square chutes.

With those new chutes, you can go thirty or forty miles. You jump at thirty or thirty-five thousand feet with oxygen. You jump and pull and start flying. They have instruments. They follow a leader. When you see 'em coming, it looks like a big snake. They do all this at night. They have strobe lights and they all have radios. It's called HAHO—high altitude, high opening.

When you make a high jump, you can feel it in the air. As you get to about eight thousand feet, you can feel the air getting thicker.

I understand your wife has made a jump.

My wife took up parachute jumping about ten years ago. She made nine jumps with somebody else, tandem jumps. [In a tandem jump, the novice is strapped to an experienced jumper who has the parachute on his back.]

Did she free fall?

Yeah, they jump at 10,000 to 13,000 feet and fall to 3,000. She had sixty to ninety seconds free fall. As you do it, he says, "Do you want me to turn some flips?" Whatever she wants to do, he does. The second time, she opened her eyes.

Why did she take up parachuting?

I don't know. She just told me one day that she's going to make a parachute jump Saturday. This was Monday. I didn't think nothing of it. Tuesday she tells me the same thing. Thursday she says, "I'm going to jump Saturday." Friday she told me, "I'm going to jump tomorrow."

I figured if she's going to jump tomorrow she probably won't even sleep tonight. She slept like a log all night. We got out there and she jumped. I couldn't believe it. A week or so later she was out there again and my daughter was out there and she was watching them make a jump. And I'm standing there with her and she looks up and she says, "I would never do that."

About three hours later, she's chuting up. She did it.

What is her name?

Barbara. We have three daughters and two jumped, Barbara and Ellen. Marjorie is my wife.

Marjorie sounds pretty adventurous.

She wants to try everything I do. For a while, I was on the navy bobsled team. I took her on the bobsled in Lake Placid. She's made parachute jumps, rode the bobsled. She skis. She does everything but diving. She doesn't want to get her hair wet.

Do many SEAL wives do these things?

Not many. A lot of them would like to but they figure they can't do it, physically. She did convince a few other wives to do it [parachute] but they only did one or two.

Has she continued to jump?

Three days before I retired [in 1990] me, her, and the guy she jumped with went out of the same airplane. A little Cessna. And since then, the guy she jumped with got killed, parachute jumping. He creamed in, went all the way in. Him and another guy, a student in front of him.

What happened?

They never did find out. The guy had over eight thousand jumps. He was a sergeant major in the army. His name was Santos Matos [Santos A. Matos Jr.].

The last one my wife made was when me and her went out of the airplane. That scared her, that guy getting killed. She was pretty close to him. The other two women who she talked into jumping, they both jumped with this guy, too. When I told her about it, she was shaken. She was that scared.

Chapter 39
"I'm Going to Jump"

For years, Marjorie E. Boesch had seen her husband, Rudy, go off to do all the dangerous things SEALs do, leaving her to raise their three daughters. And then, one day, she decided to take up parachuting herself. She tells what it was like:

Why did you decide to jump out of a plane?
After the girls were in high school, I started to work at the beach hospital here [in Virginia Beach], two days a week. This nurse took up skydiving.

She said, "You've just got to try it, Marge."

I said, "You know, Rudy has done it for so many years, I would like, just once, to try it. Yeah, I'll do it."

It was a fellow attached to SEAL Team SIX that did this tandem jumping. He was an instructor.

So I told Rudy, "On Saturday, we're going to go to Suffolk and I'm going to jump."

He said, "Jump what?"

I said, "Jump out of an airplane."

He said, "Oh, I don't believe you."

He thought sure I'd be all nervous and I was the most calm person. Really. He thought I wouldn't sleep and I'd be nervous. But I really wasn't. In fact, we took one of our daughters, Barbara, with us. She's the youngest. So we jumped and I knew right away there would have to be a second jump. You couldn't take in everything in the first jump.

Danny [Doyle], the fellow I jumped with, he said, "Did you see the numbers on the bottom of the airplane?"

I said, "Well, I didn't look up after we jumped out."

It was just great.

And Barbara said, "That's something I'll never do!" Three hours later she went up in the airplane and jumped.

What got into her?

I don't know. Just the excitement. Everybody's packing their chutes and getting their chutes on and instructions. And this is just a little airplane where you've got to crawl out on the wing.

I said, "Rudy, do you think I'll be able to hold on?"

He says, "The thing is, are you going to let go?"

But that was no problem. It was so hard getting out there with the force of the wind. All he does is tap you on the shoulder and that's it. The hard part was crawling out there. The pilot's here and you're sitting on the guy's lap, more or less. There's room for two more jumpers [in] back of you. Getting your legs out there, both of you, because you're attached together, isn't an easy feat.

The second jump I made, my leg got tangled up. Thank God we had another jumper with us to push my leg out the door. The force of the wind is so strong. Gosh!

A funny thing happened when Barbara was going to make her jump. The pilot asked if I wanted to ride along. Danny was the only one who did tandem jumps and Danny was taking Barbara. I said, sure. I sat next to the pilot. We're on the ground yet. And this was a bigger airplane. They were just going to walk out the side door.

I'll say there were twenty jumpers on the plane. So the pilot has the engines going and we're talking away. I guess we started to go and he isn't looking where he's going and there's a building there and the wing went through a window on the building. Rudy and my friend were standing there and they thought, oh my God, Marge is flying the plane and she's hit the building. That poor pilot got razzed so much. He just backed up and we went out.

I had a total of nine jumps. The last time I jumped here, in Suffolk, was in the snow. It was exciting. And then down in Florida, it was a big airplane. All you had to do was walk out the door. You didn't have to crawl out on a wing and hang on. There were like fifty jumpers on this plane. It was just wonderful.

This Sergeant Major Matos, who since has been killed, he'd turn flips and somersaults and oh, it was just wonderful. And the scenery, it was just beautiful. You hated it to end.

Did you have a chute?

No, just him—a big one like a cargo chute. He's behind me and we're hooked together. I never got as far as wanting to do it myself. I thought there was just too much to learn. I said I'm too old for this. I don't want to learn all that. It was really exciting.

How old were you?

I was fifty-one then.

Was your first jump a free fall?

Yes. It was just wonderful. I did nine jumps in two years. Everybody got the bug, I talked about it so much. Our oldest daughter, Ellen, she jumped too. A couple of other women here decided they wanted to do it. And then down in Florida, too, there were others that went on to free-fall themselves, they liked it so much. Of course they were younger, too.

Why did you free-fall?

I didn't know there was any other kind.

You made your nine jumps and then stopped?

Rudy retired. I was with Sergeant Major Matos and Rudy, in the same airplane, the three of us jumped that last time, the day after Rudy retired [in 1990]. And then, that was it.

When was Matos killed?

The next year. In fact, we were there, down in Florida, at MacDill Air Force Base. Rudy was going to go out in the morning to help look for him. It was over at Zephyr Hills [a popular sport parachuting site]. Before they got the group together, they had found him.

Another fellow had jumped with him. I guess, to this day they don't know what happened. I mean, he had hundreds of jumps. I can't imagine what happened. I know the last few jumps with Matos, I'm the one who pulled the rip cord. I'd have to reach back here on his parachute. I don't know why the guy himself couldn't have done it if something had happened to Matos.

What does it feel like to free-fall?

When you're free-falling you can see for miles. It was just a heavenly feeling. Of course when you pull the chute, you just float. With tandem jumping, you would be the last jumpers out of the plane. And then you could see all the other chutes. Especially at Zephyr Hills, where there would be like fifty jumpers. What a sight that was. Just beautiful.

You could watch their formations. They were always doing formations. Matos and I hooked up with one formation one time. They come zooming in. I don't know how they stop, why they don't crack heads. I never learned. We got in one formation, just so he could show me— how simple he says it is. It wasn't simple at all, I don't think.

Was it difficult landing with two of you hooked together?

We never had any trouble landing. You just draw your legs up. As soon as his touched, yours touched. We always stood right up, never fell.

Is it hard getting to your target?

On the first jump, you think it's way over there. How are you ever going to get there? He'll tell you which strings to pull, which side to help pull, and you get there.

Have you done any other adventurous things?

I beat Rudy in racquetball. That's one thing I can beat him in. I like to ski. I tore two ligaments in my knee this past March. I'm not sure whether I'll be able to ski in February or not but we're going out to Montana. Of course then Rudy was on the bobsled team. That was exciting too. He was on the navy team up in Lake Placid. I went up for about ten days.

They had a half-mile run and a mile run. I did both. That was great. I enjoyed that.

I don't like to dive. That never interested me. Rudy taught the three girls. But I guess I've got claustrophobia. I can't imagine going in a submarine. I can swim on top of the water, but never under. He never pushed me. He never pushed me into anything. I think he was the most shocked person when I jumped out of the airplane. He never thought I'd do it.

Chapter 40
"I Hated Every One . . ."

Jack Macione describes his experiences as a reluctant parachutist:

I made my 549th parachute jump three days before I retired. That's a fairly low number when it comes to team members. There are guys with 3,000, 4,000, even 5,000 jumps.

I'm going to admit to you. I did it all and I hated every one of them. I never felt comfortable parachuting, but I did it all. I jumped a jet from thirty-seven thousand feet. Jumped with rubber boats tied to me. Jumped even with a nuclear weapon tied to me. A little SADM [special atomic demolition munition]—forty-three pounds. One kiloton yield.

Of those 549 jumps, all but about 50 or 60 were free fall. I went to five schools: basic airborne, HALO, light army aircraft, jump master, and parachute packing. I jumped every damn aircraft we had in the inventory up to that point.

My highest jump was 37,900 feet. There was about a five-minute free fall before we opened. It was out of an A-3D over Fort Bragg about 1963.

Everything we did was dangerous. It was like everyday breathing. We would go out and do a mission that some army guy would get a Silver Star for and we would get a thanks.

In high-altitude jumping, the danger is that it is the best way to execute somebody. All these things they're doing to criminals. If you deprive someone of oxygen, you're out. You don't feel a thing. You don't even feel yourself going out. It is not depriving someone of air. With a lack of air, you start gagging and choking. If you are deprived of oxygen, you are out. And if you continue to deprive them of oxygen, they die and they don't feel a thing.

I know because that happened to me. I didn't die. I had a lack of oxygen twice. I'm talking to you like I'm talking to you now and the next thing I know, somebody is waking me up. So you've got to be sure your oxygen systems are operating. One of the dangers in those days was, we would be on ship's oxygen. You're breathing good. When we got ready to jump, we had bailout bottles. They used to call it "pull the apple." There was a little green thing. You had to break this pin by pulling it. That pin was so hard to break! Guys would pull down on it and their minds would say, it has to be broken because you can't pull any harder. And they'd go off ship's oxygen and then pass out. They hadn't broken the pin. You'd pull down until you thought you were going to dislocate your elbow and then you would hear it snap.

You had about eight minutes of oxygen. I think we made twenty-four jumps and the lowest one was about twenty-four thousand feet, when we went to HALO school. An A-3D is a twin-engine, swept-wing navy carrier plane. It was configured to train bombardiers so it had about twelve seats in it, with the crew forward and up a flight.

In an emergency, they would blow the hatch off and you'd slide down this chute. In our training, it was locked open. And you would run up the aisle and throw yourself on this polished aluminum chute and you would slide out of the plane backwards, like going out of a sort of a bomb bay.

At that altitude, of course, you had to be on oxygen. Because one breath, and you were out.

It was about fifty below zero. Your adrenaline is pumping so hard you forget about the cold. But one thing that happens, when you go out, the humidity in your goggles freezes instantaneously. You can't see a thing. So, many days we would jump without goggles and our eyeballs would freeze.

The other thing is, the air is thin up there. It's quite a sensation. Normally in a free fall, you're falling about 120 miles an hour. At those altitudes, you're falling over 300 miles an hour. There's no air, no resistance. You have no sensation of falling. But as you get down into lower altitudes, you can actually feel the air getting thicker. You can feel yourself piling up on air.

And then you begin to get in control. At those altitudes, it was not unusual to be out of control. There was no resistance from the air so you could go into a tumble, like tumbling in a vacuum. There was nothing to reach for. I went completely out of control one day. It's an experience I'd never had and most fellows never experience. I went completely out of control. I was spinning and rapidly increasing in the whipping of it. They had told us to just snap to attention in the air. And boy, I did. I went head down and stabilized immediately and then I could get control again.

Another danger was a profound "target hypnosis syndrome." You were falling from such an altitude that you had a long, long time to get fixed on your target and that slow growing of the target is almost hypnotic. I feel that it killed some people. This target hypnosis thing, I've experienced it. You see an object on the ground and it slowly gets larger. It's very hypnotic.

In high-altitude jumps, we'd jump twelve or thirteen at a time. That's all the room we had. We jumped six or eight in the first pass and then the others, for safety reasons, so we could control it. Anyway, I had made the first pass and was on the ground packing my chute. At those altitudes, you couldn't even see the airplane, much less the jumpers. But you could hear them. You could hear them falling, rushing through the air. You can't hear the airplane but you can hear the jumpers as they start to get down to opening altitude at twenty-four hundred feet.

I heard the jumpers whooshing through the air and I looked up and saw the chutes opening and then I looked way up in the heavens and saw this little tiny thing up there. The first thing I thought of was that the hatch came off the airplane. So I ran to the marshaling area and I told them, "Heads up! The hatch may have come off."

I got a set of binoculars. I looked up and it was a goddamn guy in a parachute. It was twenty below zero and three hundred knots and we figured it broke his neck. He was just hanging, being drifted. We got in a half ton [truck] and were weaving our way toward him. We finally got to some farmer's field and there's a parachute all packed up laying there. Nobody around.

What happened was, one guy went out and kind of pushed himself off. And he hit the edge of the chute [exiting from the plane] and it armed his pins. He opened about thirty-three thousand feet. The plane was doing about three hundred knots.

What we saw when we looked at him was, he was basically just conserving his energy and his oxygen. About ten thousand feet he did a cutaway, dumped his main, and came in on his reserve. Smart fellow.

Everyplace he had harness he was black and blue.

Why did he cut away?

Two reasons. One, he was running out of oxygen. Second was, he had a piece of shit chute above him. It was all in threads, nothing more than a stabilizing anchor keeping him vertical.

Here's a little anecdote. We were in St. Thomas. We used to come over a mountaintop that had a restaurant and a bar. The mountaintop was at 1,200 feet. We used to fly over at 1,250 feet and there was this big cliff. As soon as you cleared the restaurant, out you would go.

My girlfriend at the time, I brought her down to watch the big, hairy-assed frogmen do their parachuting. I had told her I would be the guy with the red smoke flare so she would recognize me. Well, the guys, everyone of them, had a red smoke flare.

We used to jump a Caribou [small cargo plane]. It had the rear deck that opened up. We used to take brand-new guys down there and put them in the Caribou. Here you come over the mountaintop. Just as soon as you clear the mountaintop, you go out.

You have the guys backed up on the ramp. Then you slap 'em on the ass and tell 'em to get out. Of course all they saw was trees. You couldn't see the cliff that dropped off to the water. You'd slap the first guy and he'd look at you: What you talking about? We're only at fifty feet. You'd have to kick 'em and beat 'em.

Were you ever picked up by the Fulton sky hook?

Sky hook. I'm one of eighty or ninety who ever made a live pickup. I did it on the ball field out at Coronado. The other guy was R. F. Adams.

Fox took my place the day he was killed. Fox had about a thousand free falls. He didn't panic. He began to think. He started to get into positions to hit the water. He curled in a ball and then he decided to go in feet first. He hit the water at a kind of forty-five-degree angle and it split him from his ankle all the way up under his arm.

I then went to California to do a dual pickup with Adams. The first day, we set up but we didn't get picked up. The lift line went up through the clouds. I couldn't see the airplane and I didn't like that. The pilot couldn't see the ground so he didn't want to make the pickup.

Let me explain something. Normally, the only thing uncomfortable on a pickup was the wind, because you were being towed backward through the air, at 150 to 200 knots, and the wind was pushing your head down. The little guys were taking the harness and pulling it over the front of their helmet and it would help hold their head into the wind. But us bigger guys, we couldn't get the harness to come around.

So we asked Fulton if he could lengthen the harness a little. So he did. Inadvertently what happened was—normally, you're being towed from like the center of your back, so you're like a kind of sea anchor, you're stabilized. But what happened was when he moved that tow point from behind you to over your head, you're just kind of on a swivel.

Well, we got picked up. Adams was above me and I was on a pigtail. We made the usual few gyrations, the spins, the turns, and then I stabilized out. All of a sudden I make three whipping rotations to the left, in a second. I no sooner look down than it happens to me again. Now I can feel Adams above me doing the same thing.

And then the thing starts cracking the whip. It's not only spinning, it's cracking. The lift uniform you put on, the legs have gotten torn off, my arms have gotten torn off. My wristwatch is gone. My ears are lacerated. I'm bleeding in the groin. And I'm doing this violent, violent rotation. Three RPMs a second. And then just a quick breather and again.

And then the plane started flying to five thousand feet and that's a sign they're going to put a parachute on the lift line and cut you loose. But they kept pulling us up.

And then I said to myself, "When I get underneath this airplane, it's going to beat me to death. I'm going to be hamburger."

As luck would have it, the air flow [below the plane] stabilized us. I feel the line stop as they put Adams into the plane. And then it was my turn. They got me up into the airplane. I was limp. I was done for— and I was in superb shape. If someone said they'd give me a million dollars to sit up, I could not have done it. Adams was lying there and he was beat up as bad as I was.

When we got back to the airport, two guys lifted me off the plane, one under each arm. Fulton was there. I remember saying, "Mr. Fulton, there's something wrong with the system."

It had actually bruised the—I think they call them filii—the little hairs in my ears. For three weeks I walked like a zombie, like Frankenstein. If someone called my name and I turned to see who it was, I would fall over and down. I'd drive on a perfectly smooth highway a mile to the base and get nauseous.

Chapter 41
When Your Eyes Freeze Shut

Engineman Master Chief Johnny Walker is a slight, dark-haired SEAL with a neatly trimmed, reddish colored mustache. He is unmarried, which is probably just as well, considering that his profession calls for him to jump out of airplanes at high altitude as often as eight times a day.

With more than thirty-three hundred jumps in his logbook, he is the senior enlisted man in the free fall parachute school at Coronado and is in charge of a team of expert jumpers who teach the art of advanced parachuting to other SEALs.

In the early 1980s, he was one of the members of SEAL Team SIX who pioneered the technique of jumping and safely opening a chute at extremely high altitudes, enabling the SEALs to travel long distances in formation before making a surreptitious landing. This is his story:

I went to static line school in 1974. Then in 1976, when I was with SEAL Team TWO, I got my initial free fall training. Our commanding officer was Captain Marcinko. Love that guy! [SEALs refer to their commanding officer as "captain" even though he is of lower rank.]

Back then free fall training was: This is how you do it. Get on the table and show me the position, then out to the airport and out of the plane you went. It lacked in a lot of the finer arts of military free fall. We did some follow-on training down in Puerto Rico—more free falls. We went to Hurlburt Field [headquarters for air force special operations near Fort Walton Beach, Florida] to do our high-altitude training—HALO.

In 1980, when I went to SEAL Team SIX, [as one of the plank owners, or original members] I think I had sixty-five jumps. For four years, that wasn't that many jumps. When we got the team started, that's when I really got into the jumping. There definitely was emphasis on jumping. We brought the whole team up to free fall level and then we did a lot of jump training. Depending on the type of jump, a HALO mission— twenty-five thousand feet and above—we'll jump out and stay in the same airspace while we're falling. On a HAHO [high altitude, high opening] mission, we'll jump out, deploy our parachutes within about four to twelve seconds after we've left the bird (to kind of stagger the openings), and we'll fly the canopies in formation down to the target.

My highest HAHO is thirty-three thousand and my highest HALO is thirty-six thousand.

What's it feel like?

Because you step out of the bird and deploy almost immediately, you're almost in the forward throw of the bird. You haven't reached terminal velocity yet. But the bird is traveling fast. The openings were hard. We had some canopy damage, people getting hurt. We did a lot of experimenting with packing the parachutes to get a softer opening.

How does the packing affect the opening?

The front of the square parachute is called the nose. And it's actually open. Looking from the front you can see different cells. The air is forced in through the front, the back is closed. So the air turns around and comes back out and creates a false front up there that gives us the ability to go through the air. It makes it just like a wing. The parachute opens from the nose to the back and then from the middle out. We roll the nose and close it off. We can make it real tight, depending on the type of jump that's coming up. And we retard the opening that way.

When we first started, people didn't do those types of jumps. So we had a standard packing, the same way civilians always pack. We just played with it on our own until we came up with a packing method that would slow down the opening. It was strange because when we first started all this, no one had done it. We had to find out what the problems were by doing it.

One thing we weren't ready for was the cold at altitude. It is extremely cold up there. Our hands would go almost numb. The toggles on the parachute are about here [reaching up in front of and above his head]. You're taking all the blood from your hands. When you get on the ground, guys would lie on the ground. Some guys would puke from the pain of the hands coming back to life. It was almost like being frozen and coming back to life.

We started playing with toggles where you could steer from down here [indicating crotch level] and keep the blood in your hands. And we played with different kinds of gloves so you had the dexterity you needed. You had to be able to grab the rip cord or if you had a malfunction, get rid of that and pull your reserve. So you had to have dexterity. We went to sports stores to get new gloves.

How long were you exposed to the cold?

It could be thirty to forty minutes, although not in extreme cold the entire time. One of the jumps we did, the outside temperature was minus eighty-two. Another strange problem is we'd wear the goggles in the bird and they're next to your face so they're nice and warm. And you jump out into extreme cold and the goggles would shatter. Then we jumped without goggles. The initial wind blast would tear [as in crying] your eyes. Then your eyes would freeze shut because of the water on your eyelashes. There'd be big gobs of ice on there. You'd dig your eyes out and find your eyelashes still attached to the ice cubes.

Some of those jumps could get interesting. As you go through various cloud layers, it might be snowing in the cloud. We had a couple of interesting experiences with that. The control lines are in the back. If you pull these lines down, you can slow the parachute down. If you pull down far enough, you can actually stall it. It'll rock backwards, the same as an aircraft. If you get in an ice storm, you start getting ice rammed into this parachute and it starts to settle back here in the tail section. And if you get enough ice in there, it starts to pull down that tail for you.

We'd look up. We could see the ice in the tail section. And then of course the tail starts dropping from the weight and some of the canopies would start to stall.

Those were things we didn't know would happen when we started this. There was no wealth of knowledge, other than to go out and try it for ourselves.

What do you do when your parachute turns into a bag of ice?

You cuss a lot. We talk to the parachutes a lot. When it's not performing well, you end up talking to it, trying to make it feel better.

As we dropped down in altitude the ice would start to melt. Once it stalls, it tries to recover, so it rocks. It could completely stall out. For fun, sometimes, on our instructor rigs, we'll take a couple of wraps on the steering lines so we can get more pull and pull it all the way down and just fall out of the sky that way. But when you let it go, it starts flying again.

Do all the SEALs do HAHO?

No, but since we started the school here, we are bringing a lot more into the regular teams. The expertise is still at DevGru [Naval Special Warfare Development Group, a major command that develops weapons and other equipment and new tactics for the SEAL teams]. But the others are catching up rapidly. Seven of our eighteen instructors are from DevGru. Most of the others came from the jump team. [The Leap Frogs parachute demonstration team.] When I came here to start the school in 1990, I made some calls and had others calling me looking for jobs.

All of the teams have a free fall platoon that's more or less designated to go into more advanced parachuting.

How do you stay together when you jump at night?

You have to stay in the same airspace at night. We put a different colored light on one jumper to designate him as the leader. If I was the leader, I would jump first and turn around and pick up the aircraft heading. I might wear a red light on my back. The rest of the jumpers would wear green. They would form almost a half-moon on me. At a preset altitude, I would turn 180 degrees and track off. That tells the guys it's time to get separation for opening. And they'd go out and open, identify my red light again as the leader under canopy, form up behind me, and we all land on the target together.

It takes a lot of practice to do it. You have to have a team that has worked together a lot. You have to know your weak fliers in that team. You can take a weak flier and make him the leader because everyone else can get to him. If I have a big heavy guy like Rocky here [Rocky

Carlock, one of the instructors] and a light guy like myself, Rocky's going to have a hell of a time staying with me because I fall slower than he does. So I might make Rocky the leader. It's easier for me to go faster than for him to go slower. I can go faster and stay down with Rocky.

Have you used these skills in the real world?

No. Not to my knowledge. I haven't done it. I served under [SEAL Team SIX commanders] Marcinko, [Robert] Gormly, [Thomas] Murphy, [Richard] Woolard. Where I really got involved in instructing was at DevGru. We said we've got to formalize this, give the guys some better basic training. About four of us got together and started taking over all the training, about 1985. We built from there to where we had specific lesson guides to teach from. It turned into a full-time job for me, teaching free fall and the advanced techniques. When I came here I brought my course and translated it into normal navy paperwork.

Have you had any scary experiences?

Things happen to parachutes. I got into a lot of T&E [test and evaluation], testing different techniques. Some of those would get interesting. I've had around twenty parachutes that didn't work perfectly and I had to get rid of them.

My first malfunction, jump number 297, I remember it well. We were making a daytime jump into a drop zone overseas. A lot of times in your training jumps you take off and jump right there at the airport. This particular jump, from where we were taking off, we were transiting to another drop zone and jumping in. You have to set your altimeter accordingly. If that drop zone is five hundred feet higher, you have to adjust your altimeter to that drop zone altitude.

We had a mass of people—a large group of jumpers, about sixty people—so we tried to stagger the openings to the experience level of the jumper. Less experienced jumpers would open at 3,000 feet, the middle group at 2,500 feet, and the experienced level at 2,000 feet. I jumped out of the bird and there were people all over the place. I was in the experienced level. So I said, "I'm getting out of here." So I just pointed straight down and dove for the bottom to get out of the way.

Being young and cocky, of course, I took it down to about 1,800 feet and then deployed my parachute. It malfunctioned. So I played with it a little bit and finally cut it away about 1,300 feet, which is way too low. The reserve came out and it wasn't looking real good. I played with it for just a second, pulled on the risers to get it inflated, reached up and pulled my toggles, and landed, just about that quick.

It was almost a jump into the party. It was the end of the trip, the end of training. We set up and had a party there. Bob Schamberger [Senior Chief Engineman Robert Schamberger, who died in a para-chute mishap during the Grenada invasion of 1983] came over and handed me a beer, right there.

He said they were kind of worried about me.

I asked, "What's the concern?"

He said, "Look at your altimeter!"

My altimeter still read 500 feet. Through some miscommunication, we had adjusted our altimeters the wrong way. So I didn't even pull until 1,300 feet. That was pretty low. I cut away [the main chute] around 800 feet so I pulled the reserve at 700 feet or so. [At that point, he was probably only about four seconds from impact.]

For that jump, I should have pulled my main at 2,000 feet and probably would have cut away around 1,800 feet. Everybody pulled low but only one guy was hurt. He broke his ankle or arm when he landed in a bunch of cow shit and slipped.

Have there been fatalities in your chute training?

No. We've had a few who got hurt. There was one fatality but it wasn't related to training. Occasionally there's an entanglement. Some guys have had to land together, on one chute. These are techniques we've developed. You can't tell them exactly what to do. If you go through another guy's lines, the top jumper can cut away and get his reserve deployed. The lower jumper has to deal with what he has. His chute might be all screwed up. If they entangle and the bottom jumper panics and cuts away, he might tangle up that upper jumper and it's over then. The biggest thing we teach is communication: recognize, analyze, and react. You can talk to each other or communicate by radio. Even in a free fall, as instructors, we can talk to the students.

We teach what's called accelerated free fall or AFF. On your first jumps, the instructor actually goes out holding onto the student. You take a grip on his harness and up on his shoulder and you exit with the student. You help him stable out. We have hand signals. If I want his legs to move, I give him this signal. We have them practice touching the rip cord so they know where that is. It just makes those first couple of jumps a lot smoother rather than just throwing him out of the airplane and letting him flail for himself.

The instructor's right there. In the event of an emergency, the instructor can pull for the student. The AFF training is a civilian, rather than a military, rating and it is a real hard rating to get. I have all my instructors AFF trained. When our student first goes out of the airplane, the instructor is right there with him. We progress him up. We continue to go out with him on the exit and then we let him go but we stay right with him.

The instructor stays until the student pulls, then clears the distance and he pulls. On the first couple of jumps we have the student follow us in under canopy so we can show him where the wind line [the way the wind is blowing] is and the proper approach to the target.

We teach them to land into the wind. You might have eighteen knots forward speed under canopy. If I have six or eight knots of ground wind, by turning into the wind I'm down to ten to twelve knots. Then you pull your toggles to stall and flare [a sudden pull on the lines to dump air from the parachute as the chutist reaches the ground], bleeding off all the airspeed right as you touch down.

At night, it depends on the experience of the jumper. We tell them to come in with half to three-quarter brakes. Be prepared to do a PLF— parachute landing fall. We set up lights for the landing pattern. I usually try to land right near a light so I can see the ground. When we jump equipment, I lower the equipment. Then I bring it in until I hear the equipment hit and then do a dynamic flare.

When the student can land on his own, the instructor will fall down almost to the bottom, about 2,000 feet, mainly because we've got to get down, get our chutes packed, grab our next student, and go back up. We'll make eight jumps a day during the initial part of the training.

Then we let them start exiting on their own and flying. They tend to progress a lot faster. The way we used to teach, the instructor would go with him. But if the student is flipping and spinning he doesn't really learn anything. He's looking straight down to make sure the ground is there instead of at the instructor.

We have a school at El Centro, with a classroom building and berthing. The students come for four weeks and make an average of thirty-five to forty jumps. We start with basic free fall and they have twelve jumps to pass the first test. We lose a few of them. They can't pass that test. Then we throw in equipment. We start jumping at night. We bring in oxygen and take them up to a night, combat equipment, oxygen jump. That's the level we try to get them to. Once we get that accomplished, we talk about grouping and free fall. An instructor might have five students and he'll go out as the leader and teach them advanced techniques. Then we get into the HAHO, flying formations under canopy.

In training, about the time the trainees are all nice and cocky—they've done this thirty to forty times and they're all laid back in their seats— we do an emergency bailout. The pilot turns on the bells and whistles. The instructors jump up, start running around, throw the side door open. We get them out. Then the instructors jump out and have fun. I enjoy it.

I enjoy the teaching. You meet a kid the first day. You hold his hand on the first few jumps. A few weeks later you see this kid with full combat equipment, on oxygen, he's doing real good, landing right on the target. It's a real good feeling.

SEALs in Action

Chapter 42
Jump into a Dark Sea

In October 1983, the prime minister of the tiny Caribbean island of Grenada was killed after being toppled from power in a leftist coup. President Reagan, concerned for the safety of a group of American medical students studying on the island, ordered a hastily organized invasion of Grenada.

U.S. special operations forces, including the new antiterrorist SEAL Team SIX, were picked to lead the way. One group was assigned to parachute into the sea near the Point Salines airfield and go ashore to prepare for a landing there by army Rangers. Four SEALs were lost at sea in that nighttime drop. Engineman Master Chief Johnny Walker tells of his role in that phase of the invasion:

I was on the Grenada jump—jump master in the lead bird.

Sometimes in the team area, you can tell if something is up, the way people are moving. But on Friday afternoon [21 October] we all went on normal liberty. We had a wedding to go to the next day. The next morning [Saturday] the beepers went off and everything went pretty quick from there.

There wasn't a lot of time to brief everybody on who was where and what was going on. Our job was to get there and take orders when we got there. We had two birds involved, two different groups. [The SEALs took off from Pope Air Force Base, North Carolina, in two four-engine C-130 air force transport planes on Sunday, 23 October 1983.]

The jump was actually pretty strange. It was set up as more of an administrative jump, a daylight jump. We weren't in any particular threat area because we were pretty far off the coast. I went up to the pilots and asked them the approximate flight time to the drop so I could plan on telling my boys to suit up. I think they gave me something around three hours. [Walker recalls there were about fourteen SEALs divided between the two aircraft.]

I got the guys suited up and was ready for the aircraft to start giving me time warnings. We didn't get any time warnings so I went back up to the pilots to ask and they said it was going to be another couple of hours. So I got the guys undressed and we had them take their parachutes off. We waited for the aircraft to give us time warnings.

The weather report we got was the seas were calm, the winds were calm. When we did finally start getting our time warnings, we got everybody suited up. When the ramp opened up, I noticed it was pitch-black outside. We couldn't see a thing.

I grabbed a flashlight off the air crewman and tried to stick it on the boat. [Each plane carried a fiberglass Boston Whaler loaded with equipment, to be dropped with a cargo chute.] We had no lights rigged anywhere. We were told it was going to be a daylight drop.

The boat left the bird and we jumped behind it. When we hit the water, the seas were large and the wind was very strong. We weren't prepared for this at all. We had all done water jumps before. But we didn't know we were jumping into high seas. I don't know whether we would have done anything different knowing the conditions, but it might have been nice to know.

My jump, I got out, had a couple of twists. We were supposed to be around fifteen hundred feet. I think it was a lot lower than that. I got out of the line twists and shortly after that I hit the water. Hard! I never turned my parachute into the wind because I didn't have time.

I ripped a lot of equipment I had on my body, ripped it off. We were jumping with full equipment, our combat equipment—load-bearing harness, magazines, canteens, first aid kit. Most of the guys had their rifles. I was the 60 [M60 machine gun] gunner at the time so my 60 was in the boat.

When I hit the water, my fins got ripped off, some of the pouches I had on my load-bearing equipment got ripped off. The parachute never deflated. It remained inflated and started dragging me through the water, almost from wave to wave, dragging me facedown, swallowing water rapidly. I reached up and grabbed the lines of the parachute and started dragging them in, trying to collapse the parachute. I remember, I knew I was on my last second there. The parachute collapsed.

You felt like you were drowning?

Oh, yeah, because I couldn't get any air. It was just forcing water into my mouth. And I had a lot of the lines all around me. I just set there for a brief second, almost in awe of what had just happened. Then the parachute started to reinflate. But I had time to get to my knife and start cutting lines and got enough of them cut so it didn't start dragging me again. The knife that I used to cut myself free with had just been bought for me as a pseudobirthday present from [Quartermaster First Class] Kevin Lundberg, one of the guys who died on that jump. He and I were best friends.

I just started swimming in the direction I thought the boat might be. Obviously, the light I had clipped on the boat had come off. I was groping in the dark, trying to call out for other people.

How high were the seas and wind?

Say the waves were six to eight and the wind at least twenty knots.

Would you normally not jump under those conditions?

Actually, for a combat jump, we probably would have. But the guys would have been more prepared as far as what to do when they hit the water.

You're all alone?

I just swam in the direction I thought the boat might be. I lost my bearings. There was a ship down there. They were there to assist as necessary. I knew my job was to find the rest of my group, find the boat, and get on with the mission.

I could see the ship; it had lights on it. I swam around for an unknown amount of time. The ship was moving around a little bit. I was worn out from swimming so I headed toward the ship. As I got close to it, I heard someone fire three shots. My instinct was, everyone's on the boat except me and they're looking for me. So I swam in the direction of the shots I heard. I was still pretty worn out from swimming with all those clothes on [camouflage greens, boots, and a life vest, but no fins] so I decided to head for the ship and get to safety.

Right as I got to the ship I ran into one other jumper out there. They had a cargo net rigged over the bow and we climbed up. We were the last two to be recovered that night. Which means somebody was alive, one of those four guys, was alive until the last minute because we

316 SEALs IN ACTION

questioned everybody and it wasn't anybody who was on the ship who fired the three rounds. Someone was alive until almost the very end.

Everyone had recovered back to the ship from both drops when I got there. One boat was recovered and one was lost. We put a group together—eight or ten of us, enough to fill one boat. We got some weapons from the ship and ammunition, that were lost in the other boat, and launched out for the mission.

We were right there, almost to the island—we could see the island, see the lights of the city—and we got spotted by a patrol boat. Well, not spotted; I think they may have heard the motors, saw the white water from our wake, something like that. We came off the throttles to slow down, almost dead in the water, and of course we lost an engine then. [The boat was powered by two outboard motors. They had a tendency to quit running if the throttle was pulled back too far.] We never really got that engine back.

Were there air force people with you?

Yes, we had some CCT with us. [CCT stands for combat control team, an air force unit that controls air traffic under combat conditions.] They were on the ship waiting for us. I'm not sure how they got to the ship.

What was the original plan?

We were going to get in our boats, go over and pick up the CCT guys, and head in to the island and take a look at the runway where the actual landing was going to happen, to see if the runway was clear and if it would hold a 141 [C-141 jet transport]. Our job was to take them in, get them to the runway so they could make a determination if 141s could land, if they hadn't strung wire across the runway. Basically, our job was to take them in, get them to the runway, and provide security for them.

Once we lost the engine, we decided to go back to the ship and regroup. We got picked up next morning about first light. They came in and dropped two more boats for us. We made an attempt the second night. We went in that night with two boats and all the people we could get together.

The SEALs jumped into the sea Sunday night and made their first attempt to reach the island during that night. They returned to the ship Monday morning and made their second attempt Monday night.

\

On the way in, we lost another boat. The engines went down on it. We transferred as many people as we could. Idling around, circling around, we lost the other boat. The boats were old and tired. We were just in the process of acquiring new boats.

Did you get close to shore the second time? Did you see the air-drop by the Rangers?

Close, but not close enough to swim in. We were in the boats, dead in the water. We watched the birds come over. They were coming over us and starting to drop over the island. We finally got communications and the ship came and found us and recovered us. That was the end of the war for us.

We stayed on the ship that day, that night. The ship was right off the coast then, pretty much off the harbor. We watched one of the helos get shot down, I think it was a Cobra. They [the Grenadians] had patrol boats but they weren't a big threat.

Other members of SEAL Team SIX were embattled ashore. One unit was trapped at the governor-general's mansion, on a hill overlooking the city of St. George, where they had gone to rescue the governor-general, Sir Paul Scoon. Another unit, whose assignment was to take control of a radio transmitter, became involved in a furious firefight with Grenadians armed with heavy weapons and armored personnel carriers.

We recovered some people from the radio station. The SEALs naturally headed for the water. Some swam out to the ship, probably a couple of miles. A couple of them stole a small boat and came out that way. There were helos in the area that we had some SEALs on. They recovered guys out of the water.

From the ship, the SEALs could see and hear, on the radio, the air force AC-130 Spectre gunships supporting the members of Team SIX trapped at the governor's mansion. The battle at the radio station occurred so quickly that the SEALs had to escape to the sea before the gunships could come to their aid.

The Spectre gunships, we could hear them talking to the guys and the support the Spectre was giving them, which was excellent.

I remember listening on the radio. One of them [Spectres] was running out of fuel. There was going to be a delay between when he had to leave to go back and get fuel and the bird to come in and relieve him, to take up support. I remember the pilot feathering some engines to save fuel so there wouldn't be that lapse, for fear that if there was that lapse, the guys at the governor's mansion would have been overrun. Those guys did a hell of a job. [When the fighting died down, members of SEAL Team SIX all reported to the airfield ashore.]

We gathered up our whole team, put 'em on a bird, and sent them home.

Of the people on your plane, how many didn't make it?

It's been so long. I think it was two, maybe three. I'm trying to remember where Kenny Butcher [Machinist Mate First Class Kenneth Butcher] was. I know Lundberg was on the other bird, I think Butcher was on it too. I had [Senior Chief Engineman Robert] Schamberger and [Hull Technician First Class Stephen] Morris on my bird.

What happened to those four men?

It's just speculation that they drowned from being drug in the water. One guy survived right to the very end. No telling. It could have been sharks, for all we know. We never found them.

Chapter 43
A Beautiful Day to Go to War

Lieutenant Bobby McNabb, now assigned to a SEAL team at Little Creek, was an E-6, a midlevel enlisted man, and a member of SEAL Team SIX at the time of the Grenada invasion in October 1983. This is his account of the team's baptism by fire:

I was having breakfast with my wife and kids—I'm thinking it was a Saturday or Sunday—and I remember the beeper going off.

I thought, "Damnit, another drill. I'll be back later."

Shoot, I came back two weeks later. She was kind of used to it. She was broke in already. We just didn't come back. But they [the wives] had figured it out, what was going on. In reality, she thought we were going to Beirut because, a week or so before Grenada was the Beirut bombing. [Actually, the bombing of a marine barracks in Beirut, in which 237 Americans were killed, occurred on Sunday, 23 October. The members of SEAL Team SIX had been called to duty the previous day.]

The wives, they get together. When everybody takes off, at first they don't think about it. The beeper goes off, you go in to work. They wait around until the afternoon to see if the boys are just getting together to have a beer. Marcinko [Richard Marcinko, who had just been relieved as commander of SEAL Team SIX] was notorious for that. He wanted somebody to come over and watch football. But by the afternoon, the wives would start calling to find out who's gone and who's not.

Before you know it, they say, whoa, all these guys are gone! Then they all get together over at somebody's house and gab with each other and then keep the net going until people start returning. Well, after the first night when nobody returns and there's no word from anybody, they kind of start thinking something's up. Then they started watching the news and here everything's on Beirut. One and one equals four and so they say, "They're going to Beirut."

The OpSec [operational security] was pretty good, until the news came out with the four guys drowning.

Hell, in '83, nobody knew where Grenada was.

We're all going, "Where the hell is Grenada?"

I said, "I think it's a Caribbean island."

So I got some aeronautical charts I had because I was a pilot. [McNabb dropped out of the navy in 1978 and qualified to fly both fixed-wing aircraft and helicopters before returning to the service and joining SEAL Team SIX in 1980.]

I said, "Well, here it is. It's down by Barbados."

It was so comical. During one of the initial briefings, I'm trying to be the dutiful type guy and ask the right questions. In charge of our little group was [Lt. Wellington] "Duke" Leonard.

And I go, "Duke, what kind of uniforms have they got?"

He goes, "I don't know."

"What kind of weapons do they have?"

"Well . . . I don't know."

"How many are there going to be?"

He holds up this yellow piece of legal pad with chicken scratches on it and says, "This is all we've got."

We all started laughing. We said, "Well, there's no sense asking any more questions." We realized right away that the intel was not what it was supposed to be.

I remember hearing Duke's famous line, "Oh, they'll probably just throw their guns down." Well, when we landed, they sure as hell weren't throwing their guns down.

We were told, there's like six APCs [armored personnel carriers] on the whole island. From my vantage point I must have counted twenty going by us. Six! They must be going around us in circles. It was a hell of a lot more than six.

After our initial stop at Barbados, we flew to Grenada and fast-roped in at the back of the governor's mansion. [The assignment for these SEALs was to land at the mansion of Governor-general Sir Paul Scoon, on a hill overlooking the city of St. Georges, to protect him, his wife, and aides.]

We were crammed in the back of the helo en route to Grenada. We had just crossed over land. We were maybe twenty minutes out at that time. The crewman, I remember him tapping me on the shoulder and having the feed-tray open on the 60 [M60 machine gun] on the door of the HH-60 helo, the Blackhawk. He's standing there with a belt of ammo in one hand, shrugging his shoulders. Oh, great, he doesn't know how to load the gun.

I've got all my belted ammo around me, my gun sitting like this. [In his lap.] I had to hand my gun to someone else, push everyone out of the way so I could turn around and get up and load the gun for him. It turns out they were short of crewmen and he was another pilot and didn't know how to load the gun. I found that out afterward. God only knows if he used it.

When we were flying in, I was up on ICS [intercom] with the pilots. I remember hearing on an AM transmitter, that they were well aware we were coming.

"The Americans are coming. Get your arms."

That had a sort of disheartening note to it. We—the SEALs— wanted to do the op at night but were unable to because it had to coincide with the marine landing, which had to be in the daytime. At least this is what I understood.

Actually, it worked out kind of well, due to the hard time finding the house. We had flown over the house and had to circle back to fast-rope in. It would have been extremely difficult finding it at night.

On the way in, the helo took sixty-three rounds. One of the pilots and two SEALs in the back were hit. That was the helo that had to be taken out to the Wasp. They had to put a fire hose in the exhaust side of the engine to get it shut down. They couldn't shut the helo down.

The guy who was flying it was a warrant officer—an ex-Ranger. He just sat there while we were getting shot up and made sure we could all get out before he moved. We wound up getting shot at by a quad .51 [caliber machine gun], which was back behind the mansion. We had a hard time finding a place to fast-rope so we had to hover looking for a place, all the time getting shot at. It was kind of bad from that perspective. It couldn't have been any worse.

The helicopter carried two ninety-foot ropes. The SEALs, wearing heavy leather gloves, grabbed the rope with their hands and slid down as though it were a flexible fireman's pole, about a second apart.

With all that shooting, we were just trying to get the hell out of the helo.

I was to be the last guy of our squad to exit the helo. The worst part of it was there was a guy in front of me, [Lt.] John Koenig, the officer in charge of our group. The guy in front of him, [Petty Officer] Larry Jackson, had got his MX radio caught on the fuel bladder webbing in the back of the helo. So Jackson's holding the rope and trying to get out. Koenig is trying to push him out. I'm trying to push out Koenig and Jackson and the helo is getting shot to hell.

So I said, "Screw this!" I just put my shoulder into Koenig and drove him and Larry out. Finally his MX radio broke off his web belt. Larry went out, John went out, and I just leaped out. I think we just got our ninety-foot fast ropes and there was about three foot of rope on the ground. I was doing about 100 miles an hour down the rope and landed on top of Koenig, knocked the dog shit out of Koenig. John still swears I did it deliberately.

I was weighing 215 and carrying a thousand rounds of 7.62 and an HK-21 [German-made machine gun] and a 9mm pistol as backup. I had a total of 135 pounds of gear on. We knew we weren't moving far so all I carried was bullets and guns. We just had a couple of canteens of water. No food or things like that.

Gormly [Comdr. Robert Gormly, who had taken over as commander of SEAL Team SIX from Richard Marcinko a short time before] was still in the helo. The plan was he would land after everything was secure. The problem was the helo was so shot up and it had to be used to medevac the copilot, who was shot in the leg and the face. So Gormly never actually made it in to the mansion. The next time I saw Gormly was when we got back to the airfield a day or two later.

The securing of the house was relatively uneventful. There were a couple of good shoot-outs but nothing of super significance. I got into one shoot-out when two Cubans or Grenadians jumped out of the bush about twenty yards away and started shooting at me. I was surprised and pissed that they were shooting at me. So I opened up with my HK. Three- to four-round bursts, bullshit! I shot about seventy-five to one hundred rounds. It was just like the *Predator* movie.

We spread out around the house about ten or twenty yards apart and about twenty-five yards away from the house. It was a real pretty place. Beautiful view. There was a hedgerow I kind of cut out and sat in the shade. It was a beautiful October day, a nice comfortable temperature. You couldn't ask for a better day to go to war. If it had been August, it would have been miserable. It would have been 110 degrees.

Did you have any food?

We anticipated it would be only a few hours. I figured, hell, I'm not going to starve. We didn't think about it until a day or so later. Then we were powerful hungry. Our biggest worry was batteries for the radios.

During the first day, one of our guys pissed me off. A bad guy shot an RPG [rocket-propelled grenade] over the top of us. It hit the house and blew up.

Our guy says, "I saw him right over there, probably about a hundred yards away."

"Well, why didn't you shoot him?"

"Well, he was a hundred yards. I didn't figure I could hit him."

Hit him? Hell, I could hit him with a pistol that far.

Most of us stayed in the perimeter during our entire time there. We didn't have anyplace to go. One guy was the relieving watch. He'd come out and you'd go in the house and take a combat nap for an hour.

Duke Leonard, the funniest thing I recall, was he called in a 105 strike 360 degrees around the house, twenty-five meters out, from an AC-130. He's up six to ten grand. [Six thousand to ten thousand feet.]

I'm listening on my radio and I hear Duke pass, "Yeah, call in a 105 strike 360 degrees around the house." I look back to the house. I'm about from here to where that lady is from the house [indicating a woman walking by].

I go, "Hell, I'm twenty-five meters from the house. Holy shit!"

I recall lying down. You could hear the bullets start to go around the house. I was along the driveway in the hedgerow. The branches [from nearby trees] are falling down right around me. So I'm lying down behind a little curb, scared shitless. Well, real concerned. And then I thought, boy are you stupid. They're shooting from above. What are you going to do? So I sat up. I figured at least I'll give less of a target for the plane.

Duke still swears to this day that they were shooting the 105 and I still argue with him. I later talked to the pilot who got the call and he said he wouldn't shoot the 105 that close to U.S. troops. What he did shoot was the 20mm. He zipped it around the house for what seemed like an hour but was probably thirty to sixty seconds.

What Duke was hearing was the 40mm shooting back up from the APCs that had surrounded us, trying to hit the Spectre.

There was one [APC] on my side [of the mansion] less than from here to the road, a hundred yards, seventy-five yards. Later that night, we called in a 20mm strike on him and oh, man, it was eerie.

Needless to say, no one got hit from our side. They did kill something like twenty-three guys later that day on the other side. There were a bunch of guys trying to come up and we called in an AC-130 strike on them. They smoked 'em. They must have shot three thousand rounds of 20mm at them. I don't know if you've ever heard how those things shoot—20mm? God, they're brutal. It just went on and on and on. I'm going, man, I'm glad I'm not on the receiving end of that.

That was in the daytime. The only night shoot I saw was when we called in a strike on an APC on my side. He was probably fifty to seventy-five yards away. He wasn't shooting at us. He was trying to hit the plane. You could hear the plane, kind of see it outlined up there. The plane shot the 20mm at him. Every time one of those rounds hit they kind of give off a spark. Well, he was hitting dead on top of the APC. The Spectre hit the APC so many times it had a hellish glow over the top of it. You could see the bodies getting blown about. Oh, man, it was brutal. They really messed that thing up. It was pretty good from my perspective. I thought it was neat.

There was always something going on. That first morning, the one marine Cobra that got shot down and landed on the beach? Oh, if you want to talk about a heroic job of landing, find that guy. I ran into him a couple of years later and he had a helacious story about how he flew that thing.

The marines are notorious at doing everything doctrinal, follow the book, no variations.

The Cobras were making strafing runs at this building. I remember watching them flying in, always the same pattern. And then they'd do a 360 and come back. They were just doing a donut. I watched the Cobra get hit and head for the shore. As the helo flew over the top of us, I heard this sickening sound. Being a helo pilot, I thought, boy, he's been hit bad. He was doing an auto rotation heading toward the shore. The helo caught fire after he landed. Then we heard what sounded like a huge firefight, but it was the helo caught fire and all the rounds started cooking off. Unfortunately, we just didn't have enough people to send and help.

[Petty Officer] Timmy Prusack was there with us. Real funny guy. The most jovial SEAL you'll ever meet. When the bad guys were coming at us, Timmy came around to each of the positions. He's a big, barrel-chested guy. One of those jovial laughs, ho, ho, ho. He comes up, goes, "Bobby, there's twenty-five guys coming from the other side, ho, ho, ho." I go, "Oh, great, Timmy."

I figured we were going to get overrun. So I took another hundred rounds and linked it up to the machine gun.

"Thanks a lot, Timmy. Thanks for telling me."

Did the soldiers ever attack you?

They never were given the opportunity because Spectre took them out prior to getting to our position.

One of the biggest problems we had was communications. A lot of that was just lack of equipment. Bob Gormly had the comm guy in our helo. But because the helo didn't land, the radioman who had the UHF/SatCom radio never made it. We didn't own all the radios we had wanted or needed. We still had comm, but only with MXs, so we didn't have the ability to talk directly to the Spectre. The comm link had to go back to the airfield, down to the marines, and they would call in the strike. We had our own AC-130—sometimes two—overhead most of the time. Except one time, they both took off because they were running out of fuel. Also, those guys were flying like thirty hours straight. They were ordered to land and get some sleep.

Under the original plan, the SEALs would secure the mansion and they, along with Scoon, his wife, and aides would be taken out by helicopter. But the heavy firing prevented the helicopters from coming in. The SEALs thus remained at the mansion all day Tuesday and Tuesday night, growing increasingly worried about their dwindling ammunition supply. Finally, on Wednesday morning, a marine company reached the SEAL perimeter.

The marines came to our outer perimeter. It was kinda anticlimactic. We just took the people down to the soccer field and flew to the airfield.

The
Innovators

Chapter 44
Birth of the STAB

SEALs and the UDT before them have always prided themselves on their ability to improvise and, often, innovate, creating new pieces of equipment to meet their special needs.

In 1966, after having served in Vietnam, Lt. Roy Boehm, who had been the first commander of SEAL Team TWO, developed an ingenious sensor system for keeping track of the movement of Viet Cong units in the Vietnam delta.

At that time, the U.S. military, in great secrecy, had begun using sensors that could detect the movement of enemy forces. Some of the sensors detected sounds. Others detected reverberations in the earth. Some even "smelled" the scent given off by the human body. But the information the SEALs received from these sensors often came too late to be of use. Boehm wanted real-time intelligence.

Working in California's Sacramento Delta, an area somewhat similar to parts of Vietnam, he set up two sensor vans with a long antenna carried aloft by a balloon. When a sensor detected movement, the signal would be picked up by one van and flashed to screens in the neighboring van.

Two sets of vans were sent to Vietnam and, Boehm says, quickly proved their worth—even if the $1.5 million cost was double his budget.

Boehm's one concern was that the Viet Cong would defeat the system by shooting down the balloons. He concluded that they didn't shoot them down because they came to rely on the balloons as a navigation aid themselves.

Another major contribution was made by Jack Macione. He tells how he developed the STAB (SEAL team assault boat), that proved a mainstay of SEAL operations in Vietnam:

Before the Cuba crisis, we had bought these trimaran hulls—a commercial hull called a Tricat. We were going to stand in this thing and fire 3.55-inch rockets.

After the Cuba mission was canceled, I went to the skipper.

I said, "Hey, the way this is envisioned, it is going to be insanity. We're going to kill more of our own people with back blasts than the guys we're shooting at. I've got the design ability. What I'd like to do is grab a couple of guys and we'll put together a prototype and come up with a good SEAL team boat."

At that time and right to this day there is a void in boats between the rubber boat and the MSSC [thirty-six-foot medium SEAL support craft used in Vietnam] or whatever the hell they are using today.

What I envisioned was a lightweight, outboard-driven boat that would be helicopter-transportable and could go in the back of a C-130.

You could pick it up and move it. Certainly the crew could move it off a sandbar.

It would be very versatile. It would be a package boat, come as a kit. You would configure the boat in a matter of minutes or an hour or so for your mission configuration.

I saw no reason this boat could not have the firepower of a destroyer plus the versatility of a high-performance craft.

We came up with a twenty-foot six-inch trimaran about seven feet wide. It was a good platform. Eventually we had twin 150-hp Mercs on it—Quicksilver racing units. We sent our guys to Mercury outboard motor school to learn to hot-tune these Quicksilver units.

The boat, fully loaded, would get up on the step in about five seconds and she'd do about eighty miles an hour with a full load.

It could be configured in many configurations. I kept the problem items down to a minimum. We didn't have any onboard computers. We didn't have any exotic electronics. It was just pure bones. The boat could carry fifteen or sixteen guys but the crew consisted of a maximum of three people—coxswain, gunner, and what I called the backup man in case one of us gets hit.

We had a flat area six feet by fourteen or fifteen feet. Off to the right side as you look forward we had a little cocoon the coxswain got into and it was a kevlar [armor] cocoon to fend off light fire.

The boat had ten gun positions, pintel mounts. If you had two M60s [machine guns] on each side they could be moved into any position you wanted. Literally, you could have ten guns.

For our main battery, we had configured it so we could actually put six 106mm recoilless rifles on the boat, firing forward. And they could fire all at once. The idea was, if we had to sink shipping at the pier, we'd act like an old PT boat and fire those 106 recoilless.

Now the 106 recoilless has the firepower of a five-inch gun. So we literally had more firepower than a destroyer on this twenty-foot boat.

We needed a fire aiming system. In order to be on target, what I designed was, we had two .30 caliber fixed mounted and bore-sighted machine guns. They fired by a foot lever. The recoilless fired by another foot lever. The .30 calibers fired full tracer. They were bore sighted at five hundred yards or whatever else we wanted. So when the tracers were on target, the 106s were on target.

The coxswain controlled the speed of the boat with his right hand, steered the boat with his left, and fired the .30 calibers or the 106s with his right or left foot.

You aimed the boat by steering left or right and you played the ups and downs of the waves. That twenty-foot boat was bouncing all over the place so it took some training. We took it out and tested it and you could get real good with it. It was just a matter of timing, of training.

One of the problems we had is that the 106 round was going to pass eighteen inches from the coxswain's head. We had plenty of information on what happens when you're behind a recoilless. But we had no information on what happens when you're in front of a recoilless.

So we took it down to Dam Neck [a naval installation south of Virginia Beach, Virginia] to do some testing. We weren't exactly a test lab. We were doing it all by the seat of our pants. We took a tin can, a C-ration can. We stretched a condom over it to kind of simulate an ear drum. We put it in the place of the coxswain's head and we fired the recoilless. It blew that condom right to shreds.

We figured we had a problem. We didn't have the technology. We didn't have the time. We didn't have the knowledge. So I just got in the coxswain's seat, put a football helmet on, or a motorcycle helmet, and I fired. And we found out there was no problem whatsoever for the coxswain.

In the center of the boat at that time we had a .50 caliber [heavy machine gun]. The .50 caliber was more of a problem than the 106. The .50 caliber had a hard crack to it. So you could feel it on your ears.

The coxswain had a helmet with a boom mike and earphones connected to the radio system. The radio was nothing more than our backpack radio. The whole idea of the boat was, if you took a hit and the radio got shot, another backpack could be put in.

If the boat got a hole in it, it was a one-hour patch with fiberglass. If the engine stopped, take it off, put a new one on. If you want to dick with it, do it later. I used to tell guys to take the engine off and throw it in the river. We didn't have time to work on them when you could get new engines for three thousand dollars.

Another innovation we had was a minigun—a 7.62mm minigun. We were the first boat to have one. I literally stole the minigun from a firm out of Washington. I was told by a navy commander if I took that gun he'd court-martial me. We got the gun, through legal ways, but we stole it.

We had the first minigun in the world mounted on a boat. The gun would fire two thousand to four thousand rounds a minute.

Another thing we had: we designed a wire cutter on the front of the boat. One of the dangers I felt was that they could string wire across the stream and it would decapitate you if you were going at high speed and hit that wire. But we never encountered any wire.

The boat was parachute deployable. You kick out the boat with all the gear on board and then the guys go out. We actually knew we could parachute the boat with a crew in it.

We had also designed to do a LOLEX, a low-level extraction, of the boat. [This is a tactic in which a cargo plane flies close to the surface and a load is dropped out the cargo hatch as the plane flies on.] There was no reason we couldn't have LOLEXed that boat onto the water with a crew in it. It is not one of those things you want to practice. You practice it with dummies. But when you have to, you do it.

The boat could do 100 to 150 mph and be okay. We never went that fast. So to LOLEX it at one hundred or ninety knots was well within its capability. It would be like going over a wave. There would be seatbelts. I would have been willing to do it.

Another thing we tested was a helo lift. We were doing one test over Little Creek [the naval amphibious base near Virginia Beach, Virginia]. The helicopter was at about one thousand feet. The boat started fish-tailing. The pilot got panicky and he pickled the boat.

As it fell, it got forward lift and she started flying. It was falling but also moving at a high rate of speed horizontally. It flew in and almost made a perfect landing in the parking lot. But the engine caught a car and she went nose down and destroyed about five or six cars. The boat stayed together so well we eventually used it as a target boat in some of our other testing.

One thing we worried about was, the Viet Cong had B-40 rockets with armor-piercing antitank rounds. We had high-tech armor plate that could be bolted inside the boat. One of the things I inadvertently came up with and didn't realize was, this gave us the first stand-off system for armor-piercing rounds.

What I came up with inadvertently was what ended up on all the armored vehicles. And that was a stand-off or triggering shield. If the round hit us, it would trigger on the fiberglass. The armor plate on the inside would catch all the shrapnel. Because it was triggered six inches away from the armor plate, the whole effect of the shell was defeated.

We took a boat to Dam Neck, put six silhouette targets in it, and we fired rounds at it from recoilless rifles. It was concluded that any injuries sustained in the boat would be from flying debris, not from the round itself.

We took ten STABs to Vietnam. We used them every day and never sustained one injury in the STABs. We had many people shoot B-40s at the boat but never hit it. It was a dot out there when she was running high speed. In fact, except for one occasion, we never even got hit at all. I had the rare opportunity of being there the only occasion where we did take fire.

We were making insertions off a river. I think it was the Mekong. We had put the teams in. It was about seven or eight o'clock the next morning. I got a call on the radio. We had a team in trouble.

They said, "We're surrounded. We're taking automatic fire. Get us out."

We were tied up to a landing ship, out on booms. You walk out on the boom and then down a rope into the boat.

We scrambled. We ran out the boom, down the rope, and kicked it in the ass. I was the coxswain. We're doing seventy or eighty miles an hour, just that quick. We had two M60s, plus the .30 calibers out front.

So I was hauling ass downriver and I was talking to Rick Trani [Lt. Frederick E. Trani] with my boom mike. Rick got killed later. Actually, he didn't get killed. He died of an improper transfusion, wrong blood. He was a new officer on the scene. He had his crew in and he was in trouble.

So coming downriver, I said to Rick, "Give me a flare so I can find you."

"Okay, here it comes!"

I could hear it. It's one of those you bang and they fire.

He says, "Shit!"

"What's the matter?"

"The goddamn thing hit a palm tree. It didn't clear the area."

"Give me another flare."

Bang, he popped another.

"Son of a bitch, it hit the damn palm tree again."

So just at that point I saw the water alive with live rounds.

So I says, "Never mind, Rick, I got you spotted."

What was happening was, he was backing up to the river and the enemy was unloading on him and the bullets were coming through the jungle and into the river.

Wait a minute. I know what I had on board. Besides my two crew members I had a reserve officer who was a combat artist. He had been put on a couple of months of active duty to come over and do artwork on Vietnam. Well he had a .45 strapped to him.

I kicked the STAB in the ass, made a ninety-degree turn right into the embankment. I had my M60 machine gun laying down fire left and right. And Rick's crew came over the bow and into the boat.

The combat artist, he was unloading his .45 into the jungle. He was having a ball.

We got everybody on board, kicked the thing around, put it up on its tail, knocked it down, and headed back upriver.

I turned around to see how everybody was. Across the stern of the boat there was a stitch of machine-gun bullets on the inside of the stern. They walked across the stern and right up onto one engine, went through the cover, hit the flywheel, and just died in the engine. It didn't stop the engine. Those bullet holes were like six or eight inches apart. The bullets had to have come over the bow and had to have come over when we had all the people on board. Not one person got hit. I mean, bullets had to be going between legs, under arms, over shoulders. I mean, it was an absolute miracle nobody got hit.

We had some tricks we would do with the STAB boat.

The Viet Cong would put a sentinel at the mouth of a tributary. A boat like a PBR [patrol boat, river] would come up the river and then turn into a tributary. All the tributaries, for the most part, were one way. You couldn't go up and come out somewhere else.

So the Viet Cong would put a sentry on the tributary, hidden. When the boat went by, he would beat the tom toms, literally, and they would set an ambush where the boat had to come back downriver.

One of my favorite tricks, using the STAB, was to have a Huey [UH-1 helicopter] lift us. Now a Huey could lift the boat and that was part of the design.

It would lift the boat, fully loaded with the crew in it, and they would set us in up a tributary.

Then we would come downriver. Here is a situation where no boat went upriver so there was no alert. And our motors were quiet. The motors were so quiet that, on night insertions when we were idling in, we used to keep a guy back there with one hand on each engine so he could tell the coxswain if either of them shut down. Sometimes those big engines would just shut down and you wouldn't know. That's how quiet they were.

We would come downriver and we could catch the Viet Cong sunbathing, swimming, bullshitting, playing cards, all on the riverbanks. Of course with the miniguns and the M60s we just cleaned clock, real quick. And then we'd haul ass.

Chapter 45
Dogs on Patrol

The SEALs' innovations extended beyond inanimate objects. One of their most intriguing experiments was the use of dogs in Vietnam. Bill Bruhmuller pioneered the use of dogs by SEAL Team TWO and Bo Burwell, who later served with the team in the delta, valued the use of dogs on patrols in the northern part of South Vietnam.

Bruhmuller tells how the SEALs found the dogs a mixed blessing:

When we first went to Vietnam, we didn't know the terrain or anything like that. I got the idea that maybe having a scout dog would be a pretty good idea. We heard about the army using them to get success. Our CO, who was Bill Early, agreed to give it a try.

Because time was so short, the only place we could go for training was the Norfolk Police Department. The trainer was a super guy in the department named Bob Bouchard, who was later killed on a night surveillance. They said sure, they would be glad to take us in, but the only training they could give was attack training and a little bit of surveillance.

They gave me a dog, Prince was his name. He was a good dog, very alert, very aggressive, very easily handled. Prince was a perfect SEAL. He could work hard and he could play hard. He was just one of those dogs that, at the end of the day, he could turn it off. And at eight o'clock in the morning he would go back to work again.

We went through about a six-week training period. When we completed the training, Prince graduated number one. I graduated number two. He was smarter than me.

We brought him back to the team and took him over to Vietnam. We did use him a couple of times, but what we found out in the delta was that it just really made trying to perform your own mission and trying to control the dog, too, very difficult. They needed a little better territory than the territory we were operating in.

But he was great on ambushes. That dog would just lay right there next to you. He would alert five minutes before anybody even came into view.

Some movement or some noise would alert him. He would just look in that direction and you knew someone was coming that way.

There just weren't that many missions we could take him on. But we thought there was still a place for dogs. They just needed to be better trained. So when we came back to the States we did a report on the thing.

Prince was turned over to another handler. That was the beauty of this particular dog. Most attack dogs or dogs of that sort, you can't transfer handlers. But Prince was just that kind of a personality. He could transfer over to another guy. He transferred over to Mike Bailey. Mike took him down to official military training and then took him in country.

That time, the dog did an excellent job. He was wounded once. He saved their platoon on numerous occasions by alerting.

Mike was telling me, one time they took a break and let the dog take a break, just like people do. Prince wandered off a little way and he came back. He was playing with something. He always liked to play with a ball. He came back and he was throwing this hand grenade around. The guys were just scattering!

Someone got it away from him and Prince took off again and came back with another one. They decided maybe this dog has found something. So they followed him and he went right back and they found a large cache of enemy weapons. So Prince had done his job in that respect.

There was one other story on him up in I Corps [the northernmost military area in South Vietnam]. The SEALs were running a point element for a marine group. Mike was at the point. The dog alerted to a couple of sand dunes.

Mike said to the marine in charge, "The dog is alerting to something over here. Hard to tell what it is but we need to go around this way."

The marines elected not to do so. But the SEALs went the other way. The marines all got ambushed.

We ended up with four or five dogs. We parachuted with them, in a harness underneath the reserve chute. The dogs weren't all that crazy about parachuting. When I jumped with Prince, I had to muzzle him.

He would pretty well go anywhere I wanted to go. But he wasn't too cool on jumping out of airplanes. He never really raised hell about it. He was an unusual dog. You could keep him calm. All you had to do was talk to him. Prince would stay calm.

This wasn't going to be his lifestyle, jumping out of airplanes, but it seemed that he accepted it as part of the job. We were still together. He had that confidence in me. If I was doing it, it would be all right.

When you jumped, did he squirm?

Not too much. When I jumped I would try to hold my hands close to his neck and his hind quarters and try to concentrate on jumping and scratching at the same time. He'd squirm a little bit but not much. Once we got out of the blast of the plane and the parachute was open, it was easy to calm him down.

How did you land?

You'd try to do a good PLF [parachute landing fall] so you didn't hurt the dog. We later rigged up a harness where you could lower the dog down so he would land before you did. You could release him. The dog wouldn't run off. He would stay right there.

It was all trial and error, test and evaluation of our own ideas.

Some of the after action reports indicate you had trouble with another dog.

There was one dog that was really spastic. He wasn't very big but he was very skittish, very unpredictable. He would never stay calm on ambush. That was the biggest thing you wanted. If you used a dog for an alert on ambush, you wanted to make absolutely sure he was not going to start barking or start jumping around.

And when the shooting started, you wanted to make sure he would stay calm. This one dog just wouldn't do that. You had to play with the dog to try to control him. He wanted to get out of there. It wasn't the handler's fault. It was just his personality.

Before he began operating with SEALs in the south, Bo Burwell was a hospital corpsman who operated with marine reconnaissance units in the northern part of Vietnam. His experience using dogs was much more encouraging than that of Bruhmuller and others in the delta:

The dogs weren't that effective down south. We used dogs with the recon unit and they were so much more effective up there. Down south, if you got into deep mud, you'd end up carrying that dog. Another way they could help you was with the smell. And if something's been underwater, they're not going to be able to track it.

But up north I have seen these dogs, if the wind was blowing right, I have seen them alert on a signal literally a mile away. You could see the people there. And you would see him zoom in on it.

One dog saved my life on two occasions. His name was King—service number K9–37. He was probably the prima donna of the dogs. That dog was so good, I used to let him curl right up next to me at night. He would never bark or growl. But you would feel him move and you could see where he was looking and know where the threat was at.

One time I was out walking on the point and I had actually walked by—the rest of the patrol was back on the tree line and I had gone out to scout an area. The dog was also working out there. The handler, he could give signals and move that dog.

Apparently I had walked by somebody. But when this guy made a move in the bush, the dog picked up his trail and went in behind him and that dog was on him, boom, just like that.

Did the dog grab him?

He wasn't one of these dogs trained to grab a person by the arm and watch him. There's no contest when you have a 110-pound shepherd and a 120-pound Vietnamese. The dog will win. I think that guy was dead before he hit the ground.

On another occasion, he saved me when he alerted on a booby trap that we probably wouldn't have seen. There were many other occasions when he picked up booby traps.

He later got killed.

I wasn't there when he was killed. They were running a scouting operation for another marine company. They had forced this recon officer to do something that was against his nature. He had been up and down this trail three or four times. The lieutenant had been wounded the day before and they ordered him up there again.

King took the most of a claymore. It was a command-detonated thing and the dog was right on top of it when it fired off. The mine messed up the whole patrol but the majority of the shot hit the dog. In his last action, he saved some people.

Chapter 46
What Do You Wear to War?

One thing most military people never have to worry about is what to wear. Someone decides on the uniform of the day and that's it. But the SEALs are different. They have a long tradition of adapting both their clothing and weapons to the demands of the job they are given.

But, among the SEALs there are still vigorous differences of opinion on what the well-dressed frogman wears to war. Three veterans of the war in Vietnam told about their own preferences.

Command Master Chief Rudy Boesch, who arrived in Vietnam right after the Tet offensive of 1968, takes the most conventional approach:

Some of the guys wore Levis. But, to begin with, you're always wet. You put a pair of Levis on and get 'em wet and try to bend your leg. You can't do it. You lose all your flexibility.

Nobody in our platoon wore Levis. We wore the regular jungle greens. That's the best clothes we had. Everybody wore boots. We just ain't used to walking around barefoot. You're stumbling over stumps, bumping into trees. It's dark out there at night; real dark.

We'd come in off the river at night. It would look just black. We'd plow into the trees with a Mike boat or a PBR, go right into the trees until the boat hit land and then we'd jump off. As soon as we jumped off, we'd get right down in case the boats had to shoot, in case somebody was in there. And then we'd just lay there for half an hour or an hour.

We wouldn't move. The boat would back off and leave and we'd just stay there and listen, make sure nobody's around or heard us. If we thought we were compromised, we'd call the boat right back in and leave.

Some SEALs said they went barefoot because, if they encountered a wire attached to a booby trap, they could feel it.

If you feel it, it's too late.

Bo Burwell was one of those who had a different answer to the question of what to wear:

What did you wear?

Lots of times I wore camouflage outfits. But they made so much noise, and the mosquitoes could bite through them. I started carrying blue jeans with me. I'd wear those for operations. The huge pockets [in the clothing issued by the navy], whenever you came up out of the water, they made so much noise. And when your legs rub together, it makes noise.

I'll demonstrate. [He rubbed his legs together.] At night, that noise right there, you can hear that seventy-five meters away. You can hear a sound and you can point right back at it. You can go by something and without even looking, you can put your finger right back on it.

A lot of times they would shoot at sound. That right there could get you killed. Moving out there at nighttime, the quieter you can move, the better off you are.

And that's the reason a lot of us went barefoot. I've done a lot of barefoot work. If we got into briars and stuff, I had shoes—coral shoes—I could put on. I carried one in each hip pocket.

For walking on the point and moving in and out through mud, you couldn't hardly beat going barefoot because of the quietness you could move with. You never make a sound, hardly. If the ground has been dug out, you can feel the soft areas where there might be a booby trap or a mine.

I carried blue jeans with a big heavy set of suspenders to hold them up. I wore them kind of tight. And then I wore one of the blue and gold shirts, a heavy T-shirt.

I carried my machine-gun ammunition in belts, usually about a thousand rounds, and then I had one of these camouflaged vests that

I wore over that ammunition. I'm sure you've seen the famous picture of the guy with the bandanna on his head and the belts of ammunition. Why in the world camouflage yourself if you're going out there with this big mirror? I'm sure that was probably for picture purposes. That man in the picture, Tom Keith, was a top-notch performer.

Did you wear underclothes?

No. Why? You're going to be wet all the time anyway. I didn't wear anything that I didn't need. And underclothing was just something that kept you wet and gave you jock itch.

What about panty hose?

I know of some people who did that to keep the leeches off. I've been eaten up by the leeches up in the mountains. Of course you have a different leech up there than in the wetlands. I had thirty-one leeches on one leg one time, when we were sitting in an ambush. You could put insect repellent on them and they would drop right off.

They were bad up north. They weren't as big as the water leeches and they were a brown color instead of the blue.

Leeches, they would give you an uncomfortable feeling. I've been sitting in ambushes and you could feel those things getting on you. Of course in an ambush you don't even blink an eye. If you start swatting mosquitoes or fighting leeches, a guy out there may not know just what you are. But once you swat, he knows. He might have you right in his sniper's scope.

There were other things there that bothered me a lot more than the leeches and mosquitoes. I kind of tuned them out.

In the Rung Sat, you would be sitting out there and you would see all this trash because of the swiftness of the water and all of a sudden you see this log going this way [indicating upstream].

They had those crocs there. They lose quite a few people to crocs in the delta region each year. In fact we had a West Coast guy attacked by a croc. And he whipped it.

One of our groups shot one of them. It was sixteen–eighteen feet long. Big. They definitely demanded respect.

If you saw one coming, at that time you stop worrying about what's that over there and you keep your gun on this thing in case it turns toward you.

There were other things over there. I've been stalked by tigers around Khe Sanh and the A Shau Valley region. [Where he operated as a medical corpsman with marine units.] Wild boar was another thing that was very difficult.

Another thing we had to worry about down in the southern region was dogs and geese. They were one of the best early warning systems that made it difficult to sneak up on people. And believe it or not, hogs. They're more intelligent than a dog, I guess. I have actually seen hogs go in the house and wake people up. You're sitting there watching with binoculars and you can't believe what you're seeing. This thing actually alerted them.

Those geese, they did double duty. They eat the larva of certain insects that would damage the rice crops and if you get a goose excited, you never had so much noise in your life. They'll tell everybody in the world where you're at.

Thomas Holmes, another medical corpsman, had an unpleasant experience that resulted in a quick change in what he wore on patrol:

We used to wear Levis with the button front. I liked Levis better because they were thicker material. They fit better than the baggy fatigues and you didn't always have this shh shh shh [rubbing sound].

They had pockets, but you usually wore your equipment up high anyway, rather than trying to reach down when you were in the water. It was also harder for mosquitoes to bite through that than the other material.

Some SEALs said they didn't wear jeans because they were uncomfortable when they got wet.

I think it depended on the type of operations and the duration. Ours were half a day to a day, as opposed to some that might be in the jungle for a long time.

In the UDT and SEAL teams back then, you just didn't wear skivvies. So here we are operating with Levis. And that's when leeches got in and nailed my crotch.

On one evolution we were working with OV-10s and Sea Wolves. We were going on a skirmish line through a hootch complex to another hootch complex and then we were going to extract. And, being the radio operator, I was working two Wolves and two OV-10s.

They were all circling. This was at night and they all had the same lights. You couldn't tell a plane from a helicopter.

We had gone through one hootch complex and were moving to the next one. Well, there was a third hootch complex and our air assets were looking at two different ones than we were looking at.

We called for a strafing run to hose them down before we assaulted them. The OV-10s were working one area and the Wolves were working another and the assets were getting screwed up. We're all coming on line. Everybody is looking forward and figuring we're going to watch this show, like being at the movies. And all of a sudden it opens up behind us.

How far?

We were a safe distance. We had let them know we were leaving our first objective and moving toward the second. So we were in between the hootch complexes.

We were basically walking through a swamp up to these guys. That's when the leeches got me. As we patrolled in, they nailed me and it was pretty painful. At first I thought it was a snake that got me. I pulled it away.

On extraction, I asked if anybody had any mosquito repellent. I had been giving lectures on leech bites, never having had one. My first reaction was to do what I had been teaching.

Rick Nepper, he was one of these guys, if you wanted something, he would have it. If you needed a kitchen sink, he would have it. Good old Nepper whips out a whole bottle.

I ripped open my Levis and just hosed them down. I pulled like three of them off. I had two right on the penis and three right at the head of the scrotum. I've got pictures of it. It looks like a claymore went off in my lap.

After I ripped it open and hosed it down, it's like a cartoon where you see the road runner and the coyote and the coyote realizes he's done something really stupid? That's when it was instant flame.

You thought the insect repellent would get rid of them?

Well, it did. They flat came off. But it got me too.

Rick Nepper, he was on his second tour and he used to wear panty hose. He said they would keep the leeches off and we all razzed him. But after that experience, that's when I went to panty hose. The leeches were actually coming in between the buttons.

Did the panty hose prevent them from getting in?

I guess so. I didn't have any more problems.

Chapter 47
SEALs: A New Generation

SEALs gained their first—and lasting—fame in Vietnam. But most of those who served in SEAL Teams ONE and TWO in that decade-long baptism of fire have now retired, and a new generation is learning how to fight in new places: Panama, the Persian Gulf, Somalia, Bosnia—wherever the nation needs a small, hard-hitting commando force trained to strike from the sea.

In January 1991, "Joe Baxter," a twenty-one-year-old hospitalman third class, was part of a unit from SEAL Team ONE assigned to Naval Special Warfare Task Group Central, stationed at Ras al-Mishab in Saudi Arabia, about forty miles south of the border with Iraqi-occupied Kuwait.

When Baxter (he asked that his real name not be used because he might later be involved in secret SEAL operations) returned home to Coronado, he enrolled in an English class at the local community college. As a class assignment, he wrote the following account of his introduction to war as one of the new generation of SEALs in the first U.S. land combat operation of the Persian Gulf War on 31 January 1991:

I jumped from the top rack onto the cold linoleum floor in a fearful panic. My heart was pounding against my chest. I instinctively reached for my weapon, inspected it to make sure both my CAR15 assault rifle and the attached M203 grenade launcher were loaded. I slung the multipurpose weapon over my shoulder before putting on my gas mask and boots. I didn't have to check my Sig Sauer 9mm pistol; it was loaded on my hip as it had been for the past three months.

The high-pitched scream of the missile raid siren was deafening as my three roommates and I scrambled out our door and into the barracks hallway. We made it outside and into the underground bunker in less than a minute and a half. I grabbed the handheld Motorola radio and listened to the watch officer relay his missile sightings from his observation post on top of the one-hundred-foot grain silo.

"Five missiles incoming. Estimate thirty seconds to impact . . . five, four, three, two . . ." The watch officer took cover before they hit. The explosions were close. The bunker walls were buffeted as the pressure from the blast inflated my lungs as if they were balloons about to burst. The explosions were so loud they hurt my ears even with my hands cupped tightly over them. The Iraqi missiles hit closer every time. This time, a missile exploded only fifty yards from the grain silo. There won't be many volunteers for the next watch up there!

The morning following the attack of the loud-but-not-so-accurate rockets, the four of us left for the border. We were excited and ready. The whole idea of war was new to us, and we were thrilled to be living this adventure. My fire team had the next three-day shift on the border, and I was looking forward to it. Even though we would be closer to the enemy, it was more peaceful there. At the border, the menacing missiles only streak overhead like toy bottle rockets as they make their way toward the targets farther south.

Upon arrival at the sand-swept border station, we relieved our buddies in Fire Team Four. They looked tired and worn but said things had been quiet, except for the usual radio warnings of a possible raid by Iraqi assault forces. We joked about the Iraqi troops not knowing the difference between an assault force and a herd of camels. Then we warned our buddies to wear ear plugs when they went to sleep that night. They thanked us and gave us the finger as they drove south in one of two humvees we named our battle wagons, due to the .50-caliber machine gun they each sported. [The high-mobility, multipurpose, wheeled vehicle—abbreviated HMMWV and familiarly called the humvee—is an all-terrain vehicle, successor to the jeep.]

For the next three nights we would trade off sleeping, two at a time, to keep a twenty-four-hour vigil on the border zone nearest the Persian Gulf. We would notify the southerly bases of those pesky bottle rockets headed in their direction and attempt to call in air support to destroy the mobile launchers. We also reported any enemy movement in our area of responsibility, which usually consisted of a few truck convoys and the monotonous ritual of the Iraqi guards across the border praying to Allah five times a day.

It was the third night of our rotation on the border. Things were heating up at other border stations. Several marines were killed a few kilometers inland where two Iraqis posed as defectors and then signaled approximately fifty men to ambush the unsuspecting marines. Nightly bouts of ineffective small-arms fire were the norm for inland border stations, but our station on the coast had remained calm.

We were all awake that last night, talking about how bored we were, when a mortar flare suddenly illuminated the border station nearest us. I was peering through binoculars at the other station when I suddenly realized our station was illuminated. I looked up and saw a mortar flare slowly parachuting down, casting odd, dancing shadows all around.

"Hey, Tony, what the hell is going on?" I whispered to our sniper.

"I don't know, Doc. Maybe we should pack up some of this gear just in case."

"Yeah, I think you're right. I'll get ready to go."

Suddenly we heard the rumble of tracked vehicles, traveling at high speeds, closing in on us from the north. We all instinctively dove to the ground, a result of endless training. As I hit the ground, the Iraqis opened fire. I found an Iraqi armored personnel carrier in the crosshairs of my M203 grenade launcher. Tony grabbed a handheld antitank missile and took aim. Wayne and Joey did the same.

My safety was off, and I was ready to fire. But I didn't. None of us did. Orange tracers as big as beer bottles were zipping right over our heads, but we knew [the Iraqis] couldn't see our camouflaged bodies. If we fired back, it was sure to bring a hail of devastating fire directly into us.

I knew at that point we were going to attempt to slip out of this situation as fast as we could. I crawled up to the radio to notify our base that the Iraqis had decided to pay Saudi Arabia a visit, but I couldn't reach anyone on my first two tries, and I wasn't about to wait around for someone to answer. My buddies were on their hands and knees already gathering our gear. We had enough gear for an entire platoon and only four guys to load it. I disconnected the radio from the eight-foot high-gain antenna as bullets continued to whiz over my head. I quickly crawled toward the humvee with the radio in one hand and two antitank missiles in the other. We couldn't leave anything for the Iraqis.

My buddies were waiting for me in the humvee. Tony was in the driver's seat and I jumped in next to him, yelling at him to go! He slammed his foot on the gas pedal and sent the humvee bouncing over a twenty-foot sand dune. We kept the lights off, hoping the Iraqis wouldn't see us attempting to escape. We were all screaming at Tony, telling him which way to go, and he was screaming at us, telling us to shut the hell up.

Tank rounds began to explode near us. The Iraqis had seen us, and their rounds were getting closer. Tony swerved left and right, dodging explosions as the flying dirt splattered against the windshield. It was exactly like a scene from a war movie I had seen: total chaos and danger. But somehow we were escaping. I was breathing so hard my lungs stung from the rush of cold air that I kept sucking in. We stopped at an army safe house a few miles south of our bunker to warn them of the attack, but they had seen the one-sided firefight and were already evacuating. Tony kept the speedometer pegged until we reached the first Saudi checkpoint, about five miles south of the border. We warned the wide-eyed Saudi guards of the Iraqi assault headed their way, then drove further south to our base.

The entire base was mobilizing for a quick evacuation if the Iraqis decided to continue south. We left our gear packed while Wayne briefed the skipper on what had just happened. We finally got word to stand down, so my buddies and I headed back to the barracks for a couple hours' sleep.

I still had a surplus of adrenaline running through my body as I lay on my rack and stared at the ceiling, recalling what had become a blur of memory. As the adrenaline diluted itself, I began to question our actions. Maybe we should have held up behind a sand dune and attempted to destroy a tank or two. We might have been able to stop the entire assault.

But we knew the loss of our hole-in-the-ground bunker would not turn the tide of the war, and we also knew we had no immediate air support. I guess that was our rationale for the actions we took, but I still wondered if we did the right thing.

I began to think about war in general. It was so different from what we consider a normal experience, but it was made up of many incidents that are very normal and only a few that are not. War became more of a complicated job to me than an adventure. Slowly reliving the experience kept me up the rest of the night.

The Iraqi forces were repelled the next day by U.S. armor and air support, while my buddies and I readied ourselves for future operations. It was reported to us that more than ten tanks and multiple armored personnel carriers had rolled right through our position. Good thing we left when we did. Still pondering what had happened the night before, I inspected my gear for the next mission.

Chapter 48
Letting Go

Mike Bennett served in both UDT and SEAL units and remained in the teams until 1990. And then, thousands of miles and twoscore years from Vietnam, he had a strange experience. He tells what happened:

This was in 1990 or 1991. It wasn't long after I had retired in March 1990.

My wife, Nina, and I went in this art store in Washington and I saw this painting—*Reflections in the Wall*. It's a picture of a fellow at the wall at the Vietnam Memorial. He's leaning against the wall with one hand and, instead of seeing names, you see the faces of people looking out from the wall.

But the reflections, the faces in it, were not looking at him. They were looking straight out at me. And they were mad! The faces looked mad. I recognized a couple of them. They were mad because we haven't let them go.

All the guys in the teams that got killed, in our minds, we just put them on another cruise. When we were in country, they were back stateside. When we would go back stateside, they were in country. We never really let them go.

And the hair on the back of my neck stood up. I couldn't breathe. I couldn't take my eyes off it. I broke out in a sweat and then I had to get out of the store. And I walked out.

They were telling me to let them go.

And then I finally decided, that's what I've got to do and that's what they're telling me to do. I said, okay. And I thought about all the guys in the teams that I knew that had died and were killed in Vietnam.

And I said, okay, they're dead. They're gone. It's over. And that's when the faces turned around and looked back at the guy in the picture. And that, I believe, was a real turning point for me, just turning it all loose.

I could breathe and it was like a huge weight, the whole world, came off of my shoulders.

Had you been to the wall itself before this?

Yeah.

And you hadn't had this kind of reaction looking at the names of your friends?

Right. Because the reflections—the faces—weren't there. Later on, after I had come to terms with it, Nina bought the painting for me. It's hanging in the upstairs family room. I look at it every once in a while and it's a relief. It's a relief.

Isn't it strange that a picture would trigger that kind of reaction when the wall itself didn't?

We all have to have our triggers, somewhere. A lot of these guys just haven't found theirs yet. And they hang on and hang on until they die. They never really get over it. I'm not sure why that happens. I'm not sure whether it's because they're weak or maybe it's because they were in too deep.

Glossary

AC-47   A twin-engine gunship, based on the DC-3 commercial plane, used in Vietnam. Nicknamed Spooky or Puff the Magic Dragon.

AFF   Accelerated free fall, a technique in which an instructor holds on to a trainee and instructs him as they fall from high altitude before opening their parachutes.

AK-47   Infantry rifle, comparable to the American M16, developed by the Soviet Union and originally used by communist forces, including the Viet Cong and North Vietnamese. Now in wide use throughout the world.

AO   Area of operations of a military unit.

APC   Armored personnel carrier.

APD   A destroyer converted for use as a small troop carrier.

Apollo   The U.S. moon-landing program and the spacecraft used.

AR-15   Early version of the M16 rifle used by U.S. forces.

ASW   Antisubmarine warfare.

AWOL   Absent without leave.

B-40   Rocket launcher.

Barndance card   A report on operations kept by SEAL platoons in Vietnam.

Black Ponies   OV-10 Bronco fixed-wing planes used in Vietnam.

BOQ   Bachelor officers' quarters.

Boston Whaler   A small, high-speed boat used in Vietnam and later in the Grenada operation. Still in limited use today.

Bright Light   Code name for SEAL efforts to free American prisoners in Vietnam.

Bullfrog   The longest-serving SEAL.

C4   Plastic explosive.

Can Tho   City in the far south of the Vietnamese delta where SEALs often operated.

capewells   Parachute quick-release fasteners.

cast and recovery   The procedure for dropping a SEAL into the water from a helicopter or boat and picking him up again.

CCT   Combat control team, an air force unit that controls air traffic under combat conditions.

claymore   A directional mine that can be detonated by a soldier some distance away. It sprays a fan-shaped area with projectiles with a lethal range of more than fifty yards.

Cobra   Helicopter gunship.

Combat Talon   MC-130 combat transport plane used to insert, resupply, and retrieve SEALs and other special operations forces.

CTF-116   Commander Task Force 116. In Vietnam, a unit responsible for enforcing curfews on the water, interdicting Viet Cong infiltration, preventing taxation of waterborne traffic by the Viet Cong, and countering enemy movements and supply efforts on inland waters. TF 116.1 was assigned duties in the Mekong Delta. TF 116.2 was responsible for the Rung Sat Special Zone.

DevGru   Naval Special Warfare Development Group. A major SEAL command that provides centralized management for the test, evaluation, and development of technology applicable to naval special warfare forces.

DMZ   Demilitarized zone between North and South Vietnam.

Dong Tam   Army base near My Tho in the Vietnamese delta, from which SEALs operated.

Draeger   German-made underwater breathing apparatus, also known as a rebreather, in which carbon dioxide is passed through a canister of lime and cleansed. This, plus an oxygen cylinder, provides a fresh supply of oxygen to a swimmer.

driver   In a two-man swim team, the driver memorizes the course and uses a compass to chart the course underwater.

E&E   Acronym for escape and evasion.

Flintlock   Name for annual special operations exercises in Europe.

Fulton sky hook   System in which one or more persons attach themselves to a line that is lifted by a balloon and snagged by an airplane, which then lifts the men from the ground to the plane. It is named for Robert E. Fulton, its inventor.

Gemini   Second phase of the man-on-the-moon program and the space capsule used.

Grayback   USS *Grayback,* a diesel-powered submarine converted for use by frogmen. On its deck were two large hangars originally designed to carry the Regulus missile.

HAHO   High altitude, high opening parachute jump.

HALO   High altitude, low opening parachute jump.

HSSC   Heavy SEAL support craft used in Vietnam.

Hell Week   An intensive period of physical and mental testing during SEAL training.

HH-60   Blackhawk troop-carrying helicopter.

Huey   UH-1 helicopter used in Vietnam, and since, as a troop carrier and gunship.

I Corps   Pronounced "Eye Corps." The northernmost of the four military regions into which the U.S. divided its Vietnam operations. SEALs operated primarily in the far south of the country in IV Corps, the south-central area in III Corps, and in I Corps near the border with North Vietnam and Laos.

IBS   Inflatable boat, small. A rubber boat capable of carrying seven men. Propelled by paddle or a small outboard engine.

Jackstay   Name for the operation in which SEAL and UDT units first operated with other military forces in a major operation in Vietnam. It was held between 26 March and 7 April 1966.

K-bar   A combat knife used by SEALs.

Kampf swimmers   German frogmen.

Khmer Rouge   Communist rebels in Cambodia.

Kit Carson scouts   Units in Vietnam made up of former Viet Cong.

LAAW   Light antiarmor weapon.

lai day   Vietnamese for "come over here," used by SEALs to stop and question suspects.

LCM   Landing craft, medium, also known as a Mike boat, used for river operations and beach assaults.

LCPL   Landing craft, personnel, light.

LDNN   *Lien Doc Nguoi Nhia,* Vietnamese for "soldiers who fight under the sea," the Vietnamese counterpart of the SEALs.

Lock out   To put a diver on a submarine into an antechamber that is then flooded before the diver leaves the ship.

LPD   Landing platform, dock.

LSSC   Light SEAL support craft.

LOLEX   Low-level extraction, a tactic in which cargo is dropped from an open hatch as the plane flies on.

LST   Landing ship, tank.

LZ   Helicopter landing zone. A hot LZ is a landing zone under enemy fire.

M80   A small explosive device like a cherry bomb, used for signaling swimmers underwater.

M16   Rifle used by American forces.

M60   Light man-portable machine gun. Designed to be fired from a tripod or pintel, it can be fired from the hip.

M79   Grenade launcher.

MACSOG   Military Assistance Command Studies and Observation Group, the unit that carried on covert operations in Southeast Asia during the Vietnam conflict. SEALs were often involved in secret operations under MACSOG command.

MACV   Military Assistance Command Vietnam, the American command.

MC-130   *See* Combat Talon.

McGuire rig   An emergency procedure in which one or more persons are attached to a line dangling from a helicopter and transported while hanging below the craft.

Mercury   The first phase of the man-on-the-moon program and the space capsule used.

Midrats   Midnight rations. A meal served in the middle of the night.

Mike boat   Landing craft, medium.

MSSC   Thirty-six-foot medium SEAL support craft used in Vietnam.

My Tho   City in the central Vietnamese delta, an area where SEALs often operated.

NCDU   Naval combat demolition units, originally trained during World War II to clear the way for landings in Europe. Many of the NCDU men later became members of underwater demolition teams in the Pacific but one small unit, operating in the South Pacific, retained the NCDU designation.

NVA   Acronym for the North Vietnamese Army.

O₂ table   A table that tells a diver how long he can safely remain at various depths while breathing pure oxygen.

OAS   Obstacle avoidance sonar, part of the navigation system in a SEAL delivery vehicle.

OINC   Officer in charge.

Operation Thunderhead   Code name for an unsuccessful effort to free American captives in North Vietnam in June 1972.

OpSec   Operational security.

PBR   Patrol boat, river.

PLF   Parachute landing fall. The technique used by parachutists to spread the shock upon landing.

Puff the Magic Dragon   Nickname for the AC-47 gunship used in Vietnam.

Regulus   Submarine-launched cruise missile developed in the 1960s. When it was phased out, the USS *Grayback,* a diesel submarine designed to carry the missile, was converted for use by the frogmen.

RPG   Rocket-propelled grenade.

RPG7   A type of rocket-propelled grenade.

ruff puffs   Nickname for Vietnamese regional force soldiers.

Rung Sat Special Zone   *See* RSSZ.

RSSZ   Rung Sat Special Zone. An area between Saigon and the South China Sea where the SEALs conducted many of their operations, keeping open shipping lanes to Saigon.

SADM   Special atomic demolition munition. A forty-three-pound device small enough to be carried by a parachutist or delivered by a swimmer.

SAR   Search and rescue and the designation for a helicopter involved in such operations.

SatCom   *See* UHF/SatCom radio.

scrubber   The lime canister that removes carbon dioxide from exhaled gas in a closed-circuit diving rig.

SCUBA   Self-contained underwater-breathing apparatus. Applied most often to the air tanks used by recreational divers but also applicable to more sophisticated systems used by SEALs.

SEAL   Name for navy frogmen, derived from Sea, Air, Land.

SDV   SEAL delivery vehicle, known earlier as swimmer delivery vehicle. A small vehicle capable of carrying up to eight combat swimmers.

They are not shielded from the cold of the sea and must use breathing rigs.

Sea Wolf   Navy UH-1 helicopter gunships that often supported SEAL operations in Vietnam.

Seafloat   A SEAL base near Can Tho, in the southernmost part of Vietnam. It was based on barges anchored in a river. The base was later moved ashore and was known as Solid Anchor.

slick   A UH-1 Huey helicopter without the armament carried by a gunship.

Solid Anchor   A SEAL base near Can Tho, replacing the barge-based Seafloat.

Spectre   An AC-130 four-engine gunship carrying a 105mm howitzer and other guns. It succeeded the earlier AC-47 gunship.

SpecWar   Naval Special Warfare Command.

Spider hole   A concealed foxhole employed by VC or NVA soldiers.

Spooky   Nickname for the AC-47 gunship. Also known as Puff the Magic Dragon.

STAB   SEAL team assault boat.

Starlight Scope   A night vision device that intensifies ambient light.

static line jump   A parachute jump in which a line attached to the plane pulls the person's rip cord, opening the chute. Also known as a rope jump.

Stoner machine gun   A light rapid-fire machine gun often carried by SEALs in Vietnam. It was not issued to other troops because of the care needed to maintain it properly.

Swedish   Swedish-made light machine gun used by SEALs in Vietnam.

T-10 Area   The northeastern section of the Rung Sat Special Zone, an area so dangerous that few Americans, except for SEALs, entered it.

T&E   Test and evaluation.

TOC   Tactical operations center.

turtle back   Term used when a swimmer lies on his back on the surface, swimming slowly and conserving his energy.

UCMJ   Uniform Code of Military Justice.

UDT   Underwater demolition team, the name given to navy frogmen in World War II in the Pacific. The first SEALs were drawn from UDT ranks and the UDT units were incorporated into the SEALs in 1983.

UHF/SatCom radio   A radio capable of using both ultra high frequency and satellite communications channels.

Uzi   An Israeli-made light machine gun.

VC   Viet Cong, local military units in South Vietnam allied with North Vietnam.

VCI   Viet Cong infrastructure.

Viet Minh   The Vietnamese force that opposed the French.

wet suit   A rubberized suit that helps keep a swimmer warm even though it is permeable to water.

XO   Executive officer. Second in command in any command.

Index

America, USS, 227
A Shau Valley, 313
Aberdeen Proving Ground, 37
AC-47 gunship, 89
Achille Lauro, 227, 228
Adams, R. F., 270, 271
Admiralty Islands, 13, 14, 17
AFF (accelerated free fall), 277, 278
Aitape, 14
Anderson, Lloyd G., 13
Angkor Wat, 174, 175
Antoine, Frank, 144–46
Apollo 11, 54
Apollo 12, 58
Apollo 13, 58
Apollo 14, 54–56
Armstrong, William J., 13
Atkinson, Solomon D., 87
Australia, 13

Bahrain, 64, 196
Bailey, Larry, 109–11, 117–21
Bailey, Mike, 307
Baltic Sea, 231–33, 236, 237, 246
Banfield, Roger C., 62, 63
Barndance card, 88, 90, 91, 115, 162
Barnes, Jim, 73, 76
Bassac River, 116
Beck, William G., 168
Beirut, 289, 291
Bennett, Michel, 54, 155, 195, 321
Bent, Christopher O., 51

Berry, Fred T., 202–4
Biak, 17
Binh Thuy, 123, 134, 147
Birkey, Sam, 214, 216, 217
Birtz, Pierre, 38
Black Ponies, 134, 169
Blackhawk helicopter, 292
Boehm, Roy, 299
Boesch, Rudy, 38, 258, 262, 311
Boesch, Marjorie E., 262
Borneo, 13, 17, 20
Bosiljevac, T. L., 1
Bosnia, 316
Boston Whaler, 73, 192, 284
Bouchard, Bob, 307
Boynton, Mike, 38, 39, 105
Bracken, Tommy, 198
Braly, Sam W., 112, 113, 120
Brewton, John C., 85–88, 91–101
Bright Light, 165
Brown, Rick, 188, 192
Bruhmuller, William N., II, 33, 43, 112–18, 306, 310
Bryson, A. Y., 96, 98, 99
Bucher, Lloyd M., 203
BUD/S (basic underwater demolition/SEALs training), 140, 190
Bump, Charles, 40, 199
Burwell, Lowell E., 85, 91, 94–96, 100, 309, 312
Butcher, Kenneth, 288

C-4 explosive, 154, 166, 203
Camau, 95
Callahan, John, 73

Cambodia, 173, 175, 176, 184, 185
Camp McGill, 32
Can Tho, 114, 117
Cape Kennedy, 48, 51
Carlock, Rocky, 276
Carter, Jimmy, 226
Cavala, USS, 225
China, 33, 86, 96, 150, 151
Chinese, 30, 33, 34
Chinnampo, 30
Cho Lach, 128, 129
Christopher, Robert D., 97–99
Chuting Stars, 251, 252
CIA, 39, 40, 201
Clapp, Roger, 132, 133
Clark, Robert P., 85, 97, 255
Clendenning, Robert, 199
Combat Talon, 232
Conger, Bob, 210, 214
Coral Sea, USS, 227
Coronado, 28, 29, 75, 123, 128,
    131, 195, 198, 220, 223, 227,
    252, 253, 270, 272
Cousins, James C., 198, 199
Crumbo, Kim H., 138, 139
CTF-116, 127
Cua Viet River, 159

d'Avout, François, 230, 232, 246
Da Nang, 71, 159, 160, 165
Dam Neck, 301, 303
Das Boot, 237
Davis, Hershel, 2, 6, 170
Dawson, William L., 11
DevGru (Naval Special Warfare
    Development Group), 275, 276
Devine, John A., 23, 24
Devine, David E., 125, 126

DeVries, Cornelius C., 13
Dien Bien Phu, 183, 202
DMZ, 67, 70, 71
dogs, 36, 88, 306–10, 314
dolphins, 195–97
Dominican Republic, 37, 42
Dong Tam, 107
Dow, Neil G., 48
Draeger breathing apparatus,
    233, 234, 246, 252
Dry, Melvin, 206, 210–13, 215,
    216, 219
dry deck shelter, 207

Early, Bill, 73, 306
East Germany, 239
Eckernförde, 246
Edwards, Tom, 206, 213, 214,
    216, 217, 218
El Centro, Calif., 278
82d Airborne Division, 37
Ellis, Doug, 96
Eskridge, Harrison G., 13
Esmoil, Caleb, 244

Farmer, Lance G., 138, 139, 140,
    167
fast-roping, 243
Fetzko, Frank, 188
fishnets, 32, 33
Fisher, Robert, 25
Flying Fish, USS, 201
Flynn, Cathal, 198
Flynn, Frank, 136, 203
Folman, James J., 98
Fort Pierce, 12–14, 22, 29, 111
Fox, James Earl, 254, 269
Fox, Ronald G., 111, 112, 117

frogman, 6
Fulton, Robert E., Jr., 253, 254, 270–72
Fulton sky hook, 253, 269

Gallagher, Robert T., 38, 103–6, 115, 117, 120
Gemini, 47–49, 51
Glorietta Bay, 198, 199
Gormly, Robert A., 121, 198, 276, 292, 295
Grabowski, Ted, 134
Grayback, USS, 200, 207–12, 214, 216–19, 224
Greenland, 35
Grenada, 277, 283, 289, 291, 292
Grissom, Virgil I., 47, 49
Gulf War, 196

HAHO (high altitude, high opening), 259, 273, 275, 279
Haiphong, 200, 202, 206, 220
Haise, Fred, Jr., 59
HALO (high altitude, low opening), 252, 256, 267, 273
Hamilton, William, 195
Hawkins, Thomas, 159, 162, 187
Hell Week, 29, 140
HMMWV, 317, 319
Hoist, USS, 228
Hollandia, 17
Holmes, Thomas, 314
Hornet, USS, 54
Hulse, Joe, 258
humvee. *See* HMMWV

Inch'on, 31, 33
Iwo Jima, USS, 62

Jackson, Larry, 292
Janecka, Stan, 257
Japanese, 11, 16, 18, 21–26, 32, 75
Johnson, Lyndon B., 37

Kaine, Francis Riley, 11, 13, 16, 19
kamikaze, 18, 32
Kampf swimmers, 231, 240, 246
Kauffman, Draper L., 12, 22, 26
Keith, Roy, 147
Keith, Thomas H., 98, 313
Khe Sanh, 313
Khmer Rouge, 173, 175–85
Khy Hak, 174–78, 182, 183
Kiel, 246
King (dog), 309, 310
Kit Carson Scouts, 136
Klinghoffer, Leon, 229
Kochey, Fred, 111
Koenig, John, 292
Kompong Thom, 173–76, 178
Kopeln, 232
Korean War, 28–30, 34
Kurit, Cheryl, 100
Kuwait, 316

Lai day, 87, 127, 133
LDNN, 144
Leap Frogs, 251, 252, 275
leeches, 313
LeMoyne, Irve C., 199
Leonard, Lt. Wellington, 290, 294
Leyte, 17
Libya, 223
limpet mine, 224
Lippe, Brian, 227
Little Bit (dolphin), 195, 197, 198

LOLEX (low-level extraction), 302, 303
Lovell, James A., Jr., 59
Luksik, Jack, 67, 144
lunar module (LM), 59
Lundberg, Kevin, 285, 288
Lutz, John, 206, 210, 212–14
Lynch, Frank, 24, 26

MacArthur, Douglas, 16, 17, 33
MacDill Air Force Base, 264
Macione, Jack, 35, 37, 43, 149, 153, 171, 266, 300
MACSOG (Military Assistance Command Studies and Observation Group), 165
MACV (Military Assistance Command Vietnam), 149
Maguire, Joseph, 231–40, 242–47
Marcinko, Richard, 109–22, 255, 272, 276, 289, 292
Mark 8 hose, 71, 156
Mark 8 SDV. See SDV
Martin, Philip, 205, 220, 222
Matos, Santos A., Jr., 260, 264, 265
McConnell, Steve, 214
McCoy, Alvin F., 94
McDivitt, James A., 48
McGrath, Tom, 214, 216
McGuire rig, 145, 146
McNabb, Bobby, 289
Mekong River, 129, 303
Mercury, 47, 322
Messall, Edward A., 13
Mike boat, 74, 76, 92, 109, 111–15, 117, 118, 121, 155, 311

Military Assistance Command Studies and Observation Group. See MACSOG
Military Assistance Command Vietnam. See MACV
Morris, Stephen, 288
Moscow, 232
Murphy, Tom, 276
My Tho, 102, 116, 126

Naval Coastal Warfare Center, 28
naval combat demolition units, 12, 13
Naval Special Warfare Task Group Central, 316
Nealy, Richard C., 151, 155
Nepper, Rick, 315
New Guinea, 13, 14, 19
Nha Be, 85, 96, 123, 125, 145–47, 159
North Island, 222
North Korea, 33
NVA, 69, 80, 94, 143, 166, 167

OAS (obstacle avoidance sonar), 189
Oceana, 256
Ogden, USS, 67
Okinawa, 11, 21, 24–27, 205–7
Olpenitz, 231, 232, 236
Olson, Norman, 72, 251
Operation Jackstay, 72, 73, 76
Owl, Everett W., 48

Palma, Luco W., 61, 62
Panama, 231, 316
Panama City, Fla., 28, 117
Pandopony, Sam, 13

panty hose, 313, 315
parachute, 3, 52, 54, 56, 62, 172, 173, 233, 251–53, 257, 259–61, 264, 266, 267, 269, 271–78, 283–85, 302, 309
Paracommander, 255
Parks, James L., 28, 201, 202
Patrick, Donny, 126
Pensacola, USS, 228
Pentagon, 91
Persian Gulf, 316, 318
Petersen, Robert W., 102, 105
Philadelphia Naval Hospital,108
Philippines, 11, 15, 17, 18, 28, 206
Phnom Penh, 173, 180, 182, 183
Pierce, Alan H., 13
Pierce, Ron, 235, 240, 244, 245
Point Man, 110
Pope, Walter, 124–26
Port Hueneme, 13, 196
Prince (dog), 307–9
Prout, James Gregory, 92, 93
Prouty, Sandy, 132–35, 138, 139, 142
Prusack, Timmy, 295
PTSD (post traumatic stress disorder), 127
Pueblo, USS, 204
Puerto Rico, 187, 201, 225, 232, 273
Pusan, 30
Putman, Bobby, 192, 193
P'yongyang, 33

Qaddafi, Mu'ammar, 223–25

Ras al-Mishab, 316
Reagan, Ronald, 226, 283

Red Cell, 110
Rhinebolt, Henry J., 115, 121, 122, 149
Robinson, Kenneth C., 117
Rodger, Ronald J., 116
Rogue Warrior, 110, 115, 121
ROK (Republic of Korea forces), 161
ruff puffs, 128, 130

Sabino, Michael, 193, 194
Saigon, 72, 86, 96, 99, 133, 152, 159, 183
San Clemente, 29, 196, 201
Sandy, James D., 13
Saudi Arabia, 316
Schaible, Dave, 131
Schamberger, Robert, 277, 288
Schropp, Jack, 187
Schwartz, Paul T., 150, 151
Scoon, Paul, 287, 291, 295
Scott, Lenny, 144, 145
SCUBA, 52, 252
SDV (SEAL Delivery Vehicle), 187–94, 198, 199, 206, 209, 210, 214, 218, 224, 225, 227, 228
SDV Team TWO, 187, 225, 228
Sea Wolf, 89, 99, 105, 106, 129, 134, 135, 139, 145, 163, 164, 314,
Seabees, 16, 21
Seafloat, 133–36, 142, 155
SEAL Delivery Vehicles (SDV), 28
SEAL Team ONE, 67, 123, 127, 131, 136, 144, 165, 203

SEAL Team TWO, 37, 38, 39, 42, 43, 85, 88, 96, 102, 109, 126, 159, 230–32, 255, 273, 299, 300, 306
SEAL Team FIVE, 1
SEAL Team SIX, 2, 110, 229, 262, 272, 273, 283, 287–89, 291, 293
SEAL Team EIGHT, 1, 200
Seoul, 33
sharks, 15, 289
Sick, Roger, 156
Siem Reap, 173, 174
Simmons, Larry W., 1
Slimpa, Peter, 253
Somalia, 316
South China Sea, 87
South Vietnam, 62, 67, 86, 159, 202, 204, 306, 308
Soviet Union, 32, 223, 232, 236
Special Forces, 38, 39, 253
Spectre gunship, 287, 289, 294–96
spot report, 105
STAB (SEAL team assault boat), 109–18, 120–22, 299, 301, 304, 305, 306
Starlight Scope, 37, 38, 42, 44, 132
Stoner, 7, 89, 90, 110, 124, 125, 139
Subic Bay, 28, 73, 209
submarine, 3, 12, 14, 18, 32, 189, 197, 200–205, 207–11, 220, 223, 224, 225, 231–34, 236–38, 240, 241, 265

Swigert, Jack, 59

T-10 area, 86, 91, 92, 96
target hypnosis syndrome, 268
Tan Son Nhut, 78, 149
Teap Ben, 174, 177–81
Tet, 146, 147, 311
Thailand, 184
Thomas, Tony, 165
Tollison, J. P., 114, 123
Tonkin Gulf, 220
Trani, Frederick E., 304
Tripoli, 299
Troy, Mike, 75
turtle back, 238, 241
Tuure, Richard J., 39, 104, 106, 109

U Minh forest, 134
U-boat, 233, 234, 237, 239, 241
UDT One, 29–31
UDT Eleven, 21–23, 25, 26, 30, 56
UDT Twelve, 30
UDT Thirteen, 21, 59
UDT Sixteen, 21, 22, 24–26
UDT Eighteen, 21
UDT Twenty-one, 48
United Nations, 33, 38

Van Hoy, 125
VCI (Viet Cong infrastructure), 125, 132, 137
Viet Cong, 63, 72, 78, 79, 86–89, 97, 109, 110, 117, 132, 138–41, 144, 147, 148, 150–55, 159, 165, 171, 299, 300, 303, 306

Vung Tau, 132

Walker, Johnny, 272, 283
Wallace, Mike, 50
Wardrobe, James Eugene, 123, 131, 132, 136, 138, 141
Wasp, USS, 49, 51, 52
Watson, James, 111, 112, 114, 115, 119, 120
Westmoreland, William C., 70, 149, 150
Weyers, Maynard, 202–4, 208
White, Edward W., 49
Wilhide, Jonny N., 13
Williams, Charles, 232–46

Williams, Dillard, 13
Williams, Lawrence C., 63
Willis, Claude, 125
Wolfe, Richard, 139, 140
Wonsan, 30, 33, 35
Woolard, Richard P., 85–92, 95, 96, 100, 230, 276
Wright, Bill, 200

Yeaw, Ronald E., 2, 102, 106, 108
Young, John W., 47, 49

Zephyr Hills, 264, 265
Zumwalt, Elmo R., Jr., 100, 133